# The Philosophical Mysticism of Gerard Manley Hopkins

Through the lens of Hopkins's 'masterwork', *The Philosophical Mysticism of Gerard Manley Hopkins* readdresses Hopkins's frequently overlooked mysticism as an interior narrative within his corpus. Drawing on a range of religious, literary and visual traditions from Augustine's *Confessions* to the seventeenth-century spiritual emblem, this book demonstrates the ways in which the Wreck deliberately constructs and conceals a mystical and contemplative narrative. Typology and allegory are some of the important hermeneutic tools used in this re-rereading of Hopkins, relating the poet to the discursive tradition surrounding the Old Testament *Song of Songs,* the philosophical theology of the Greek Fathers and, perhaps most intriguingly, the meditative and visual tradition of the baroque heart-emblem. On the centenary of the publication of Hopkins's poems, this book places the writer firmly within a mystical tradition, necessitating a fundamental reconsideration of the legacy of this major Victorian poet.

**Aakanksha Virkar Yates** is a Lecturer in English literature at the University of Brighton, specialising in nineteenth century and modern literature. Her research is fundamentally interdisciplinary, placing literary works in dialogue with theology, philosophy, visual culture and music. Working in the growing field of inter-art studies, Dr. Virkar Yates is also the recipient of several awards, from the Nehru Trust for Cambridge University, the J. N. Tata Fund and recently a Rising Stars award from the University of Brighton.

**The Nineteenth Century Series**
Series editor: Joanne Shattock
*Professor Emeritus, University of Leicester, UK*

The series focuses primarily upon major authors and subjects within Romantic and Victorian literature. It also includes studies of other nineteenth-century British writers and issues, where these are matters of current debate: for example, biography and autobiography; journalism; periodical literature; travel writing; book production; gender; non-canonical writing.

Recent in this series:

**Life Writing and Victorian Culture**
*Edited by David Amigoni*

**Pre-Raphaelite Masculinities**
*Edited by Amelia Yeates and Serena Trowbridge*

**Thackeray in Time**
History, Memory and Modernity
*Edited by Richard Salmon and Alice Crossley*

**The Philosophical Mysticism of Gerard Manley Hopkins**
*Aakanksha Virkar Yates*

# The Philosophical Mysticism of Gerard Manley Hopkins

Aakanksha Virkar Yates

Routledge
Taylor & Francis Group
NEW YORK AND LONDON

First published 2018
by Routledge
711 Third Avenue, New York, NY 10017

and by Routledge
2 Park Square, Milton Park, Abingdon, Oxon OX14 4RN

*Routledge is an imprint of the Taylor & Francis Group, an informa business*



*Library of Congress Cataloging-in-Publication Data*
CIP data has been applied for.

ISBN: 978-1-138-09390-4 (hbk)
ISBN: 978-0-429-50627-7 (ebk)

Typeset in Sabon
by codeMantra

For Elizabeth, Thea and Elias

# Contents

# Acknowledgments

All material from the *Collected Works of Gerard Manley Hopkins* is published by permission of Oxford University Press (OUP). Permission to reproduce journal content from *Literature and Theology* is granted by OUP Journals. Reproduction of emblem images from *The Devout Heart* (1634) is by permission of the Provost and Fellows of Eton College. Thanks also to the editor of *Victorian Poetry* for permission to reproduce an article that first appeared in the journal.

I owe special thanks to Norman Vance for his continuing guidance, encouragement and kindness. To David Jasper, for his helpful comments. To my parents, Elizabeth and Jeevan, for a lifetime of love and support. To my husband and friend Robert Yates who enabled me to pursue this work and whose fine eye and honesty the original thesis benefited from. I am grateful too to the remarkable teachers who have inspired me, in the nearer and more distant past – Con Coroneos, Stephen Heath, Alison Hennegan, Shefali Balsari-Shah, Eunice de Souza, Bubla Basu and Shirin Darasha. This book is dedicated to my mother and my children, Thea and Elias.

# 1 'Rare-Dear Gerard'
## Hopkins and the Early Fathers

> There have been in all history a few, a very few men, whom common repute, even where it did not trust them, has treated as having had something happen to them that does not happen to other men, as having *seen something*, whatever that really was. Plato is the most famous of these... human nature in these men saw something, got a shock; wavers in opinion, looking back, whether there was anything in it or no; but is in a tremble ever since...in Wordsworth when he wrote that ode human nature got another of those shocks, and the tremble from it is spreading. This opinion I do strongly share; I am, ever since I knew the ode, in that tremble.[1]
>
> (23–24 October 1886. Hopkins's own italics)

Hopkins's letter to R. W. Dixon is energetic, dramatic and tending to persuasion. But what remains unsaid here is that Hopkins counts himself amongst those very few men, as one who has 'seen something'. Hopkins's 1876 ode *The Wreck of the Deutschland* is his testament to this vision. The poem portrays an experience of mystical vision and testifies to the very possibility of such vision, predicated on a faculty of intuitive or mystical knowledge. In this way, Hopkins places himself in that idealist, Platonic tradition which links early Alexandrian theology with Augustinian tradition, finding its most immediate expression in the writings of John Henry Newman. In this tradition, Hopkins finds what will be the centre of his spirituality and poetics, a model of love, knowledge and vision that derives from an ancient religious discourse on contemplation. The practice of contemplation in Alexandrian Christianity is developed from the Platonic *theoria*, originally understood as the intellectual vision of the truth. For Clement of Alexandria, writing in the second century, contemplation becomes the perfection of *gnosis*, the 'higher knowledge' of God; it is the soul gazing upon divinity, the direct intuition of the divine described by St Paul in his Hymn to Love: 'We see now through a glass in a dark manner; but then face to face' (1 Cor. 13.12).[2] Both Clement and the third-century father Origen portray contemplation as the goal of mystical life; the journey of the soul is an ascent to a vision of Christ or God. For Hopkins, as for these

Alexandrian Platonists, the physical world (with the text as its representative) becomes an economy by which the soul ascends to heaven and to the divine vision promised in Matthew 5.9: 'Blessed *are* the pure in heart, for they shall see God' (KJV).

Why does Hopkins writing in the nineteenth century turn to the contemplative theology of the early church? The answer lies both in his Tractarian roots and in the important figure of Newman. As critics and biographers have pointed out, Hopkins's conversion to Roman Catholicism has frequently obscured his High church background. In his 1991 biography, Robert Martin notes that for almost exactly half his short life, Hopkins was a member of the Church of England. By the time of his conversion at 22, his intellect and spiritual cast of mind were firmly established.[3] Hopkins's early Tractarianism turned his attention to patristic tradition. It perhaps also prevented the poet from later aligning himself with that tendency of the Roman church identified by Newman, which in claiming infallible authority, failed to refer to the ancient church as the source of this authority.[4] For Hopkins, much of the continuity between his Anglican upbringing and Catholic adulthood derives from the patristic and medieval tradition of Christianity revived by the Tractarians. The important influence of Tractarian theology on Hopkins is explored in detail in Chapter 2. This chapter brings to view what is often obscured in studies of the Oxford Movement – its inherent mysticism, as seen in the Tractarian doctrine of the divine indwelling and the sacramental mysticism that issues from this. For Hopkins, after his conversion of 1868, it is the contemplative teaching of the early church that will enrich and expand his meditative practice as a Jesuit. A number of critics have noted Hopkins's dissatisfaction with the discursive methods of St Ignatius's *Spiritual Exercises*. This study goes further, suggesting that Hopkins uniquely attempted to unite the meditative practice of the *Exercises* with the mystical theology of contemplation. Only in this way can Hopkins satisfy the mystical desire of his soul, which, like the psalmist, yearns to 'appear before the face of God' (Ps. 41).

Since the publication of the First Edition of Hopkins's poems in 1918, a few early and influential studies of Hopkins as a Jesuit have suggested his indebtedness to the meditative methods of the *Spiritual Exercises*. Louis Martz's early study, *The Poetry of Meditation* (1954), argues the impact of Roman Catholic methods of meditation on English poetry written in the seventeenth century. In his list of meditative writers, Martz includes the Victorian example of Hopkins, suggesting that the poetry of Hopkins together with that of John Donne best shows the imprint of Jesuit methods of meditation. Ignatian meditation is threefold, comprising the practice of composition (or proposing of the subject), analysis and colloquy (when the reformed soul speaks with God). These exercises correspond to the three powers of the soul defined by Augustine, namely memory, understanding and will. Martz suggests that the movement of meditative poetry resembles this threefold method; the structure of Ignatian meditation functions as a fundamental organising impulse deep within the poetry. Martz suggests this method as readily apparent in Hopkins, and he draws particular attention to the poet's dramatic 'composition' of scene in the opening lines of many sonnets. Yet, despite the fact that the Ignatian method derives in part from the medieval mystical progression of purgation, illumination and union, Martz remains wary of the appearance of mystical vocabulary in meditative poetry. Although meditative writers frequently use the threefold way of mystics, Martz suggests that their meditations nevertheless end in the realm of devotion and stop short of mystical contemplation.

Another early book to examine Hopkins's work in relation to the Ignatian tradition is David Anthony Downes's *Gerard Manley Hopkins: A Study of His Ignatian Spirit* (1959). This full-length study closely examines Hopkins's poetry in the light of his Jesuit training. Downes focuses largely on the Ignatian content of Hopkins's verse, except in the final chapter, which develops some of Martz's meditative and structural arguments. The *Spiritual Exercises* itself comprises four weeks of meditation – the First Week a consideration of sins, the Second Week a meditation on the Life of Christ, the Third Week on the Passion and the Fourth Week a meditation on the Resurrection. Downes traces these themes in Hopkins's work, identifying in the poet a fundamentally Ignatian perspective. He also relates Hopkins's sacramental world view to the principles of Ignatian spirituality laid out in the 'Foundation' of the *Exercises.* In identifying parallels between the *Wreck* and the *Spiritual Exercises*, Downes draws on Hopkins's spiritual notes dating from 1881 to 1883. These notes were intended by the poet as a treatise on the *Exercises*, though they remain unfinished. The *Wreck* itself represents Hopkins's personal experience of the *Exercises*, and an important theme in Downes's analysis is the operation of grace as understood by the poet through the medium of this devotional manual. Neither Downes nor Martz, however, explore the relevance to Hopkins of the *scala mystica* from which the *Exercises* themselves derive.[5]

John Pick in *Gerard Manley Hopkins: Priest and Poet* (1966) provides a further detailed account of the influence of Ignatian spirituality on Hopkins's life and work. Pick develops many of the arguments made by Downes, similarly suggesting the importance of the 'Principle and Foundation' of the *Exercises* in Hopkins's thought. The 'Foundation' teaches that human beings are created to praise and glorify the divine, and that all of creation exists to assist in the pursuit of this end. In this way, Hopkins finds in the *Exercises* a path to God through the created world. Interestingly, Pick is one of the very few critics to note, if in passing, the affinity between the objectives of Ignatius's four weeks of spiritual exercises and the three traditional stages of ascetical life. As the contemplation of sins, the exercises of the First Week may be compared with the purgative stage; the Second and Third Weeks, which focus on the life and Passion of Christ, may be seen as analogous with the illuminative stage; the Fourth and last meditation on the Resurrection may be compared with the unitive stage. But Pick also highlights the explicit cautioning *against* such assumed parallels as given in the *Directory*, a body of instructions drawn up in the 1590s for teachers or directors of the *Spiritual Exercises*.[6] Pick's study itself ultimately denies the reading of Hopkins as a contemplative or mystical poet. Dennis Sobolev, in his article 'Gerard Manley Hopkins and the Language of Mysticism', notes the disappearance of any discussion of Hopkins's mysticism from the 1950s onwards. Sobolev argues that Pick's study, first published in 1942, was influential in ending any tentative speculation on the subject. As Pick unequivocally asserted, 'only by using the word in a very loose and inaccurate sense may Hopkins be called a mystic'.[7]

Overall then, studies of Hopkins's meditative influences have been mainly concerned with the relation of the poet's sacramental vision to the meditative techniques of the *Exercises*, with a frequent focus on the Ignatian method of harnessing sensory experience for religious understanding. This application of the senses relates to the Ignatian 'composition' of place, the opening meditative exercise Martz first suggested to operate so dramatically in Hopkins's sonnets. As a secondary emphasis, meditative studies of Hopkins have examined the Ignatian content of his poetry; its treatment of the themes of Christ's life, Passion and Resurrection. Yet, none of these studies have significantly shifted critical attention from the techniques and themes of Ignatian meditation to the older contemplative tradition from which they take their origin. Rather, there has been on the whole an attempt to separate the practice of meditation from the mystical realm of contemplation. Yet such a division would be artificial to someone such as Hopkins, with his theological training and his familiarity with patristic tradition. It would have also have been dissatisfying for the poet on account of his 'Platonic impulses', suggested as one reason for Hopkins's attraction to the highly intellectualised Jesuit order.[8] These impulses likely also explain Hopkins's affinity for the Alexandrian Platonists and the Augustinian tradition, which continues their idealist epistemology.

The threefold method of Ignatian meditation, we noted, is based on Augustine's three powers of the soul. In Augustine's Trinitarian theology, these three powers of memory, understanding and will are assigned to the image of the Trinity in the soul (*The Trinity* 10.11.18). It is in this way that Augustine understands the individual to be made in the image of God (cf. Gen. 1.27) – the divine image is found not in the body but in the incorporeal soul. The perfect operation of the soul's powers is implicitly understood to perfect the divine image in the soul. Until the sixteenth century, the practice of meditation had an ultimately contemplative end – the mystical knowledge of the inner presence of

Christ. In his *Treatise de Quantitate Animae*, Augustine describes seven grades of the soul; the final three stages are *tranquillitas*, *ingressio* and *contemplatio*, and these anticipate the medieval mystical progression of purgation, illumination and union.[9] Throughout his writings, Augustine propounds an ultimate knowledge or vision of God that is interior to the mind and presented as the perfection of the soul's powers. For Augustine, knowledge is finally remembering; God is sought and found within the mysterious recesses of the mind. Augustine's *scala coelis*, or ladder to heaven, similarly charts the soul's search for God through the ascending grades of creation. In the final stages, the mind must once again turn inwards in order to find the divine. Ignatian meditation derives from this Augustinian foundation; its discursive emphasis, however, obscures its relation to the medieval *scala mystica* and to Augustinian theology more broadly. As we will see, Hopkins reads the *Exercises* in a contemplative light, in a way that challenges contemporary Jesuit practice but is at heart truer to an older Catholic tradition.

An important figure to shape and inform Hopkins's contemplative attitudes is Cardinal Newman. The idealist nature of Newman's belief is apparent, and he is often seen as the modern reincarnation of the true Augustinian spirit.[10] Also prominent in Newman's thought is the influence of the Alexandrian theologians, particularly Clement and Origen. The Alexandrians were the pre-eminent early proponents of the idealist tradition in orthodox Christian thought and their idealist epistemology is continued and developed in Augustinian tradition. Alexandrian philosophy finds an important place in an early work of Newman's Tractarian phase, *Arians of the Fourth Century* (1833). In his book, Newman discusses the Tractarian principle of economy that he derives from Clement and Origen. He explores this principle in considerable detail, suggesting two ways in which it may be understood. On the one hand, it is a primarily exegetical technique; in a broader sense, however, the 'economy' comes much closer to the word 'symbol' and is understood as divine action in the world. In his much later *Apologia pro Vita Sua* (1864), Newman returns to a powerful and moving consideration of the principle of economy and its origin in Alexandrian sacramental mysticism. The *Apologia* was published when Hopkins was a student at Oxford, and despite an astonishing lack of references to the work in Hopkins's undergraduate records, it is likely he was familiar with it by 1865.[11] In the *Apologia*, Newman describes a personal transformation effected through his reading of the Alexandrians. He describes himself as having found in these theologians the 'mystical or sacramental principle', which would so centrally shape his thought.

> The battle of Arianism was first fought in Alexandria; Athanasius, the champion of the truth, was Bishop of Alexandria; and in his writings he refers to the great religious names of an earlier date, to

> Origen, Dionysius, and others who were the glory of its see, or of its school. The broad philosophy of Clement and Origen carried me away...Some portions of their teaching, magnificent in themselves, came like music to my inward ear...These were based on the mystical or sacramental principle, and spoke of the various Economies or Dispensations of the Eternal. I understood them to mean that the exterior world, physical and historical, was but the outward manifestation of realities greater than itself. Nature was a parable: Scripture was an allegory... ...And thus room was made for the anticipation of further and deeper disclosures, of truths still under the veil of the letter, and in their season to be revealed.[12]

The economical or sacramental system described by Newman transfigures the visible world into a parable read by the enlightened. Newman relates this system to that found in Bishop Joseph Butler's *Analogy of Religion* (1736) and John Keble's *The Christian Year* (1827). The 'mystical or sacramental principle' effectively implies a simultaneous concealment and revelation; the visible both offers and withholds the invisible, and the seen becomes symbolic of the unseen. Such a system bears out the ultimately mysterious nature of grace and the incapacity of mere reason to fathom divine mysteries. Clement in the *Stromateis* repeatedly asserts the truth contained within the visible by means of an economy or 'mystery'; gnostic vision is the discernment of this truth. This same mystic idealism is systematised in Origen's conception of the two heavens and two earths. These he understands as sacramentally related; the visible is a blurred imprint of the invisible, showing God as in a glass darkly. For Clement and Origen, the knowledge of Christian revelation in the Incarnation is the key to interpreting the world of matter. This world and all of creation becomes an economy by which the soul ascends to the divine. In other words, such an economical system demands a contemplative ascent; the obscure vision offered by the economy of creation is ultimately paralleled with the perfect vision of God. To be a 'gnostic' of the kind Clement extols, one must practise contemplation, and the *Stromateis* 7.3.13 gives a representative text relating gnosis and *theoria*. Here, Clement describes gnostic souls who

> keep always moving to higher and yet higher regions, until they no longer greet the divine vision in or by means of mirrors (1 Cor. 12.13), but with loving hearts feast forever on the uncloying, never-ending sight...This is the apprehensive vision of the pure of heart.[13]
>
> (Matt 5.8)

For Origen too, the contemplating mind is the 'divine sense' that sees the invisible;[14] the 'sheer contemplation' of God is the end goal of religious life and human aspiration.[15] In the writings of both Alexandrians, contemplation is aligned with both earth and heaven, present and future. The activity of contemplation is the means by which the soul ascends and the end goal of this ascent. Naturally, there are differences too in the contemplative theology propounded by the two fathers.[16] What is clear, however, is that the highest spiritual development is seen in the exercise of contemplation, and this contemplative faculty is the soul's highest correspondence with a sacramental or economical creation.

A number of critics have noted the importance of the Tractarian principle of economy for Hopkins. Yet, this has been viewed in a primarily formal sense, in relation to Hopkins's use of the multiple meanings associated with typology. The economical system in this sense is connected with Tractarian poetics – the typological principles seen in Keble's *Christian Year* or in the poetry of Newman himself. Such an application of the principle has not, however, looked to its origins in patristic theology. In Clement and Origen, the system of economies is emphatically given meaning by the discourse on contemplation that accompanies it. Hopkins's poetry and prose must also be read in relation to this discourse. Contemplative theology is at the centre of Hopkins's theopoetics and has yet been neglected in discussions of his Tractarian poetics. George Landow, for example, argues for a typological reading of Hopkins. In his important book *Victorian Types, Victorian Shadows*, he suggests that much of what is difficult in Hopkins can be explained in relation to the poet's application of a typological or economical system. At the same time, Landow asserts that this principle provides a better explanation of Hopkins's verse than the tradition of gnosticism (he refers here to James Cotter's study, *Inscape: The Christology and Poetry of G. M. Hopkins*, which argues the gnostic tradition as key to a reading of Hopkins). Yet, the economical principle and the tradition of gnosticism are intimately related, as Hopkins would have known from Newman and from his own reading of the fathers. The mystical or sacramental principle elicits and is accompanied by the activity of contemplation. As the higher activity of the soul, this practice of contemplation is central to gnosticism; for the Alexandrians, the spiritual faculty that reads or contemplates the mysteries of this world, may also attain to an intuitive apprehension of the divine.[17]

Hopkins's poetry undoubtedly makes extensive use of typological and economical representation. But it is important to appreciate that in Hopkins's poetics, as in patristic exegesis, the typological supports the mystical. Hopkins finds in Newman and the Alexandrians not only a sacramental method, but a broader contemplative theology. Newman's development of Alexandrian idealism plays a key mediating role here. As Harold Weatherby notes, Newman's conception of two systems, one physical and one moral, is clearly indebted to Origen's idea of the relation between the visible and invisible worlds.[18] This Origenian idea strongly appealed to Newman. Indeed, that this enthusiasm for Origen serves as common ground between Hopkins and Newman is an intriguing point neglected by scholars and one that merits closer attention. Interestingly, the sole recorded reference to Origen in Hopkins's writings is found in a letter written in the year that followed the publication of Newman's *Apologia*. In a letter dated Epiphany, January 6, 1865, Hopkins declares Savonarola to be 'the only person in history (except perhaps Origen) about whom I have a real feeling'.[19] Hopkins's effusive affirmation is similar to Newman's emotive accounts of Origen in the *Apologia*, where Newman declares that he 'loves the name' of Origen. Origen's economical system receives its fullest exposition in his *Commentary on the Song of Songs*. The erotic imagery of the Song, if read literally, can lead to error; but contemplated by the spiritual sense, an understanding of the Song raises the soul to a knowledge of divine and heavenly mysteries. Origen's *Commentary on the Song* is woven into the mystical, interior narrative of Hopkins's *Wreck of the Deutschland*. As a veiled account of the soul's ascent to the divine, Hopkins's ode owes much to Origen's threefold exegetical system, as we will see in Chapter 6.

The principle of economy is suited not only to the subject matter of *The Wreck of the Deutschland*, but also to Hopkins's vocation and temperament. Commenting in later years on the histories of earlier members of the Society of Jesus, Hopkins writes to Dixon: 'I quote these cases to prove that shew and brilliancy do not suit us, that we cultivate the commonplace outwardly and wish the beauty of the king's daughter the soul to be from within.' (1 December 1881)[20] The dangers of pride, fame and the temptations of art found the young Hopkins caught between the conflicting pulls of poetry and priesthood. He famously destroyed his early experiments in verse, and, consequently, the *Wreck* was written after years of artistic abstinence. In his ode, Hopkins takes refuge in a typological language of shadows and similitudes – not an ostentatious or flamboyant style, but one that (for the most part) 'cultivate[s] the common-place outwardly'. The gravity of the subject matter demands a great measure of religious reserve. Only in the obscurity of an economical system is Hopkins able to reconcile the paradoxical demands of art, as it strives for expression, and a mysticism that reaches towards silence. The *Wreck of the Deutschland* becomes an unparalleled exercise in economy, accommodating the needs of both poet and reader. As Newman observes, economy, in the interpretation of scripture, is the principle of 'accommodation to the feelings and prejudices of the hearer, in leading him to the reception of a novel or unacceptable doctrine'.[21] In the Victorian times in which Hopkins lived and wrote, contemplation was a dangerous activity, unattainable and undesirable for ordinary Christians. To lead his readers to the vision of God centrally inscribed within his ode, Hopkins must write the poem as sacrament or mystery. To do so, he uses a typological and allegorical language, inscribing multiple levels of meaning. Each level leads to a deeper or more elevated apprehension of the truth – yet a truth that never ceases to be a mystery. Hopkins's text must be contemplated as Hopkins contemplated the world, ascending from the visible to the invisible, from the corporeal to the divine. Like Newman, Hopkins derives from Origen and patristic tradition a sacramental and mystical system whose culmination is the highest love, vision or knowledge to which the mind or heart can attain – the divine vision.

The immediate knowledge or vision of God is an idea at the centre of Newman's *Grammar of Assent* (1870). In his earlier *Apologia,* Newman had given a personal testimony of the direct relationship between the soul and a luminous mental image of God, experienced without mediation of the intellect. Newman's *Grammar* is again centrally concerned with this intuitive apprehension of God as the sustaining principle of faith. Newman writes: 'what I am directly aiming at, is to explain how we gain an image of God and give a real assent to the proposition that He exists.'[22] For Newman, a real faith can only be one that is based on an immediate knowledge of the object of faith, and not on mere abstractions or 'notions'.[23] Faith must be based on real assent, and Newman develops his argument through an important set of interrelated terms. Real assent is to 'things or images' and brings immediate intuitive awareness; it is aligned with implicit reason. Notional assent is to conclusions and abstractions and is aligned with explicit reason. Newman's implicit reason (analogous to Coleridge's 'philosophic imagination') is the higher faculty, able to apprehend God in 'a complex act of intuition'. It is this intuitive and immediate knowledge of God that Newman suggests to be at the heart of religion. Only the image of God can sustain the soul, not mere reason or abstraction. For Newman, the image of God is imprinted directly upon the conscience, which alone can achieve a real apprehension of God. It is in Newman's development of his idea of the conscience that his Platonic idealism becomes apparent. The image of God imprinted on the conscience is not knowledge acquired through the senses in a Thomist sense, but is instead akin to a Platonic doctrine of innate ideas or to Augustine's conception of infused grace (for Aquinas, Newman's real assent or real apprehension would be possible only in heaven).[24]

Newman's argument for the image of God intuitively apprehended as the ground of faith continues the idea of contemplation developed in Alexandrian theology. At the same time, Newman's conception of 'real apprehension' modifies Alexandrian teaching, bringing to bear contemporary Romantic attitudes. The change lies in an 'affective' modification of traditional neo-Platonic idealism, a modification seen also in Coleridge (who, however, derives his idealism from Plotinus). For Clement and Origen, it is the mind enlightened by Christian doctrine and instructed in the discipline of contemplation that is the primary faculty for the intuitive apprehension of God. For Newman, neither the mind nor affections in themselves but the conscience as the union of these faculties becomes the medium by which divine images and ideas are imprinted in the soul. Contemplation for Newman is not a purely intellectual activity, but one that is involved as much with feeling as with cognition. In this, he is in keeping with the contemporary merging of idealism and sensationalism that had followed from Wordsworth and Coleridge. In both these Romantic poets, traditional Neo-Platonism and idealist conceptions of intuition and illumination merge with eighteenth-century theories of sensation; their poetry seeks to affirm the spiritual without denying the affections or the experience of the senses.[25] Similarly, for Newman, real apprehension is the achievement not only of mind and memory, but also of the passions and the imagination. In the *Grammar of Assent*, it is the conscience, the intellect in conjunction with the imagination and the affections, that becomes the locus of a mental image of God.

*The Wreck of the Deutschland* inaugurates a moment of assent. 'I did say yes', Hopkins writes in the opening section of the poem. This moment of assent, we will see, is accompanied by an intuitive or mystical apprehension of God that has important connections with Newman's *Grammar* and with patristic and contemplative theology more broadly. Few critics see Hopkins as a mystic, although Alison Sulloway observes that Hopkins, writing to Bridges, hints that Christ appeared to him at one time or another.[26] Yet, *The Wreck of the Deutschland* is at its centre a poem about seeing God. A complex narrative of faith and conversion, Hopkins's poem conceals an inner narrative that follows Newman's *Grammar* in celebrating the mystical presence of God and the intuitive apprehension of his image. Curiously, Hopkins began reading the *Grammar of Assent* in August 1873, only two and a half years before he began work on the *Wreck*. The abiding influence of Newman's philosophical opus on Hopkins may be gauged by his request to Newman in February 1883 to publish a sixth edition of the book with a commentary. When declined, the request was made again, two months later. Newman's *Grammar* may be seen to provide Hopkins with a contemplative framework with which he is able to extend the meditative discourse of the *Exercises*. That the two works are linked in Hopkins's spiritual imagination is perhaps intimated in a coincidence of timing. As noted, Hopkins's unfinished writings on the *Exercises* span from 1881 to 1883. Much of this writing was done during a Long Retreat of November–December 1881. But the creative year, Christopher Devlin suggests, was 1881–1882.[27] Hopkins's request to Newman to write a commentary on the *Grammar*, at the beginning of 1883, follows very shortly on the heels of his incomplete treatise on the *Exercises*. Hopkins's affective, contemplative modifications of Ignatian meditation indeed bear much affinity to Newman's conception of the conscience as the organ of divine intuition; for Hopkins, Newman's contemplative insights as based on patristic theology offer a remedy for the purely speculative and discursive emphasis of Ignatian meditation.

A number of critics including Downes and, more recently, Jude Nixon and Margaret Johnson, have noted Hopkins's familiarity with Newman's arguments for the role of intuition and the affections in matters of faith. Downes points to Hopkins's letters to his father at the time of his conversion, noting that Hopkins's entire argument and explanation of his decision suggest that he clearly understood 'the workings of Newman's illative imagination'.[28] Johnson similarly points to Hopkins's discussion of his conversion in a letter to Liddon, observing that Hopkins uses categories that closely approximate Newman's distinctions between real and notional assent, faith and reason.[29] Newman's 'illative sense' is virtually interchangeable with 'implicit reason'; both are the grounds of real assent. But these readings do not relate Newman's idealist epistemology to the contemplative discourse of Alexandrian theology. In fact, Newman's 'conscience' can be understood as a substitution for the Alexandrian conception of 'gnosis'.[30] Deriving from the gnostic and contemplative tradition of Clement and Origen, Newman's 'conscience' is similarly concerned with a mystical apprehension or intuition of the *imago Dei*. No doubt this 'image' plays on the central paradox of contemplative discourse: to contemplate God is to see the unseen. But it is precisely Newman's formulation of the intuitive apprehension of the divine that becomes the centre of Hopkins's enigmatic *Wreck of the Deutschland*. This is Hopkins's paradise within: the image of the divine in the soul, not only known through Christian doctrine, but also *felt* and *contemplated* through the ultimately mystical faculty by which belief is born.

Hopkins in his powerful account of the idea of vision in Plato and Wordsworth describes the men who had 'seen something, whatever that something really was'. Hopkins's relation of Wordsworth and Plato points to the very yoking of spiritual intuition and affective experience that is the Romantic modification of Neo-Platonic tradition. Perhaps Hopkins has something of this in mind when he declares the 'shock' of Wordsworth's *Intimations of Immortality*. Hopkins recognised too that Newman drew on this Romantic inheritance, and in a letter dated December 1, 1881, he describes the poetry of Keble, Faber and Newman as the expiration of the Lake School.[31] As Nixon observes, Hopkins is probably the first critic to read the Tractarians as Romantics.[32] *The Wreck of the Deutschland* offers a further insight into this relation and suggests Hopkins's recognition of the fact that Newman's illative sense and his argument for the intuitive apprehension of God had much to do with a Romantic epistemology.

28

But how shall I ... make me room there:
Reach me a ... Fancy, come faster—
Strike you the sight of it? look at it loom there,

Thing that she ... there then! the Master,
*Ipse*, the only one, Christ, King, Head...

29

Ah! there was a heart right!
There was single eye!
Read the unshapeable shock night
And knew the who and the why;
Wording it how but by him that present and past,
Heaven and earth are word of, worded by?—

This passage functions as a key semantic nexus in Hopkins's complex synthesis of typological and allegorical meaning. Hopkins inscribes here a mystical vision, and the odd use of the word 'Fancy' can in part be explained by Newman's real apprehension. Real assent, as Newman describes it, is a response to 'things or images'. Belief, which is synonymous with real assent, apprehends the object of faith in an act of intuition – a vision brought about by the imagination and affections. At this enigmatic climax of the *Wreck*, Hopkins jarringly describes a vision of a 'thing'. In some respects, this is the Kantian thing-in-itself, but Hopkins's language also echoes Newman's *Grammar of Assent*. This 'thing' is itself the divine image, apprehended as an object of contemplation. Hopkins critically links this vision with the operation of 'Fancy', calling up those famous Romantic categories of Fancy and Imagination. Coleridge's categories of these two faculties show a close kinship with Newman's argument for the role of the imagination and affections in religious belief. Coleridge was an important influence on Newman's conception of conscience, and Hopkins's use of the term 'Fancy' effectively calls up a whole Romantic epistemology – an appeal to the imagination, the passions and the heart. For Newman, conscience and heart are closely related. In his *Grammar of Assent*, Newman argues for an intuitive knowledge of God 'in my conscience and heart'; the two are effectively equated too in Newman's description of God as seen by a '*right* heart [my italics]'.[33] Hopkins similarly suggests this divine vision as the achievement of a 'heart right' (29). The passage is a central moment in Hopkins's theopoetics. It is his testimony to a vision seen through a faculty akin to Coleridge's philosophic imagination and to Newman's conscience. Even the word 'shock' (29) suggests a sudden 'impression on the mind', an intuitive act of apprehension; notably, it is the same word Hopkins uses when describing the 'shock' of reading Wordsworth's *Intimations*, the poetic legacy of a man who has 'seen something'.

It could be argued of course that Hopkins's use of the word 'Fancy' places him on the wrong side of Coleridge's philosophic distinction. For Coleridge, fancy is the lower power and imagination the higher.

Fancy is a mere aggregating faculty of mind; imagination is the modifying and co-adunating faculty (more closely akin to Newman's 'conscience'). However, Coleridge also uses the terms interchangeably, and what is most important is that both terms denote the mental faculty opposed to reason and implicitly aligned with Newman's affective understanding of the conscience. Indeed, Fancy is linked by Coleridge to 'images' and 'impressions', and Hopkins's use of the word intimates (as does the stanza taken as a whole) that metaphor of seeing, which lies at the heart of contemplative discourse. Ultimately, 'Fancy' in *The Wreck of the Deutschland* functions largely as a literary cue, intimating a non-reasoning faculty or illative sense, which alone can apprehend the divine. Newman's conception of conscience, as we have seen, draws on the Alexandrian idea of gnosis as linked with contemplative practice. Where Clement speaks of the 'true gnostic', Origen speaks of the 'spiritual' or 'perfect' Christian who possesses a real and 'visual' knowledge of Christ (this is the union with God suggested in 1 John 3.2: 'now are we the sons of God...when he shall appear, we shall be like him; for we shall see him as he is', KJV).[34] Through the *Grammar of Assent*, Hopkins reaches back to a patristic theology of contemplation. But, as for Newman and Augustine, it is no longer a purely intellectual model of contemplative ascent. Hopkins's 'heart', like Newman's conscience, participates in that affective modification of neo-Platonic tradition that is the achievement of Newman and the Romantics before him. At the heart of the *Wreck* is a powerful affirmation of personal belief and an intuitive apprehension of the divine, which alone can be the grounds of such assent.

## Notes

1 G. M. Hopkins, *The Collected Works of Gerard Manley Hopkins*, vol. 2 *Correspondence 1882–1889*, ed. R. K. R. Thornton and C. Philips (London: OUP, 2013), 821. All material from this title is published by permission of Oxford University Press.

2 Perfect contemplation is naturally reserved for the blessed in heaven, but patristic discourse on contemplation importantly suggests that the vision of God may be glimpsed even during mortal life; see Bernard McGinn, *The Foundations of Mysticism*, vol. 1 *The Presence of God: A History of Western Christian Mysticism* (New York: Crossroad, 1991), 71–72. Unless otherwise specified all biblical citations are to the Douay-Rheims Bible. Following his reception into the Jesuit order in 1868, Hopkins would have been expected to consult the Latin Vulgate, or the Douay-Rheims English translation, with its emphasis on the Latin. Naturally, Hopkins would also be entirely familiar with the 1611 King James Version of his Protestant youth, and the Greek New Testament of his classical training.

3 Robert Bernard Martin, *Gerard Manley Hopkins: A Very Private Life* (New York: G. P. Putnam's Sons, 1991), xv.

4 This is the subject of Lecture 2 of Newman's *Lectures on the Prophetical Office of the Church*, entitled 'On the Roman Teaching as Neglectful of Antiquity'. Here Newman writes, 'They profess to appeal to primitive

Christianity...Whatever principles they profess in theory...yet when they come to particulars...they supersede the appeal to Scripture and Antiquity by putting forward the infallibility of the Church...', Lecture 2.1, www.newmanreader.org/works/viamedia/volume1/lecture2.html.

5 Louis Martz points out that meditative treatises of the seventeenth century did not in general make explicit the underlying theology of the three powers of the soul as analogous to the Trinity; these theological implications were either seen as too theoretical to be discussed in meditative treatises, or knowledge of these implications was assumed on the part of the reader. See Louis L. Martz, *The Poetry of Meditation*, rev. ed. (1954; repr., New Haven, CT: Yale University Press, 1962), 34.

6 John Pick, *Gerard Manley Hopkins: Priest and Poet,* 2nd ed. (London: OUP, 1966), 28. This injunction perhaps goes some way toward explaining why Hopkins might choose to submerge the operation of this threefold mystical structure in his own work. Hopkins's use of this structure of ascent is seen in his incorporation of meditative emblems as discussed in Chapter 7.

7 Pick, *Gerard Manley Hopkins*, 131, quoted in Dennis Sobolev, 'Gerard Manley Hopkins and the Language of Mysticism,' Conference on Christianity and Literature (22 June 2004), www.encyclopedia.com/doc/1G1-125407680.html. Sobolev refers to the 1942 edition of Pick's study.

8 This observation is made by David Downes, cited in Jude V. Nixon, *Gerard Manley Hopkins and His Contemporaries: Liddon, Newman, Darwin and Pater* (New York: Garland Publishing, Inc., 1994), 104.

9 For a fuller discussion of this, see Dom Cuthbert Butler, *Western Mysticism: Augustine, Gregory, and Bernard on Contemplation and the Contemplative Life,* 3rd ed. (London: Constable & Co Ltd, 1967), 28.

10 It is Eric Przywara who suggests Newman as a reincarnation of Augustine; Przywara is cited by Harold Weatherby in *Cardinal Newman in His Age: His Place in English Theology and Literature* (Nashville, TN: Vanderbilt University Press, 1973), 71. My discussion of the influence of Newman's idealism on Hopkins is indebted to Weatherby's insightful reading of Newman.

11 Alison Sulloway is the first to observe that Hopkins's 1865 eucharistic poem has for its title a phrase used in the *Apologia* – 'The Half-way House'; see Alison Sulloway, *Gerard Manley Hopkins and the Victorian Temper* (London: Routledge, 1972), 18.

12 John Henry Newman, *Apologia Pro Vita Sua & 6 Sermons*, ed. F. Turner (New Haven: Yale University Press, 2008), 154–55.

13 McGinn, *The Foundations of Mysticism*, 105.

14 A. N. Williams, *The Divine Sense: The Intellect in Patristic Theology* (Cambridge: CUP, 2007), 82.

15 Ibid., 81.

16 Clement's conception of contemplation is in many respects less rarefied than Origen's; see Williams, *The Divine Sense,* 81.

17 The importance of an Augustinian-Origenian view of exegesis within Hopkins's poetry is also suggested by Jeffrey Loomis in his study of Hopkins's sacramental poetics. However, Loomis seems not to engage with the contemplative discourse that is traditionally allied with such a system.

18 Weatherby, *Cardinal Newman,* 95.

19 G. M. Hopkins, *Collected Works*, vol. 1 *Correspondence 1852–1881*, ed. R. K. R. Thornton and C. Philips (London: OUP, 1938), 78. All material from this title is published by permission of Oxford University Press.

20 Hopkins, *Collected Works,* vol. 1 *Correspondence*, 504. This letter of December 1881 is the very one in which Hopkins reflects on the 'obscure' but

'brilliant' Polish Jesuit, whose little emblem book on the life of St Stanislaus is 'much in the style of Herbert and his school', ibid., 503. Emblematic imagery is one of the primary means by which Hopkins builds his interior narrative in the *Wreck*; see Chapter 8.

21 Newman, *The Arians of the Fourth Century*, quoted in Weatherby, *Cardinal Newman*, 84.

22 John Henry Newman, *An Essay in Aid of a Grammar of Assent*, ed. I. T. Ker (Oxford: Clarendon Press, 1985), 73.

23 Newman for the most speaks of the notional as abstractions from the visible or sensible.

24 Weatherby, *Cardinal Newman*, 159.

25 Weatherby here refers to the work of Claude Finney on the Neo-Platonic tradition in English poetry; Weatherby, *Cardinal Newman*, 110, 137.

26 Sulloway, *Gerard Manley Hopkins and the Victorian Temper*, 184.

27 G. M. Hopkins, *The Sermons and Devotional Writings of Gerard Manley Hopkins*, ed. S. J. Christopher Devlin (London: OUP, 1959), 107. All material from this title is published by permission of Oxford University Press.

28 Nixon, *Gerard Manley Hopkins and His Contemporaries*, 103.

29 Margaret Johnson, *Gerard Manley Hopkins and Tractarian Poetry* (Aldershot: Ashgate, 1997), 169.

30 Weatherby, *Cardinal Newman*, 107.

31 Hopkins, *Collected Works*, vol. 1 *Correspondence*, 506.

32 Nixon, *Gerard Manley Hopkins and His Contemporaries*, 87.

33 Weatherby, *Cardinal Newman*, 162.

34 McGinn, *The Foundations of Mysticism*, 124.

# 2 Divine Labour

## Contemplation, *Energeia*, Stress

> we all beholding the glory of the Lord with open face, are transformed into the same image from glory to glory, as by the Spirit of the Lord.
>
> (2 Cor. 3.18)

Christian contemplation has clear philosophical roots, deriving from the Platonic understanding of contemplation or *theoria* – the intellectual vision of the truth. In the patristic period, Christianity and Neo-Platonism meet at the level of mysticism, and it is with Origen, the most Platonic of Christian writers, that the mystical tradition begins. There are no doubt important differences. Platonist mysticism is based on the soul's kinship with the divine, whereas for Christianity after Origen, humanity is created *ex nihilo*. At the same time, the biblical idea that man is made in the image of God suggests a modified form of this kinship, and this theme receives extensive treatment by the Greek fathers. In the philosophical theology of early Christian tradition, not only Plato, but also Aristotle and the Stoics are equally important. Middle Platonism, which takes many of its emphases from Aristotle, exerts a more considerable influence on the Church Fathers than might seem likely.[1] Both Clement and Origen argue the gnosis or higher knowledge of Christ as the key to understanding the world. They emphasise the soul's journey through progressive deification to divine union, urging the practice of contemplation as the means and end of this higher knowledge. For the Greek fathers, contemplation is allied with both earth and heaven. The contemplation of God in created things is followed by the contemplation of God in the afterlife.

In Greek patristic tradition, knowledge is understood as a vision of and participation in the divine. In the last chapter, we saw that the conception of gnosis developed by Clement and Origen becomes the basis of Newman's idea of conscience and real apprehension as the intuitive vision of God. In his *Grammar of Assent*, Newman importantly acknowledges Aristotle as his master, citing the *Metaphysics* as a key influence. After completing his studies at Oxford, Hopkins wrote a short essay on Aristotle in 1868, two years after his reception into the Roman

Catholic church by Newman. At the time, Hopkins was a guest in Newman's house, and Newman himself was writing his *Grammar of Assent*. Hopkins's short essay focusses on the relation between Aristotle's metaphysics and ethics, reflecting on Aristotle's analysis of being in terms of *kinesis* (motion), *dynamis* (potentiality) and *energeia* (activity). In the *Metaphysics*, it is *kinesis* or motion that first suggests the notion of *energeia*, but while *kinesis* remains incomplete (as process) *energeia* is itself complete (as activity).[2] Commonly translated as 'activity, operation', *energeia* can also be understood as 'actuality', having its end within itself. The word derives from *ergon*, 'work, function, action'; *energeia* is 'being at work', from which derives the modern day 'energy'. Hopkins in his essay reflects:

> There are three stages in the conception of all Beings – the potential, the actual, and the passing fr. the one to the other: these answer to the Not-being, Being, and Becoming wh. appear in various philosophies fr. Heracleitus to Hegel.

The passing-over or becoming, Hopkins reflects, is called by Aristotle "process" or "motion", defined as *energeia*.[3]

Hopkins goes on to observe that in the concrete world, potentiality and actuality relate to matter and form. Human beings cannot apprehend either pure matter or pure form. But between these two is a spectrum of being that comprises 'matter in various degrees of form. The change or passing fr. the one to the other is motion and its meaning is form [,] the realisation of form in matter.' So, 'form is called the end or final cause, motion is called the outworking or [*energeia*].' In nature, the action of some efficient cause drives matter to its fullest or highest form. Man too, Hopkins reflects, may be understood as matter and form, 'mind being the form of man'. Hopkins writes:

> the absolutely highest end of man; it must be the fullest *action* of his mind – that is contemplation, and that on the purest attainable forms, namely what is eternally and unchangeably true. But for many reasons this is only possible to a few...[4]
>
> (my italics)

Hopkins, like Aristotle, regards seeing, thinking and understanding as instances of *energeia*, these activities being the characteristic function of the human mind. In the Greek tradition, mind is *nous*, understood as the ability of the soul to contemplate form. Of course, the ultimate *energeia* is the Prime Mover, whose absolutely pure *energeia* is *noesis* (intellectual apprehension). Put differently, God thinks himself and this thought is the proper function of God and man; in practising contemplation, man most closely approaches the life of God. Becoming, for Hopkins, is motion as *energeia*. In man, the activity of contemplation brings union with God, fulfilling the highest potential of the individual soul.

In another 1868 essay, Hopkins discusses the idea of being in the work of Parmenides. The pre-Socratic thinker is widely regarded as the father of metaphysics and was an important influence on Plato and Aristotle. In this essay, Hopkins translates the original Greek of Parmenides' poem while simultaneously commenting on it. Hopkins writes:

> Thou couldst never either know or say / what was not, there wd. be no coming at it. There wd. be no bridge, no stem of stress between us and things to bear us out and carry the mind over...[5]
>
> To be and to know or Being and thought are the same. The truth in thought is Being, stress, and each word is one way of acknowledging Being and each sentence by its copula is (or its equivalent) the utterance and assertion of it.[6]

It is in Hopkins's Parmenides essay that he first uses the much-discussed terms 'instress' and 'inscape'. Critics have often written on Hopkins's association of stress and being. But what is striking here is the similarity between Hopkins's description of a 'bridge' or 'stem of stress' that can 'carry the mind over' and his discussion of *energeia* as 'motion' or 'outworking' in his Aristotle essay. That Hopkins himself explicitly relates 'stress' to *energeia* is briefly noted by Bernadette Ward in her study of Hopkins's philosophical theology. Ward makes an interesting observation. She writes:

> Considering that stress is also identified with "efficacy" as *energeia*, and considering that he wrote these notes in Newman's household... it seems likeliest that stress refers to the real in the sense of Newman's Real Apprehension, rather than the fully ontological meaning of real being.[7]

Ward refers here to Hopkins's equation of 'efficacy' and 'stress' in his 1880 notes, relating this to the Parmenides essay. But what remains implicit in Ward's discussion is the relation between contemplation and *energeia* as it developed in Greek patristic tradition. This is a tradition Hopkins knew directly and also through Tractarians such as Newman and Pusey. Hopkins's discussion of matter, form and motion in Aristotle's *Metaphysics* at a time when he was reading Newman and the Greek fathers strongly suggests that this discussion relates to similar considerations in patristic philosophical theology. Greek writing on the subject of *energeia* was based on St Paul's use of the term and this conception of activity or energy, as developed by Paul and the fathers, is key to Hopkins's extraordinarily dynamic view of being. From this patristic tradition derives the heart of Hopkins's spirituality and poetics, and the heart of his mystical world view.

Although there is no single doctrine of the energies in Greek Christianity, this theme is anticipated in Clement and Origen, and was more explicitly examined during the later stages of the Arian controversy when a clarification of the role of the Holy Spirit came to the fore.[8] Origen himself suggests contemplation to be the defining activity of the Trinity and of all spiritual beings, the unifying principle of the cosmos. In his *De Principiis*, Origen describes Christ gazing upon the Father, painting a striking picture of a world in which all beings are sustained through their contemplation of God. Origen suggests that when these minds fell from their contemplative state they became embodied souls who must liberate themselves from bodily existence to become minds again, ascending to contemplation of the divine. Origen's theory of the pre-existence was deemed heretical in light of the Nicene doctrine of creation *ex nihilo*, yet his writings remain the basis of western contemplation. In his Commentary on the *Song of Songs*, Origen suggests a threefold division of philosophy into ethics, natural contemplation and finally 'enoptics' (inspective contemplation). According to Origen, the individual first learns virtue, then understands the natural world and finally ascends to divine contemplation through contemplation of the soul.

Aristotle's argument for the hylomorphism (from the Greek *hylē*, 'matter'; *morphē*, 'form') of all created things is upheld by Origen and other Greek fathers. Eastern fathers use the term *hylē* or matter to refer to what Aristotle calls prime matter, 'a substratum of pure potentiality'.[9] The terminology of *energeia* is employed by Athanasius when he refers to the Holy Spirit as the activity of the Son, during the Arian controversy of the fourth century.[10] While Arius understands the Son as an immutable creature, Athanasius contests this on the basis of an Aristotelian ontology. Such a creature, Athanasius argues, implies a metaphysical impossibility even God cannot surmount. For the Greek fathers, as for Augustine in the West, any creature is that which comes from non-being and can therefore return to non-being. Athanasius' argument effectively employs the distinctions between God and creatures discussed by Aristotle in *Metaphysics* XII.[11] Aristotle's Prime Mover argument suggests that creatures that are *moved* from non-being into being must be moved by something immovable – not inactive but perfect, a perfect being with no potential for change. Having no potentiality, God has no prime matter, being instead pure *energeia*. Like Aristotle, the early fathers understand God as truly immaterial, immutable, atemporal and infinite or aspatial. Critically, as Nathan Jacobs points out, such a God 'cannot know the potential for either increase or decrease in goodness. Hence, whatever he was is what he is and always will be. In short, God is necessarily incorruptible.'[12]

Arguing for the divinity of Christ and the Holy Ghost, Athanasius was responsible for the first work devoted specifically to the Holy Spirit.

In *Letters to Serapion*, he writes: '...the activity (*energeia*) of the Trinity is one...For there is nothing that is not originated and actuated [*energeitai*] through the Word in the Spirit.'[13] Athanasius's argument moves from the unity of activity to the unity of *ousia* or substance; his use of *homoouisios* becomes the key Christological term of the debate and is discussed at length by Newman. At the same time, Athanasius suggests that the divine activity has a certain structure; God the Father does all things 'through the Word in the Spirit'.[14] Athanasius's response to the Arian controversy would become the basis of Trinitarian orthodoxy, and Greek patristic writing on *energeia* was based on the use of the term in the writings of St Paul. As David Bradshaw notes, Athanasius effectively brought together the properly metaphysical (or Trinitarian) and religious (or Pauline) strands of thought and this became a distinguishing feature of Eastern theology.

In order to describe how human life can participate in the life of God, the fathers turn to the union language of scripture. The Pauline language of baptism describes corruptible flesh putting on the incorruptibility of God. This is particularly the work of the Spirit, who is the operation of God in the created world. Participation in the divine life is participation in the divine activity or *energeia*. Hopkins reflects on these ideas when writing his 1880/1881 notes on the concluding meditation of Ignatius's *Spiritual Exercises*, the 'Contemplation for Obtaining Love'. He observes:

> The second point is to consider how God dwells in creatures: in the elements giving them being; in the plants giving them growth; in the animals giving them sensation; in men giving them understanding; and so in me giving me being, life, sensation, and causing me to understand; making likewise of me a temple, since I am created to the likeness and image of his Divine Majesty.[15]

To contemplate the outer world is, in Hopkins's words, to contemplate the manner in which God

> works and labours for me in all the created things on the face of the earth, [even as a workman], as in the heavens, elements, plants, fruits, flocks. etc., giving them being...growth and sensation, etc., and then to reflect on myself.[16]

Here, as elsewhere in his spiritual notes, Hopkins describes God's 'working' in a manner that strongly resembles the Greek fathers. In the context of early Greek Christianity, the divine *energeia* specifically comes to mean the activity by which God manifests Himself in the world. For Hopkins too, the activity of God is not merely the interventions of God in the world, but the expression of divinity as it communicates itself to and operates within the created world. In clarifying this second point of the *Exercises*, Hopkins goes on to elaborate:

> God's Power or Operation, which is attributed especially to the Third Person, is put in the second instead of the third place...because St Ignatius is dwelling on the thought of communication, and the Holy Ghost is the communication or the communion of the Father and the Son. It is by communication of his power that God operates the likeness of himself in things, so that this exertion or operation comes between his presence and his essence (or nature) – Aug. 14, 1882.[17]

*Operatio* is the Latin translation of *energeia*, and Hopkins's emphatic portrayal of God's 'exertion' or 'operation' as coming between God's presence and essence is resoundingly reminiscent of the Greek energies. As in the Greek fathers, there is here a strong focus on the Spirit as God's active operation in creation. Traditionally, the Holy Ghost is understood as the communication of the Father and Son, but Hopkins extends this idea of communication to the whole of the created order. His observations reflect the patristic understanding of the energies as that mode of divinity communicated to and shared with creation. In his spiritual prose, Hopkins describes the contemplation of the natural world as the apprehension of this divine activity in the world. In his Notes on Contemplation, Hopkins reflects on the traditional structure of an Ignatian meditation as based on the three faculties of the soul. By 'will' Hopkins clarifies that he means less the practical will than the 'faculty of fruition' by which we like or dislike, a faculty to which all intellectual affections belong. Reflecting on the three faculties of memory, understanding and will, Hopkins writes:

> For all three faculties are the mind, the intellect, *νοûς*... It should have been added that as the first faculty directed towards God is the sense of God's presence the second is that of His essence; the third that of His power, that is / the display of His hand or finger working in the world...[18]

Hopkins's analysis is critical in a number of ways. It is significant that Hopkins uses the Greek *nous*, 'mind' or 'intellect'. In the Platonic and Aristotelian traditions, *nous* is specifically the contemplative faculty through which God is apprehended. While the modern terms 'mind' or 'intellect' imply only reasoning or rational thought, *nous* suggests the intellect not divorced from feeling, but moved by desire. By means of *nous* the soul aspires to a knowledge that is a direct contact, a touch or something seen. It is clear that Hopkins similarly understands the intellect not in its narrow modern meaning, but as including the will and the affections. We might think here of Origen's description of the 'intellect', 'heart' or 'governing faculty' as contemplator, where all three refer to the higher element of the soul.

The second important point to be made here is that Hopkins clearly differentiates between God's essence, presence and 'power'. Hopkins's terminology is in keeping with patristic writing on the energies (while Clement and Origen speak of God's 'operation' or 'power', 'energies' becomes the technical term from the fourth century on). In this passage, Hopkins seems to draw out this meaning with every phrase, equating God's 'power' with his 'display' and 'finger working in the world'. Hopkins's emphasis on God's working shows strong affinities with the theology of Clement and Origen, for whom the activity of God at work in the world is the heart of their teaching. As one scholar observes, Clement and Origen possess 'a real doctrine of the continuity and energy of God's working in the world – that is, a theology worthy of the Holy Spirit.' Hopkins similarly concludes his notes on the 'Contemplation for obtaining love', writing:

> This...is the contemplation of the Holy Ghost sent to us through creatures. Observe then it is on love and the Holy Ghost is called Love ("*Fons vivus*, *ignis*, *caritas*"); shewn [in]... the works of God's finger...consisting "*in communicatione*" etc... the Holy Ghost is uncreated grace and the sharing by man of the divine nature ... All things therefore are charged with love, are charged with God and if we know how to touch them give off sparks and take fire, yield drops and flow, ring and tell of him.[19]

Most critics have opposed a reading of Hopkins as mystic, suggesting this to be a loose, easy categorisation that renders Hopkins susceptible to a charge of pantheism. Yet Hopkins's assertion that 'all things' are 'charged with God' seems uncomfortably close to the very meaning of *pan theos* – all is God. Hopkins's mystical vision finds confirmation in the Greek doctrine of the energies, centred on the Spirit. Through the activity of the Spirit creation participates in divinity – and most capable of this participation and perfection is the human soul. As Hopkins writes, 'the Holy Ghost is uncreated grace and the sharing by man of the divine nature'. This seems as close a transliteration of the patristic idea of deification as possible. For the Greek fathers, grace is specifically uncreated, that is, divine. Grace is the energy or procession of the divine nature as communicated to creation. In Hopkins's words, this is a world charged with God. Hopkins's description of 'charge', like 'stress', is closely reminiscent of 'energy'. As Bradshaw importantly points out, the divine glory of the Old Testament and the divine energies of the New Testament are one and the same. In the Old Testament theophanies, it is the glory of God that is contemplated. In New Testament terminology, this glory is the divine *energeia* or working in the world. In Hopkins's famous sonnet 'Pied Beauty' he describes creation as glorifying God, contrasting the pied beauty of the created world with the unchanging beauty of its creator. The sonnet presents a string of 'dappled things', compounds of colour and form:

> GLORY be to God for dappled things—
> For skies of couple-colour as a brinded cow;
> For rose-moles all in stipple upon trout that swim;
> ... ... ...
> All things counter, original, spare, strange;
> Whatever is fickle, freckled (who knows how?)
> With swift, slow; sweet, sour; adazzle, dim;
> He fathers-forth whose beauty is past change:
> Praise him.

As Hopkins reflects in his spiritual notes, the first intention of God outside himself, '*ad extra*, outwards, the first outstress of God's power was Christ'. Christ went forth from God not only in the intrinsic, eternal procession of the Trinity, but also in an extrinsic procession, out of which comes all of creation.[20] The sole reason for this, Hopkins writes, is to give God glory. Read in relation to the philosophical speculations of the early fathers, it is possible to understand 'Pied Beauty' as referring to an Aristotelian hylomorphism. All 'dappled things' are compounds of matter and form; all creation is in this way 'pied'. Created and sustained by the will or *energeia* of God, creation simultaneously testifies to and is a manifestation of his glory. If, as Hopkins writes, becoming is motion understood as *energeia*, only God as Prime Mover remains unchangeable. God as pure actuality is alone beyond creation, having no prime matter. In contrast with the pied beauty of this world, God 'fathers forth', divinity whose beauty is 'past change'. Man must 'praise him'. In his Notes on Contemplation, Hopkins reflects that the faculty of memory identifies and reasons; the faculty of understanding 'issues in praise', whilst the will issues in 'enjoyment, which issues in love, which issues in service'. But 'practice or action' may issue from any of the three.[21] The world for Hopkins is charged with the love of God, and it is the action of contemplation that reads the world as word of God and testament to his glory.

> God's Grandeur
>
> The world is charged with the grandeur of God.
> It will flame out, like shining from shook foil;
> It gathers to a greatness, like the ooze of oil
> Crushed. Why do men then now not reck his rod?
> Generations have trod, have trod, have trod;

And all is seared with trade; bleared, smeared with toil;
And wears man's smudge and shares man's smell: the soil
Is bare now, nor can foot feel, being shod.

And for all this, nature is never spent;
There lives the dearest freshness deep down things;
And though the last lights off the black West went
Oh, morning, at the brown brink eastward, springs—
Because the Holy Ghost over the bent
World broods with warm breast and with ah! bright wings.

For the Greek fathers, grace is a procession of the energies shining forth eternally from the divine essence. The grandeur of God, in Hopkins's poem, is God's glory or *energeia*, depicted here in images of light and flame. Hopkins's striking evocations of exertion or pressure – 'ooze of oil / Crushed' – bear out too this sense of divine activity or working; the pressure and action of God's will. In patristic writing, *energeia* is synonymous with the will of God, which sustains all of creation. Hopkins's sonnet similarly offers a vision of the natural world upheld and renewed by divine love. The poem powerfully presents a world charged with love and with the energies of the Spirit. As Hopkins writes in his notes, 'the Holy Ghost is called Love ("*Fons vivus, ignis, caritas*")'. Patristic writers often conceived the created world as filled with uncreated energies; they emphasised the universe as lying within the embrace of God, encompassed by the Spirit.[22] Hopkins too portrays the Holy Ghost as enlivening, glorifying and renewing nature; the Spirit broods over the world, giving birth and being to creation.

Much has been written about Hopkins's theory of stress and his conception of inscape. This reading locates the source of Hopkins's 'stress' in the Aristotelian conception of *energeia* as applied within Pauline and patristic tradition. For Hopkins, as for the Greek fathers, both outer and inner world are unified by the principle of *energeia* – the divine energies operate in the world at large and in the inner world of the human heart. This is the essence of Hopkins's energetic vision of the world – a world that is the activity of God, because the very being of things is the divine activity. This is what Hopkins means when he equates Being and stress in his Parmenides essay where the term 'instress' first appears. Stress is being in the sense that all things have their being through God's exertion or operation. Conversely, the act of instressing the inscape is the *action* of contemplation that reaches towards the end cause or form. In his notes on Personality, Grace and Free Will, Hopkins reflects

> [Grace] is, I say, any such activity on God's part; so that so far as this action or activity is God's it is divine stress, holy spirit, and, as all is done through Christ, Christ's spirit; so far as it is action,

> correspondence, on the creature's it is *actio salutaris*... It is as if a man said: That is Christ playing at me and me playing at Christ, only that is no play but truth; That is Christ being me and me being Christ.[23]

In this critical passage, Hopkins describes grace as 'action or activity', renaming this activity 'divine stress'. What Hopkins describes here is a dual conception of the operation of grace closely akin to that described by Paul. Paul is the only New Testament author to use the term *energeia*, which he does frequently, writing about this divine activity at both a cosmic and personal level. Paul was Hopkins's favourite scriptural writer, and Hopkins often quotes from his epistles in Greek. The belief that God is active in human beings is rooted in the Old Testament where God's Word or Spirit is the vehicle of divine indwelling. But as Bradshaw points out, 'here the suggestion is one of external control. Paul's use of *energeia* and related terms, such as *sunergein* (to cooperate) and *sunergos* (co-worker), shifts the emphasis from one of external control to one of cooperation.'[24] In Paul and the Greek fathers, the operation of grace suggests the co-operation of the individual in his own salvation. Such an understanding of grace is emphatically dynamic and participatory. Hopkins's seemingly idiosyncratic definition is precisely such a synergistic portrayal of grace, which he describes as having two sides or parts – on God's part, this is 'divine stress, holy spirit' and on the part of the creature it is 'action, correspondence'. 'Correspondence' is a virtual synonym for that divine/human synergy characteristic of the Greek conception of grace. The term evokes too the activity of contemplation – for if 'correspondence' is '*actio salutaris*' then we must remember that for Hopkins, contemplation is the highest action of the mind, by which the human being fulfils his highest destiny.

Something of this synergy of stress and instress is described by Paul in Colossians 1.29. Here, Paul writes of the internal operation of divine activity, describing himself as 'striving according to Christ's working (or energy, *energeia*), which is being made effective (or actualized, *energoumenēn*) in me'. As Bradshaw notes, 'the divine *energeia* serves two distinct functions. It is at work within Paul, transforming him, so that from this standpoint he is the object of God's activity and, at the same time, it finds expression in Paul's struggle'.[25] In another famous passage, Paul again discusses this divine operation within the soul. In Ephesians, he describes the church as the body of Christ with Christ himself as its head. Every Christian is a part of this mystical body and Paul describes how 'the effectual working (*energeian*) in the measure of every part, maketh increase of the body unto the edifying of itself in love' (Eph. 4.16). In other words, God works within and through the individual; the salutary action of the individual is also part of the activity of the body of Christ, directed by him.

Another Pauline passage key to patristic writing on the energies is Paul's description of the spiritual gifts in Corinthians 12.4–6: 'Now there are diversities of gifts, but the same Spirit...And there are diversities of activities, but it is the same God which worketh all in all.' The word 'activities' is translated from the Greek *energemata*. For the fourth-century Greek fathers, the gifts of the Spirit *are* the energies of God, divinity given to creation. In a sermon preached at St Xavier's, Liverpool, Hopkins analyses this very passage. He writes:

> St Paul is careful to tell us that there are all sorts and varieties of spiritual gifts, each of them the *working* and *manifestation* of the one spirit. Therefore he is called the finger of the Father's right hand, that is all the fingers, for the fingers are the hand or arm as many things are to one. This, I say, is answerable to his name and the manner of his being – to his name, which is Spirit or Breath ...[26]
>
> (my italics)

Like the early fathers, Hopkins understands these gifts as the vitalising, active presence of the divine. His description of the Spirit as 'breath' calls up the Greek 'pneuma', which in early philosophical usage suggests immanent deity. This immanence is at the forefront of Hopkins's mind as he describes the Spirit as God's finger or fingers, the working of the divine energies in their plurality, shared with and communicated to creation.

The importance of the doctrine of the energies is that it forms the ground of all mystical experience. The energies are precisely a realm of reciprocity: creation shares in divinity by sharing in the glory, energies or activity of God. The activity of God's will brings creation into being and the whole of creation reflects the glory of God. But while nature does this simply by virtue of its being, it is man alone who must of his own will choose to the path of 'salutary action', the action that will bring him to the divine. Taken as a whole, it is possible to see how the metaphysical understanding of created being as composed of matter and form becomes part of the defence of free will. In divinity, freedom and moral determination co-exist; God's will and action are the same. In the creature, freedom to choose means that sinful action can move the creature away from the divine life towards non-being. So, the creature is corruptible, while God is necessarily incorruptible. In his Long Retreat notes of 1881, Hopkins reflects: 'man himself was created for Christ as Christ's created nature for God' (cf. 1. Cor. 2.22, 23). In an obscure commentary that seems to echo Origen's Platonic conception of the pre-existence of souls, Hopkins writes:

> The elect then were created in Christ some before his birth, like Abraham, some before their own, as St. Ignatius; that so their correspondence with grace and seconding of God's designs is like a taking

> part in their own creation, the creation of their best selves. And again the wicked and the lost are like halfcreations and have but a halfbeing.[27]

The 'taking part' in the creation of one's best self, as Hopkins puts it, is correspondence with grace. But if God simply determined the direction or choice of the human will this would destroy the idea of freedom. It is rather the concert of freedom and grace, characteristic of the Greek fathers, that is reflected in Hopkins. The co-operation between God and man entails a free decision on the part of the human subject. It is Origen who first suggests the idea of human synergy with God in the shaping of human destiny, strongly asserting the 'free assent' of the will. Origen writes, 'the will is free and so subject to commendation or condemnation'.[28] In Hopkins too, divine stress is met by what he describes as 'counter-stress', the human subject's assent to the will of God. In his notes on Personality, Grace and Free Will, Hopkins elaborates his idea of correspondence through a detailed discussion of the will. His argument is grounded in a declaration of the freedom of the elective will

> ...taking the matter [of correspondence] more in particular, I understand at bottom to be meant the simple act of *arbitrium*...For there must be something which shall be truly the creature's in the work of corresponding with grace: this is the *arbitrium*, the verdict on God's side, the saying Yes, the "doing-agree" (to speak barbarously)...no more than the mere wish, discernible by God's eyes, that it might do as he wishes, might correspond, might say Yes to him; correspondence itself is on man's side not so much corresponding as the wish to correspond, and this least sigh of desire, this one aspiration, is the life and spirit of man.[29]

In this passage, Hopkins relates 'correspondence' to the 'simple *act* of *arbitrium*' or will. There must be something that is truly the creature's in the work of corresponding with grace. What Hopkins describes as the wish to correspond or 'doing-agree' is the equivalent of Origen's free assent. Hopkins goes on to reflect that it is by the operation of the Spirit that souls are 'raised to the state when their deeds should be the doing of God in them'. In other words, Hopkins effectively describes a state in which the activity of the human will merges with that of God's Spirit. There could scarcely be a better rendition of that coalescence of human and divine wills suggested by Paul and developed by the Greek fathers. Elsewhere in his notes, Hopkins refers to Ephesians 3.16–19, quoting in Greek: 'That he would grant you, according to the riches of his glory, to be strengthened by his Spirit with might unto the inward man.' (Eph. 3.16) This 'display of divine power' in the 'inward man' is related by Hopkins to Ephesians 2.10 'For we are his workmanship, created in

Christ Jesus unto good works, which God hath before ordained that we should walk in them.'[30] Once again, Hopkins suggests the very being of each individual to be created first in Christ. The soul's turning to God is, in other words, simultaneously a taking part in its own creation and a participation in divinity through a sharing in the activity or 'working' of God. This synergy is based first on that free assent, the saying Yes, the 'doing-agree'. Turning to one of Hopkins's best-known sonnets,

> As kingfishers catch fire, dragonflies draw flame;
> As tumbled over rim in roundy wells
> Stones ring; like each tucked string tells, each hung bell's
> Bow swung finds tongue to fling out broad its name;
> Each mortal thing does one thing and the same:
> Deals out that being indoors each one dwells;
> Selves – goes itself; myself it speaks and spells,
> Crying *What I do is me: for that I came.*
>
> I say more: the just man justices;
> Keeps grace: that keeps all his goings graces;
> Acts in God's eye what in God's eye he is –
> Christ. For Christ plays in ten thousand places,
> Lovely in limbs, and lovely in eyes not his
> To the Father through the features of men's faces.

The 'Kingfishers...' sonnet enacts the operation of grace at two levels – the outer realm of the natural world and the inner realm of the soul. In the first part of the poem, Hopkins suggests a world charged or enlivened by the energies of God: stones ring, fire and flame emanate from kingfishers or dragonflies. As Hopkins writes in his 1868 notes, becoming is motion as *energeia*. This understanding of being as the activity or operation of something is precisely what Hopkins suggests when he describes the cry of each mortal thing: '*What I do is me: for that I came.*' This doing is a process of dealing out, for every living thing 'deals out that being indoors each one dwells'. Hopkins's words here can be read in light of his spiritual notes in which he describes Christ as the first 'intention' of God 'outside himself...*ad extra,* outwards, the first outstress of God's power'.[31] This vitalising activity of being *is* the glory of God in this world. For the human being, this outstressing of being is a co-operative activity. Hopkins, like Paul and the Greek fathers, sees the ultimate freedom and fulfilment of the self in its turning to God, its participation in the divine nature. The 'Kingfishers' sonnet is thrown into clearer relief when read alongside one of the best-known passages of the New Testament. In Philippians 2.13 Paul writes, 'For it is God that worketh in you both to will and to do of his good pleasure'. As Bradshaw points out, Paul's exhortation to act is coupled with a reminder that it is

God who is acting; both 'worketh' and 'to do' translate the same verb, *energein*, cognate with *energeia*.[32] This is the synergy between the soul and Christ that Hopkins describes here: 'the just man justices; Keeps grace… Acts in God's eye what in God's eye he is – / Christ'. The emphasis on deed and action is the unifying principle of stress or *energeia*. The best paraphrase perhaps is Hopkins's own definition of grace as activity: Christ playing at me and me playing at Christ, Christ being me and me being Christ.

## Duns Scotus, Aristotle and Actuality

In discussing the idea of *energeia* or actuality in Hopkins, it is important to consider too the role of Duns Scotus, one of the most influential philosopher-theologians of the middle ages. Hopkins's exuberant discovery of Duns Scotus is well known, though what remains little discussed is Scotus's development of Aristotle's conception of actuality. The most extensive treatment Scotus gives to Aristotle's doctrine is in Book IX of his Questions on the *Metaphysics* of Aristotle. Scotus also discusses actuality in his *Ordinatio*, the very text that began Hopkins's lifelong enthusiasm for the philosopher. Hopkins read the *Ordinatio* in 1872, two years before he began his theological studies in Wales. Here Scotus proposes his well-known formal distinction. According to Scotus, there is in each individual a principle that accounts for its being the very thing it is and a formally distinct principle that accounts for its being the kind of thing it is; the former is its individual difference, the latter its common nature. This individual difference is what Scotus calls *haeccitas* or thisness. The distinction between individual difference and common nature is that between thisness and whatness. Critically, Scotus insists that thisness flows from the actuality or *energeia* of the object in question. It is precisely the conception of thisness in Scotus that Hopkins seizes upon with great interest when discussing his notion of 'pitch':

> …*pitch* is ultimately simple positiveness, that by which being differs from and is more than nothing and not-being, and it is with precision expressed by the English *do*…So that this pitch might be expressed, if it were good English, the *doing* be, *the doing* choose… Where there was no question of will it would become mere fact; where there is will it is free action, moral action.[33]

Hopkins immediately goes on to exclaim: 'Is not this pitch or whatever we call it then the same as Scotus's *ecceitas*?' As Hopkins writes in the Kingfishers sonnet, each individual thing does one thing and the same, crying '*what I do is me: for that I came*.' This 'doing' is what comprises the individuality of every thing. Individuality is grounded in actuality. This, vitally, is the reason why Hopkins associates *haecceitas* not with inscape, as some critics have done, but with pitch or determination – that is, with stress.

Scotus himself develops his famous formal distinction mainly in connection with the Trinity, distinguishing between the substance of God and the divine attributes or perfections (goodness, wisdom, justice, for example). For the Greek fathers, God's attributes lie in the realm of the energies, and creatures participate in these perfections. That the formal distinction Scotus proposes begins with his differentiation between God's substance and attributes supports the argument that this distinction is comparable with the essence-energies distinction of Eastern theology. It has been suggested that Hopkins's enthusiastic discovery of Scotus was likely due to the fact that he found in the theologian confirmation of views he already held. This perhaps applies to Hopkins's conception of the energies of God, which finds continuation in the Scotist idea that individual difference flows from actuality.[34] As Hopkins writes in the Kingfishers sonnet, 'selves – *goes* itself, *myself* it speaks and spells'. For Hopkins as for Scotus, thisness flows from actuality or activity. Conversely, the being or stress of each individual thing as experienced in contemplation is the perception of its actuality. This means that in the contemplation of the natural world, the being of the object unites with that of the beholder. As Hopkins writes, whatever you look hard enough at seems to look back at you. In the contemplation of the 'inner man' or soul, this activity in its highest form is correspondence with grace.

The Greek doctrine of the energies goes a long way towards explaining Hopkins's peculiarly energetic vision of the world. For Hopkins contemplation is activity. It is the contemplation of the divine working in the outer world of nature and the inner space of the heart. What exactly it means to perceive this activity or actuality with respect to an inanimate object can in part be understood as a kind of radiance of the object, experienced in intuitive apprehension. Scotus emphasises that an object's individuality is apprehended in an intuitive grasp preceding abstractive, intellectual knowledge. Contemplation is that which exceeds vision; to go back to the Platonic *nous* this is a mode of knowledge that is direct contact; something seen or felt. All things are charged with God, but we must know how to *touch* them.

In 'Hurrahing in Harvest' we see this merging of vision, knowledge and love in a celebratory invocation of the divine presence in the world. Hopkins lifts up 'heart, eyes' to glean God in the surrounding landscape. Then, inverting this, it is the 'eyes, heart' that receive the response. As Hopkins writes, 'these things, / these things were here and but the beholder wanting, / which two when once they meet, / the heart hurls for him…O half hurls earth for him off under his feet'. As is clear from Hopkins's words, this is no static contemplation but instead an instressing of the divine stress that enlivens the world. For Hopkins, the world is not merely evidence of God's design. God is not simply inferred from his workmanship. Instead, the very being of things is the working or *energeia* of God. Hopkins's God is an Aristotelian one, or the *energeia* of the Prime Mover as described by Bradshaw – 'a being that is pure energy, an energy that constitutes the being of other things'.[35] To engage in contemplation is to participate in the activity that upholds the world, unifying beholder and object. This is why the act of looking or contemplating in Hopkins's poetry frequently merges with images of fire, light, lightning, sound. This explains too the emphasis on speaking, telling, uttering – all forms of *energeia*. The doctrine of the energies grounds Hopkins in Christian theology, guards against pantheism and suggests an answer to the general question of Hopkins's mysticism. If mysticism is frequently thought of as a disregard for the physical world in favour of an immaterial, spiritual realm, the doctrine of the energies provides an explanation of how Hopkins can be a mystic and yet be wholly engaged with the world. For Hopkins, the material world is the utterance and expression of God, a world whose being is defined by the metaphysical principle of *energeia* or stress.

## Notes

1 For a full discussion of this subject, see Andrew Louth, *The Origins of the Christian Mystical Tradition: From Plato to Denys* (Oxford: Clarendon Press, 1981).
2 Francis E. Peters, *Greek Philosophical Terms: A Historical Lexicon* (New York: New York University Press, 1967), 56.
3 G. M. Hopkins, 'Connection of Aristotle's Metaphysics with His Ethics' in *Collected Works,* vol. 4 *Oxford Essays and Notes,* 263–64. All material from this title is published by permission of Oxford University Press.
4 Ibid., 265.
5 Hopkins, 'Parmenides' in *Collected Works,* vol. 4 *Oxford Essays and Notes,* 313.
6 Ibid., 315.
7 Bernadette Waterman Ward, *World as Word: Philosophical Theology in Gerard Manley Hopkins* (Washington, DC: Catholic University of America Press, 2002), 117.
8 David Bradshaw, *Aristotle East and West: Metaphysics and the Division of Christendom* (Cambridge: CUP, 2004), 154. Bradshaw's book extensively examines the relationship between God's being and activity in Christian philosophy; Chapter 7 'The formation of the eastern tradition' is particularly relevant here.
9 This is discussed in detail in a chapter by Nathan Jacobs, 'Created Corruptible, Raised Incorruptible: The Importance of Hylomorphic Creationism to the Free Will Defense' in J. Farris and C. Taliaferro (eds), *The Ashgate Research Companion to Theological Anthropology* (Farnham: Ashgate Publishing Ltd., 2015), 262–75.
10 Bradshaw, *Aristotle East and West,* 154.
11 Jacobs, *Hylomorphic Creationism,* 269.
12 Ibid.
13 Bradshaw, *Aristotle East and West,* 155.
14 Ibid.

15 Hopkins, *Sermons and Devotional Writings,* 193.
16 Ibid.
17 Hopkins, *Sermons and Devotional Writings,* 195.
18 Ibid., 174.
19 Hopkins, *Sermons and Devotional Writings,* 195.
20 Hopkins, *Sermons and Devotional Writings,* 197.
21 Ibid., 174.
22 Vladimir Lossky, *The Mystical Theology of the Eastern Church* (New York: St Vladimir's Seminary Press, 1976), 88.
23 Hopkins, *Sermons and Devotional Writings,* 154.
24 Bradshaw, *Aristotle East and West,* 122.
25 Ibid., 121.
26 Hopkins, *Sermons and Devotional Writings,* 98.
27 Hopkins, *Sermons and Devotional Writings,* 197.
28 *The Westminster Handbook to Origen,* ed. John A. McGuckin (Louisville, KY: Westminster John Knox Press, 2004), 176.
29 Hopkins, *Sermons and Devotional Writings,* 154–55.
30 Ibid., 156. Hopkins quotes the original Greek.
31 Hopkins, *Sermons and Devotional Writings,* 197.
32 Bradshaw, *Aristotle East and West,* 122.
33 Hopkins, *Sermons and Devotional Writings,* 151.
34 Peter King, 'Duns Scotus on the Common Nature', *Philosophical Topics* 20 (1992), 11. http://individual.utoronto.ca/pking/articles/Scotus_on_Common_Nature.pdf (accessed 7 September 2016).
35 David Bradshaw, 'The Concept of the Divine Energies' in C. Athanasopolous and C. Schneider (eds), *Divine Essence and Divine Energies: Ecumenical Reflections on the Presence of God in Eastern Orthodoxy* (Cambridge: James Clarke & Co., 2013), 30.

# 3 Tractarian Mysticism and the Deification of the Soul

If divinity alone is purely immaterial and creatures are necessarily hylomorphic, this raises questions within Eastern patristic theology regarding the issue of righteousness. Given its metaphysical composition, how can the creature be confirmed in righteousness? An answer is suggested in 'the idea that creatures participate in the operative powers (*energeiai*) of God through union with Christ and the indwelling Holy Spirit... this feature of Eastern patristic theology supplies the centrepiece of their hope that the believer can put off corruption and put on incorruption.'[1] Hopkins arrived at Oxford in 1863, eighteen years after Newman's conversion and the official end of the Tractarian movement. This was a time of renewed struggle between the university's High Church party and the liberal, utilitarian faction. Hopkins was affiliated with the former. He became a devoted follower of Edward Pusey, Oxford's surviving Tractarian, and formed a close relationship with Pusey's protégé, Canon Liddon. The High Church faction led by Pusey was above all committed to the doctrines of baptismal regeneration and the real presence. In 1861, Pusey reissued Newman's famous Tract 90. Originally published in 1841, Newman's highly controversial interpretation of the Thirty-Nine Articles argued that justification by faith did not imply a denial of baptism as the instrument of justification and regeneration.

Hopkins's ritualist years at Oxford were an important step in his journey to Catholicism and his undergraduate reading list of 1865 includes *The Tracts for the Times*. Two biographies, by Robert Martin and Norman White, discuss Hopkins's Tractarian relations in their wide-ranging exploration of Hopkins's life and works. Both authors focus on points of personal contact and the influence of key figures on Hopkins's personal life. They are not, however, concerned with a consideration of Tractarian theology. Jude Nixon's *Hopkins and his Contemporaries* does examine Hopkins's relation to Liddon and Newman, discussing in detail the Romantic aesthetics of Tractarian poetry.[2] This theme is also taken up by Margaret Johnson in her book *Hopkins and Tractarian Poetry,* which, as the title suggests, focuses on the poetry rather than the theology of the movement. On the whole, there remains a lack of sustained attention to Hopkins's indebtedness to Tractarian religion as delineated in the primary religious documents of the movement. These documents provide a likely conduit for the patristic, sacramental mysticism evidenced in Hopkins's poetry and prose. In many ways, Hopkins's mysticism finds its beginnings in this sacramental mysticism at the heart of Tractarian religion, and in the patristic theology that had so great an influence on Tractarian thought.

From its beginnings in the 1830s, the Oxford Movement defined itself through the publication of its *Tracts for the Times*, which tackled key questions of church doctrine and government. The tracts emphasised the importance of liturgy, sacraments, priesthood, apostolic succession and the authority of clergy and bishops in the Church of England. With its emphasis on tradition and doctrine, as opposed to the Protestant belief in the Bible alone, the Oxford Movement was a rediscovery of patristic tradition. Much of the sacramentalism at the centre of Tractarian thought derived from the patristic tradition of the first four centuries. Pusey was the driving force behind *The Library of the Fathers*, a multivolume translation of a large number of patristic writings that was an important achievement of the Oxford Movement. Many of these are commentaries and a significant place is reserved for the writings of Athanasius and Augustine. Pusey's own definition of the movement as given in 1840 described it as aligning the Church of England with the ancient Catholic church, instead of the reformers.[3] This was the idea behind Newman's Tract 90 and a principle fundamental to the theology of the Oxford Movement. The Tractarians turned to patristic typology and to the sacramental religion of the Fathers to argue for the reality of supernatural grace as conveyed through the sacraments.

The discussion of baptism notoriously divided Tractarians and Evangelicals, with the parties primarily divided on the spiritual effects of the sacraments. Pusey argued the doctrine of baptismal regeneration in his lengthy and meticulous Tract 67, 'Scriptural Views of Baptism' (1835). Baptismal regeneration is also at the heart of Newman's *Lectures on Justification*. Together these works comprise the foremost theological documents of the Oxford Movement. Following Augustine and the ancient Church, both Pusey and Newman argued the sacraments to *convey* and not merely *signify* grace. They understood baptism as the instrument of spiritual regeneration, a death to sin and a birth to new righteousness. Baptism, in other words, was an effective means of spiritual renewal and not a mere symbol of this transformation. Evangelicals, on the other hand, were suspicious of the doctrine of regeneration and opposed to Tractarian notions of salvation through infused sacramental grace. They feared what they perceived as an *ex opere operato* doctrine of sacramental grace, which could lead to either a mechanistic or magical view of religion. Instead, they emphasised the need for a change in affections and inward feeling. The sacramental debates of the 1830s gained new impetus with the Gorham judgement on baptismal theology in 1850 and the Denison case concerning eucharistic theology.[4] At the time of the Gorham controversy, it was Pusey who led the Tractarian side, and disputes on sacramental theology remained at the forefront of Tractarian concerns until the end of the 1850s.

When Hopkins arrived at Oxford his early years as an undergraduate saw his affiliation with the High Church party. As previously, the party stressed the doctrines of baptismal regeneration and the real presence, upholding the importance of the sacraments against an entirely personal interpretation of faith. Hopkins, moving in Tractarian circles, would undoubtedly have been aware of both current discussions and of recent debates. His strong sentiments on the sacraments are made amply clear. Writing to E. H. Coleridge in 1864 Hopkins asserts:

> The great aid to belief and object of belief is the doctrine of the Real Presence in the Blessed Sacrament of the Altar. Religion without that is somber, dangerous, illogical, with that it is—not to speak of its grand consistency and certainty—*loveable.*[5]

Hopkins's words evoke the central mystery of faith as represented by the ancient church – the transforming grace or divine love by which Christ inhabits and conforms the soul. This mystery of love is central to Hopkins's mysticism. It is the operation of the Spirit as love, planted in the soul at baptism and increased through the Eucharistic sacrament. Tractarian religion strongly emphasised this mysterious nature of the sacraments. Transubstantiation, for example, was thought to introduce rationalism into theology and, as Newman suggested, to substitute something earthly for a heavenly mystery.[6] Pusey in his tract on baptismal regeneration similarly expounds the doctrine as a high mystery.[7] In a letter to Bridges, Hopkins offers his own paradoxical formulation of the mystery at the heart of Catholic belief. He writes, 'You do not mean by mystery what a Catholic does. You mean an interesting uncertainty… But a Catholic by mystery means an incomprehensible certainty'.[8]

Though we do not have specific evidence of this, Hopkins was almost certain to have read Newman's Tract 90 and Pusey's equally well-known tract on baptism. Also unlikely to have escaped Hopkins's attention were Newman's *Lectures on Justification* (1837), which drew on patristic theology to counter Evangelical suspicion of baptismal regeneration. The third edition of Newman's *Lectures* was published in 1874, shortly before Hopkins began work on *The Wreck of the Deutschland* in the winter of the following year. Hopkins's ode draws extensively on the patristic symbolism of baptismal regeneration and it seems likely that the publication of Newman's *Lectures* would have come to his attention. At the time of writing the *Wreck,* Hopkins was beginning four years of theological study at St Beuno's and in 1873 he had read Newman's *Grammar of Assent.* The question of justification is a central question in

Christianity and the chief dividing line between Catholicism and Protestantism. What is it that renders the believer justified or holy in the eyes of God? Certainly, this was a question close to Hopkins's heart and one he would return to at many stages of his religious journey. In his lectures, Newman suggests that the two diverging views on justification are reconciled in the ancient theology of Augustine, where justification relates to baptism. It is significant that Newman, in the third edition of his *Lectures*, can assure his readers that he still in all essentials holds the same doctrine that he held before his 1845 conversion to Catholicism. Similarly for Hopkins, the Augustinian and mystical theology at the heart of Newman's *Lectures* provides continuity between a Tractarian and later Roman Catholic faith.

Historically, the Protestant argument for justification by faith alone is made in deliberate opposition to the Catholic understanding of justification through obedience – that is grace in conjunction with good works. Luther taught that believers are righteous on account of the 'alien righteousness of Christ' – a righteousness that remains external to the believer but that is imputed to them through faith.[9] Trent on the other hand asserted that the sole formal cause of justification is 'inward renewal'; the cause of justification is the individual's inherent righteousness, whether habitual or of works. Even further from the idea of inherent righteousness was the Protestant doctrine of 'forensic justification' as developed by Luther's follower Philip Melanchthon. Melanchthon's teaching emphasised justification as a declaration made by God in the heavenly court, when the sinner is counted or pronounced righteous. Though the church from Augustine onwards had understood justification as both the declaration of righteousness and the process of being made righteous, Protestantism increasingly saw justification as an event that altered only the outer status of the sinner (this was complemented by a distinct process of regeneration and interior renewal). While to some extent this seems a matter of definition, it also hides a more profound theological divergence: where Catholic tradition identified only the hope or promise of this redemption, the reformers instead offered an assurance of salvation.

Unsurprisingly, the Protestant assurance of salvation was out of keeping with the devotional nature of Tractarian religion, with its burning desire for holiness and its moral and mystical inclination. As Newman writes in his *Lectures,* '...Protestants, have ended in the notion, that justification is the feeling of satisfaction which belief in God's mercy inspires, and nothing more'.[10] In direct opposition to this, Newman argued for 'imparted righteousness', a concept he derived from patristic sources. The Tractarian critique of Protestant justification accordingly centred on two points. First, Tractarians emphasised the central orthodox principle of obedience, the moral realisation of divine judgment through the holiness of the believer. The second more important point was their assertion of what would be the mystical heart of Tractarian theology: the doctrine of infused or indwelling righteousness, the divine indwelling, given in the Incarnation. Newman in his *Lectures* seeks a *via media*. He argues that the principle of justification by faith is faulty, as faith is not the primary instrument of justification. The principle of justification by obedience, Newman suggests, is correct but incomplete due to the one-sided stress of the later Roman Church, where inward renewal (seen in obedience) is argued as the sole cause of justification.[11] Newman proposes that the Roman view is completed by Augustine's understanding of justification as faith working through the charity of God; that is, justification as God's renewing love, conforming the soul to Himself. Augustine's understanding of justification as the regeneration of baptism becomes Newman's *via media*. And in this profound belief in the baptismal gift of the divine indwelling is the seed and centre of Tractarian mysticism. For Hopkins, the doctrine of the indwelling is central to his religious and mystical development; by this interior spirit of love the soul is raised to contemplation of the divine.

By extolling a doctrine of imparted righteousness, Newman's *Lectures on Justification* articulate a religion centred on love, and on the justifying grace of charity given in baptism. Newman develops his argument by evaluating both sides. In his first lecture, he examines the Protestant doctrine of faith as the instrument of justification. Newman notes that the word 'instrument' suggests the immediate means by which the believer is granted the gift of righteousness. This, he argues, must be none other than the sacrament of baptism. He then makes an even stronger critique of the Lutheran view that faith justifies without the exercise or even the presence of love. In this respect, he argues, the Lutheran doctrine of justification is faulty. Strongly opposing Luther's suggestion that faith justifies before and without love, he notes how far such a view differs from the language of the Homilies. Newman's second lecture is entitled 'Love Considered as the Formal Cause of Justification' and examines the older Catholic view that justification consists in love, or sanctity, or obedience, or 'renewal of the Holy Ghost'. In response to the later Roman stress on inward renewal as the 'only direct cause' of justification, Newman writes:

> does not the grace itself, as an *immediate divine power or presence* [my italics], dwell in the hearts which are gifted with this renovating principle? ...then surely the possession of that grace is really our justification, and not renewal, or the principle of renewal.[12]

Newman suggests that the Protestant and Roman arguments converge in the 'inward divine presence or grace...the presence of the Holy Ghost shed abroad in our hearts, the Author both of faith and of renewal... righteousness is the possession of that presence.'[13]

It is chiefly the language of St Paul and Augustine that Newman calls upon to suggest justification as the imparting of an inward gift. He cites Paul in Titus 3.5 'Not by works of righteousness which we have done, but according to his mercy he saved us, by the washing of regeneration, and renewing of the Holy Ghost'. Newman also quotes Augustine's comments on the passage given in *On the Spirit and the Letter*, 'This is that righteousness of God, which He not only teaches us by the precept of His law, but also bestows upon us by the gift of His Spirit'.[14] Newman returns repeatedly to this idea of righteousness as a gift, not as simply a quality of mind or person. The 'gift of righteousness' described by Paul (Rom. 5.17) is described by Newman as 'a *thing* given...a real and definite something in a person, implanted in him [my italics]'.[15] This cannot, Newman argues, be other than the gift of the Spirit received in baptism. Newman's conception of righteousness as a real presence, a 'thing' within the heart or soul is a fundamentally mystical idea, drawing on an Augustinian conception of infused grace. Paul celebrates this divine presence in his famous portrayal of the human body as the temple of the Spirit. As he asks in 1 Corinthians 6.19, 'know ye not that your body is the temple of the Holy Ghost which is in you, which ye have of God, and ye are not your own?' According to Newman, justification is this mysterious inward gift communicated to the baptised, who from this time on are made temples of God's Spirit. It is important point too that this indwelling is promised as the distinguishing grace of the Gospel. For another important theme of this debate is that justification is on account of the new law in Christ.[16] The old law was given on Mount Sinai, but the Spirit comes to write the divine law in the hearts of believers. As Newman writes, 'Can words be clearer to show that, as the Letter or External Law is that which condemns us to death, so the Spirit, that is the Law written on the heart, or spiritual renovation, is that which *justifies us?*'[17] (2 Cor. 3.3–6).

A more detailed appreciation of Tractarian sacramentalism helps us to see the ways in which Hopkins's *Wreck of the Deutschland* is grounded in the mystical and patristic imagery of baptism. The poem's narrative suggests a sacramental regeneration as the soul's justification. The flying heart that ascends to mystical contemplation of the divine is the heart that reflects the divine image within itself. This indwelling is the presence of the Trinity in the soul, most especially the Spirit, understood as love. Hopkins's notes on the *Spiritual Exercises* importantly reflect on the divine indwelling in the soul. He writes, 'God rests in man as in a place, a *locus*, bed, a vessel, expressly made to receive him...'[18] These formulations of the soul as divine resting place or habitation are at the centre of Hopkins's mysticism. Hopkins's spiritual notes also repeatedly connect the divine indwelling with the intercessory work of the Spirit (cf. Rom. 8.26–27). Like Newman, Hopkins frequently invokes the indwelling presence of the Spirit, whilst alluding also to the divine writing of the new law in the heart. At the opening of *The Wreck of the Deutschland*, Hopkins foregrounds a central subject of the poem: 'the gospel proffer...Christ's gift' (4). The gift of the gospel is the new law of the Spirit. 'Christ's gift' is the Holy Spirit, the soul's interior 'gift of righteousness' (Rom. 5.17). Through its typological and allegorical narrative, the *Wreck* traces the ascent of the baptised soul to the divine. For Hopkins, like Newman, a right heart can only be an Augustinian heart, infused with the divine Spirit.

As Newman develops his *via media* in these lectures he is at pains to demonstrate that justification is ascribed in scripture to the presence of the Spirit – 'and that immediately, neither faith nor renewal intervening'.[19] Newman turns repeatedly to Paul. He writes 'we are said by St Paul to be "washed, sanctified, and *justified,* in the Name of the Lord Jesus, and by the *Spirit of our God.*"'[20] Newman also emphasises the Pauline conception of the Spirit of adoption (cf. Rom. 8.15, 'Ye have not received the spirit of bondage again to fear, but ye have received the *Spirit of adoption,* whereby we cry, Abba, Father', KJV). The Pauline doctrine of divine sonship is an important dimension of Augustine's understanding of justification as regeneration. To be justified is to be translated from sonship of the first Adam to a state of grace and adoption as a son of God through Christ. This translation is achieved through the regeneration of baptism. In this way Newman arrives at the participation of human beings in the glory of the divine nature (cf. 2 Peter 1.4). In this context, he writes of 'the seal, mould, or stamp, with which our souls are marked as God's *coin* impresses His *image* upon them'.[21] Newman draws on both the literal and figurative meaning of the coin. As the *mark* made stands for both the instrument marking and the figure made, so the *image* of God refers sometimes to the original and sometimes to the duplicate or representation. Hopkins's 1876 ode celebrates this divine nature of man, drawing on the double sense of man as the divine image. Stanza 22 of the *Wreck* employs the imagery of the soul as God's coin, his 'dearest prized and priced' 'cinquefoil token'. Hopkins playfully instructs his readers – 'Mark, the mark is of man's make'. Through the poem, Hopkins's narrative of the inward law and mystic presence of Christ through the Spirit is in keeping with Newman's elaboration of the doctrine of justification. As Newman writes, 'though the inward law commonly stands for the new creature, yet it may be said to justify, as standing also for that Archetype of which the new creature is the copy'.[22] This Augustinian model of justification as regeneration or spiritual rebirth implies that man receives a quasi-divine nature as his second nature, becoming 'a new creature' (Gal. 5.6, 6.15); these effects necessarily depend on justifying faith working by charity, and not on 'faith alone'.

While proposing baptism as the instrument of justification, Newman's *Lectures* also emphasise that the cause of justification is above all the death of Christ. In this sense, justification becomes the raising of the cross within the heart and Newman describes the 'gift of the Justifying Cross'.[23] Once again, Newman's understanding of justification is closely bound up with Pauline theology. He specifically draws on Galatians 6.14, the soul's glory as the cross of Christ, 'by whom the world is crucified unto me, and I unto the world' (KJV). Paul's epistle to the Romans, similarly describes baptism as a crucifixion with Christ. Throughout Paul's teaching is an important emphasis on the person and work of Christ in his death and resurrection. This is further connected with a powerful theology of the Spirit central to Pauline thought. Only at Christ's death and departure does the Holy Spirit or Paraclete come into human hearts (cf. Jn. 16.7). Hopkins's sermon on the Gospel of John 16.5–14 closely considers this point. Hopkins reflects:

> You will ask, was not the Holy Ghost like this and did he not work like this before Christ left the world, nay before Christ came into it? did he not then search hearts? did he not then live in the hearts of the just?[24]

Hopkins answers this question in the affirmative, but he understands this work as that of all three persons of the Trinity and not the Spirit in particular. It is only at the time of Christ's death that the Holy Ghost comes with a special role or operation – work to do 'which is his own work and not the Son's and not the Father's. This special work is the glorification of Christ. As Hopkins writes, the Spirit glorifies Christ by inhabiting the heart's temple and making of every Christian 'another Christ, an AfterChrist'. The Tractarian doctrine of the divine indwelling, based on a Pauline theology of the Spirit, is at the centre of Hopkins's theopoetics. Nixon, like James Cotter, has pointed to Liddon's Corinthians lectures and their treatment of Pauline Christology as an important influence on Hopkins. Re-reading *The Wreck* reveals that it is specifically Paul's doctrine of the Spirit that is at the heart of Hopkins's mystical tract and at the heart of Hopkins's mysticism. Hopkins's ode is a hymn to love and to the mystical work of the Spirit who conforms the believer to Christ and brings the soul to contemplative union with God. Hopkins's emphasis on the doctrine of the Spirit aligns him with Newman, whose reading of Paul emphasises the gift of the Spirit as the ground of justification. (Paul's writings also teach a doctrine of 'justification by faith' but Newman accords faith the second place as an instrument *after* baptism.)[25] *The Wreck of the Deutschland* is a testament of mystical love that shows Hopkins, like Newman, to hold the older Catholic view of love as the soul's justification. As Newman writes '*This* is to be justified, to receive the Divine Presence within us, and be made a Temple of the Holy Ghost.'[26]

So, at the heart of Newman's *Lectures on Justification* we find a Pauline and Augustinian theology that rests on the operation of the Spirit and implies too a doctrine of participation in the divine nature. Writing on Newman's *Lectures*, the Tractarian scholar Yngve Brilioth observes, justification becomes the act whereby the human increasingly appropriates the nature of God; it is also the act whereby God actively enters into the individual, drawing him to heaven.[27] So Newman emphasises:

> *This*...is our justification, our ascent through Christ to God, or God's descent through Christ to us; we may call it either of the two; we ascend into Him, He descends into us; we are in Him, He in us... And this is our true Righteousness, – not the mere name of righteousness, not only forgiveness or favour... [but] the *indwelling* of our glorified Lord.[28]
>
> (my italics)

Brilioth notes that the difference between imputed and indwelling righteousness is a distinction between a purely personal and a quasi-physical or substantial form of grace. The latter is found in Augustine, who understands grace through physical analogies, as a divine substance or energy infused within the soul. This idea of grace as substance naturally combines with the Augustinian view of justification as *including* regeneration or sanctification. An individual cannot be granted forgiveness of sins and eternal life unless he is to some extent already a partaker of the divine nature.[29] In Augustine, the two forms of grace are in practice complementary; the mystical operation of grace is found together with a highly personal relation with God. The Tractarians, however, were battling an Evangelical, wholly personalised religion and a conception of grace related only to prayer and devotion. In this respect, they needed to stress the objective gift of divine grace and to revive through patristic doctrine an objective basis of faith, centred in the sacraments and in a mystical conception of grace. To Newman, grace is above all an infusion of the divine nature. At the heart of Tractarian religion, we find a mystical conception of charity as the grace that justifies, the indwelling of the Spirit as love.

In its foremost religious document, Tractarianism propounded an understanding of justification as the mystic presence of Christ, mediated through the sacraments. As Newman powerfully writes in these *Lectures*, 'Christ then is our Righteousness by dwelling in us by the Spirit... *This* is really and truly our justification, not faith, not holiness, not (much less) a mere imputation; but through God's mercy, the very Presence of Christ.'[30] Hopkins, in the famous lines of 'As kingfishers catch fire...', describes this very vision of the justness or righteousness of man.

> I say more: the just man justices;
>     Keeps grace: that keeps all his goings graces;
> Acts in God's eye what in God's eye he is –
>     Christ.

For Hopkins, the justice of the 'just' man consists in precisely this, that he 'Acts in God's eye what in God's eye he is – / Christ'. These lines look forward to Hopkins's notes on the *Spiritual Exercises* and his account of grace as 'divine stress, holy spirit': '[this] is Christ in his member on the one side, his member in Christ on the other...That is Christ *being me* and me being Christ.'[31] Hopkins's description of Christ in his member / his member in Christ is paralleled in the sonnet by a similar semantic doubling: 'Acts in God's eye what in God's eye he is'. Hopkins describes and enacts the soul's identification with Christ; this identification is achieved through the grace of the indwelling Spirit and it is in this way that the soul 'keeps grace'. Hopkins's vision of the 'just' man is fully in keeping with a Tractarian and Augustinian understanding of justification as the interior presence of Christ through the Spirit. Many of Hopkins's sonnets of this Welsh period inscribe this common theme of the mystical operation of *caritas* and we will return to this in Chapter 9.

The radical unity of the soul with Christ that Hopkins describes in his Kingfishers sonnet is also frequently elaborated by Pusey. In exploring the sources of Hopkins's mysticism, Pusey perhaps has an even more important role to play than Newman. Though he is recognised as the *doctor mysticus* of the Oxford Movement, little attention has been given to this mystical dimension of Pusey's thought. Yet, it is Pusey's language that is most palpably mystical, with words that often breathe a spirit of rapturous contemplation. In the Preface to 'Sermons During the Season from Advent to Whitsuntide' (1848) Pusey places the doctrine of the divine indwelling at the heart of his own preaching, which is aimed at

> the inculcation of the Great Mystery, expressed in the words to be "*in* Christ", to be "Members of Christ", "Temples of the Holy Ghost"; that Christ doth, through the Holy Ghost Whom he hath given to us, dwell really and truly in the hearts of the faithful.[32]

This emphasis is similarly found in Pusey's tract on baptism, a lengthy and meticulous scholarly study that argues the doctrine of baptismal regeneration through a forensic exploration of the patristic typology of baptism. Pusey expounds a mystical understanding of the sacrament, closely connected with Pauline doctrine; his extensive patristic quotations are specifically adapted to a Pauline view of baptism. For Pusey, the most profound gift of baptism is its grafting of the soul not only into the visible church, but also into the body of Christ. Pusey, as Owen Chadwick notes, almost *feels* this incorporation in to Christ; his preaching centres on that central stress of Pauline theology, the mystical experience of being 'in Christ'. Like Augustine, Pusey emphasises the Pauline understanding of baptism as mystical union with Christ's death and resurrection (cf. Rom. 6.3–6). Augustine frequently cites Romans 6.3–6 when writing against the Pelagians and Pusey's tract on baptism also closely considers how this passage portrays the soul as co-interred and co-crucified with Christ. As a death to sin and a supernatural birth to new life, baptism for Pusey is truly a regeneration, the generation of the soul from God through grace.

The patristic mystery of regenerating grace, the divine indwelling and participation in the divine nature is at the centre of Pusey's teaching. Like Newman, Pusey follows Augustine in describing justification as a free gift of God through regeneration by Spirit. (For example, in his Preface to *Sermons During the Season from Advent to Whitsuntide*, he quotes heavily from Augustine in this regard.) For Pusey, the individual's ability to serve God through righteousness is not through his own effort or merit but through the power of Christ's resurrection. Through the Spirit's operation the soul becomes a member of Christ, and hence

> partakes of that Sonship...so that henceforth the Father looks upon him, not as what he is in himself, but as in, and a part of, His well-beloved Son, and loves him with a portion of that ineffable love with which He loves His Son.[33]

Chapter 4 discusses Pusey's tract on baptism as a likely precursor to Hopkins's extensive use of baptismal typology in *The Wreck*. It is these expressions of mystical union and love that are at the heart of *The Wreck's* typological and sacramental narrative. In Hopkins's ode, death by drowning becomes a baptism in regenerating waters, a mysterious, mystical union with the death and resurrection of Christ. Drawing on the imagery of the baptismal seal and the resurrection imagery of fire and gold, Hopkins describes the nuns as 'sealed in wild waters / To bathe in his fall-gold mercies, to breathe in his all-fire glances.' Embedded too in the poem is an elaborately worked allegory based on the Pauline image of baptism as the 'putting on' of Christ (Gal. 3.27); the spiritual garments by which the soul is united with Christ. For Hopkins, as for Pusey and the patristic tradition, baptism is the beginning of the soul's *deification*. As Pusey writes in a letter of 1836, baptism implies 'a new nature, existence imparted; and this actual, not metaphorical, and by virtue of the Incarnation of our Lord Who took our nature that He might impart His to us.'[34]

In its emphasis on the connection between baptismal regeneration and the Incarnation, Pusey's thought reflects the crucial influence of Greek patristic theology – the idea that the individual *becomes by grace what Christ is by nature*. As Brilioth notes, Augustinian theology was in this respect key to Pusey's religious development, serving as the bridge by which he came to a full acceptance of the mysticism of the Greek Fathers.

At the heart of the Alexandrian tradition is a powerful link between the Incarnation and salvation, the condescension of God by which in turn the soul is transformed into the divine likeness. The doctrine of deification is specifically associated with the Alexandrian school. *Theosis* or 'becoming divine' is conceived as a union with the divine substance – incorporation not into the divine essence but into the person of Christ, who through the hypostatic union is the mediator of God and humankind.[35] Athanasius, whose influence on Newman is well known, stressed the central principle that God became man so that man may become God. Both Newman and Pusey, drawing on the Greek fathers, share the belief that the end goal of Christian life is participation in the divine nature, through the operation of grace. In the Preface to his 1848 *Sermons During the season from Advent to Whitsuntide*, Pusey defends this doctrine against the charge that it leads to pantheism. He argues that the orthodox doctrine of the Incarnation, is the very safeguard against pantheism. Just as the Incarnation united human nature with the divine, so the divine indwelling in the soul through Christ's Spirit implies that man is once again taken up into the divine nature. Pusey quotes, '"Mark" (says St Chrysostom) "how he has brought the whole to completion in Christ, how he hath raised us up into heaven. Ye are members of Christ," saith he, "ye are the temple of the Spirit".'[36] In another sermon Pusey similarly writes:

> To dwell in God must be by His Dwelling in us...By dwelling in us He makes us parts of Himself, so that in the Ancient Church they could boldly say, "He Deifieth me;" that is, He makes me part of Him, of His Body, who is God.[37]

There is a kinship between the Tractarian emphasis on divinisation and Hopkins's bold intimations of his own identity with Christ. As Hopkins famously writes in 'That Nature is a Heraclitean Fire', 'I am all at once what Christ is, since he was what I am, and / This Jack, joke, poor potsherd... Is immortal diamond.' There is a further affinity too, for both Pusey and Hopkins reflect not only the patristic doctrine of the soul's participation in the divine, but also the corresponding *visio Dei*. For the church Fathers, deification is linked with contemplation. The clearest Johannine reference to deification is 1 John 3.2: 'now are we the sons of God...when he shall appear, we shall be like him; for we shall see him as he is' (KJV). This is the theme of one of Pusey's Leeds Sermons, 'Bliss of Heaven "We shall see Him as He is"', which draws directly from the Greek Fathers. In mystical and ecstatic language, Pusey describes the vision of God as divine light. In his sermon, Pusey stresses that no created being can in himself have the power to see God; this vision is bestowed by God himself. He quotes from Gregory of Nazianzen, 'Be thou enlightened with David who saith to the light, "in thy Light shall we see thy Light;" i.e. the Son in the Spirit, than Which what can be more radiant?'[38] God dwells in and is himself 'that Surpassing, Unbounded, Uncreated, Ineffable Light'. As Pusey reflects,

> Oh what shall it be to range freely within that boundless bliss, to be admitted into its very depths, or (to speak with holy men) "to be translated into the glory of God;" to move, to think, to see, within God; in Himself and by Himself to see Himself...[39]

*The Wreck of the Deutschland* describes this very translation of the soul or heart 'from the grace to the grace' (3), the metamorphosis of the soul by the Spirit as it beholds Christ himself (cf. 2 Cor. 3.18). Hopkins, like Pusey and the church Fathers, describes this divine contemplation through images of light. *The Wreck* particularly recalls Paul's conversion and the 'ascent narratives' of Augustine's *Confessions.* It is likely that Pusey was an important figure in directing Hopkins's attention to Augustine and also to his medieval successor St Bernard of Clairvaux. Pusey was responsible for the English translation of Augustine's *Confessions*, which appeared as the first volume of the *Library of the Fathers* in 1838. Above all, Augustine taught that while perfect contemplation belongs to the heavenly life, glimpses of the divine may be seen even in the course of human existence. In the interior narrative of *The Wreck* is an Augustinian model of contemplation, which stresses the unchangeable nature of divinity. This Augustinian emphasis is highlighted too in Pusey's sermons on mystical union and vision. Sermon XV of the Leeds Sermons reflects on 1 John 3.2 and is entitled 'Bliss of Heaven "We shall be like Him"'. Pusey writes, '"So much the more unlike," says Augustine, "is the soul of man to Him, the Incorporeal, the Eternal, the Unchangeable, the more he loveth the things of time and change".'[40] It is this unchangeable and eternal essence of the divine that is seen and known in the bliss of contemplation. Referring to the mystical commentary of St Bernard of Clairvaux's *Sermons on the Song,* Pusey stresses the present nature of this vision of God as He *is*, not 'was' or 'shall be' (cf. 1 Jn. 3.2).[41] In words once again reminiscent of Augustine, Pusey's powerfully mystical language describes the future glory of the soul, when it will be imbued with

> the imparted light of God...when faith is turned into sight, and hope into its substance, then shall "charity abide" and be perfected; then shall we love with the love of God...ever through His love cleaving unto His love, ever borne to God, uplifted, filled, overflowing, receiving...by His love changed into His own unchangeableness.[42]

Drawing on Augustine, Chrysostom and Gregory of Nazianzen, Pusey understands salvation as a participation in the divine nature, in the form of that nature as love; this divine love or grace transforms the soul entirely into its likeness. Of the medieval mystical writers, Bernard is most prominent in Pusey, and Hopkins's devotion to Pusey is perhaps one of the factors to draw him to the mystical theology of Bernard and his famous sermons on the *Song of Songs*. Pusey introduced many followers of the Oxford Movement to the classics of mystical writing from Bernard onwards. In his sermon, 'The Will of God, the Cure of Self-Will,' Pusey quotes abundantly from Bernard and Augustine in exploring the mystic union of wills.[43]

It is for good reason that the Tractarian scholar Brilioth describes Pusey as the *doctor mysticus* of the movement, and these brief explorations show the powerfully mystical form and feeling of his writings. This ecstatic quality of Pusey's writing has been noted by scholars writing on the Oxford Movement. Yet this aspect of his work has received little sustained attention, much as the lack of the word 'mysticism' from Tractarian literature has obscured its inherently mystical character. There can scarcely be any doubt, however, that there are strong mystical elements in Tractarian religion. The doctrine of the divine indwelling, as linked with the Incarnation, is the very centre of Tractarian faith. Newman's understanding of justification by the regeneration of the Spirit is founded on Augustine's conception of infused grace (*gratia infusa*), the love of God or *caritas* that is the Spirit's operation in the soul. This mystical conception of *gratia infusa* is the doorway to the strong sacramental mysticism that is a primary defining feature of Tractarian theology. Both Newman's *Lectures on Justification* and Pusey's 'Scriptural Views of Holy Baptism' centre on the mystic presence of Christ in the soul, mediated through the sacraments. Although Newman's language is of a less intensely mystical character than Pusey's, both Tractarian leaders show in their writings a powerful sense of the divine presence and a profound awareness of that mystery of grace by which the soul participates in divinity. Both Newman and Pusey were responsible for deepening contemporary understanding of baptism, emphasising the mystical working of the Spirit as endowing the individual with a second, spiritual nature, transforming him into a temple of God. This sacramental mysticism, in connection with a theology of the Spirit as indwelling love or *caritas,* is the spiritual and mystical core of Hopkins's poetic corpus. In *The Wreck of the Deutschland* in particular, the mystical operation of God's transforming love is seen in its highest form, when the soul co-operates with the 'elevating' grace of God to attain to an ecstasy of loving contemplation. In Hopkins, the mystical and dogmatic theology of the Fathers takes up its habitation through the mediation of Tractarian religion. Following his conversion to the Roman church, it is the patristic tradition that continues to speak powerfully in Hopkins. From the mystical theology of Origen and Augustine to the affective mysticism of Bernard of Clairvaux, *The Wreck of the Deutschland* is a testament of love – the love that is the descent of God to the soul and the ascent of the soul to the divine.

## Notes

1 Nathan Jacobs, 'Created Corruptible, Raised Incorruptible: the Importance of Hylomorhpic Creationism to the Free Will Defense' in *The Ashgate Research Companion to Theological Anthropology*, 262.
2 Nixon draws attention to Keble's *Lectures on Poetry*; these he describes as being 'dedicated to Wordsworth', that 'chief minister' of 'high and sacred truth' who propounds the idea of poetry as religious expression, *Hopkins and his Contemporaries,* 88.
3 As Owen Chadwick points out it is the 'instead of' that divides the high churchmen of the Oxford Movement from the high churchmen of the seventeenth century, O. Chadwick, *The Spirit of the Oxford Movement* (Cambridge: CUP, 1990), 44.
4 Belief in baptismal regeneration was shared by Tractarians and the old High Churchmen. The Gorham controversy was initiated by the High Churchman Bishop Phillpotts who accused George Gorham, an Evangelical, of heresy in denying the doctrine of baptismal regeneration. Pusey, while believing denial of the doctrine to be heretical, was more conciliatory than Phillpotts with respect to the implicit Evangelical concern that baptismal regeneration should not deny the necessity of a personal conversion.
5 Hopkins, *Collected Works,* vol. 1 *Correspondence,* 62.
6 Geoffrey Rowell, *The Vision Glorious* (Oxford: OUP, 1983), 18.
7 Ibid., 16.
8 Hopkins, *Collected Works,* vol. 2 *Correspondence,* 619.
9 That this justification is still the gift of God and not achieved by the believer through faith is seen in Luther's description of 'justification *by* grace *through* faith'; for a discussion of this point, see Alister E. McGrath, *Christian Theology: An Introduction* (Oxford: Blackwell, 1994), 383–85.
10 J. H. Newman, *Lectures on the Doctrine of Justification,* 3rd ed. (London: Rivingtons, 1874), 251.
11 In part it is merely the 'technical' language of Trent that Newman objects to when he compares the 'cold' language of the Schoolmen with the warmer language of the Fathers, *Lectures*, 31, n. 1.
12 Ibid., 137.
13 Ibid.
14 Augustine, *On the Spirit and the Letter,* 56, quoted in Newman, *Lectures,* 31, n 1.
15 Newman, *Lectures,* 140.
16 Yngve Brilioth, *The Anglican Revival: Studies in the Oxford Movement* (London: Longmans, Green and Co., 1925), 278.
17 Newman, *Lectures,* 45. Here Newman refers again to Augustine, *On the Spirit and the Letter,* 31, 'The Old Law Ministers Death, the New, Righteousness'.
18 Hopkins, *Sermons and Devotional Writings,* 195.
19 Newman, *Lectures,* 137.
20 Ibid., 138.
21 Ibid., 170. The image of the soul stamped as God's coin signifies its belonging to God. Augustine uses this image in his Homilies; he writes, 'as the tribute money is rendered to him [Caesar], so should the soul be rendered to God, illumined and stamped with the light of his countenance'. (En. Ps., Ps 4.8).
22 Ibid., 171.
23 Ibid., 176.

24 Hopkins, *Sermons and Devotional Writings,* 98–99.
25 See Newman, *Lectures*, 240–41.
26 Ibid., 144.
27 Brilioth, *Anglican Revival,* 288.
28 Newman, *Lectures,* 219. This idea is related by Newman to St Paul's words in Colossians 3.3 'your life is hid with Christ in God'.
29 The close relation between the two is seen in Bishop Bull's 1760 work, 'Harmonica Apostolica', which expounds the doctrine of justification; as Brilioth notes, this work was of the greatest importance for the Tractarian view on the subject, *Anglican Revival,* 278.
30 Newman, *Lectures*, 150.
31 Hopkins, *Sermons and Devotional Writings,* 154.
32 Edward Pusey, *Sermons During the Season from Advent to Whitsuntide* (Oxford: John Henry Parker, 1848), Preface, v.
33 Pusey, Tract 67, quoted in Brilioth, *Anglican Revival,* 313.
34 Rowell, *Vision Glorious,* 17.
35 McGrath, *Christian Theology,* 360–61. This differs from the understanding of deification as 'becoming *like* God', associated with the Antiochene school and often conceived in terms of ethical perfection, ibid.
36 Pusey, *Sermons from Advent*, xxv.
37 'The Christian's Life in Christ', ibid., 233.
38 W. Dodsworth, John Keble, C. Marriott, E. B. Pusey, W. U. Richards and I. Williams, *A Course of Sermons on Solemn Subjects,* 2nd ed. (Oxford: John Henry Parker, 1847), 273, note c.
39 Ibid., 284.
40 *De Civitate Dei* ix. 17 quoted in Pusey, *Sermons on Solemn Subjects,* 269.
41 Pusey, *Sermons on Solemn Subjects*, 283, note r.
42 Ibid., 269.
43 Pusey, *Sermons from Advent*, 357–74.

# 4 Baptism and Ascent

## Created Corruptible, Raised Incorruptible

Augustine's model of justification based on baptism is one part of a spiritual and mystical discourse of regeneration utilised by Hopkins in his poetry. As the first sacrament of the church, baptism symbolises the entry of the believer into the body of Christ. It is a death to the world and a birth in the Spirit. A powerful symbol of renewal, baptism marks the beginning of the soul's ascent and the adoption of the believer into mystical union with Christ, and divine sonship. The sacrament of baptism is thought to imprint the divine likeness in the soul. This image is gradually restored through grace by a process of sanctification leading to final glorification, the perfect restoration of the divine image. Theological writing on baptism develops from and combines two scriptural traditions: the Johannine conception of man as 'born again' through baptism (3:3–5), and the Pauline idea of the Christian as 'buried together with [Christ] by baptism into death' (Rom 6.4). The baptismal font is both mystical womb and tomb, and it is from this powerful nucleus of mystical thought that much of the imagery for Hopkins's *The Wreck of the Deutschland* derives.

To fully discern Hopkins's poetic deployment of the language of baptism in *The Wreck* and other poems, we need a more detailed knowledge of its scriptural and historical expression. At its core, baptism evokes a twofold symbolism, signifying the destruction of the old and the creation of the new. In patristic tradition, baptism is frequently compared with the creation of the first Adam. Made in the divine likeness, yet lost to paradise through sin, the individual regains this likeness through baptism. Baptism is a remaking of the self; by destroying the old Adam, the soul is born again in the divine image. This symbolism derives from the death and resurrection of Christ. In the words of the fourth-century Eastern Father Cyril of Jerusalem, 'Baptism is not only purification from sins and the grace of adoption, but also the antitype of the Passion of Christ.'[1] So, conformity to Christ dead and risen is of primary importance, and this idea is powerfully expressed by St Paul. For the early church, this is the true meaning of the baptismal rite of immersion into water. The descent into water is a descent into death, and the triple immersion of baptism is symbolic of the three days of Christ's burial.

St Cyril is another of the early Fathers who greatly advances the Pauline doctrine of baptism as conformity to the death of Christ. He suggests that Paul's words are intended to remind us that baptism is a participation (*koinonia*) in a similitude (*mimesis*) of Christ's sufferings. As Paul writes in Romans 6.5, 'For if we have been planted together in the likeness of his death, we shall be also in the likeness of his resurrection.' Cyril observes that this *likeness* of the death of Christ implies the imitation (*homoioma*) of Christ's suffering. Yet, paradoxically, while there is imitation on the one hand, there is on the other the reality of salvation.[2] As Jean Danièlou notes, the death and Passion of Christ has two aspects: the historical fact and the content of saving grace. The historical event is imitated or symbolised in the sacrament, but the content of saving grace allows for true *participation*. Baptism is accordingly a figure of both the Passion and the resurrection. Sacramental conformity to the death of Christ brings the resurrection of the dead and the restoration of true sonship. Yet if biblical and patristic writing on baptism is filled with the symbolism of death, it is equally filled with the symbolism of rebirth. One of the key scriptural passages here is John 3.5, where Christ says to Nicodemus: 'Except a man be born of water and [of] the Spirit, he cannot enter into the kingdom of God' (AV). This scriptural passage is discussed at length by Edward Pusey in 'Scriptural Views of Holy Baptism.' John 3.5 is a central text in the argument for baptismal regeneration, and Pusey reflects:

> ...Baptism is spoken of as the source of our spiritual birth, as no other cause is, save God...[we are] "born *of* water and the Spirit," in contrast to our birth *of* the flesh...and in order to express that this our new birth *of* God is, as being of God, a deathless birth, it is described as a birth *of* seed incorruptible.[3]

Also implicit here is the conception of the church as mother, giving birth to the sons of God. The birth of the Christian is accomplished in baptism, and this baptismal rebirth takes place only with the one bride of Christ, the church. The font is thus the womb and birthplace to eternal life, the baptismal bath in which the children of God are begotten. This baptismal symbolism of death and rebirth is central to Hopkins's *The Wreck of the Deutschland*. Also important in Hopkins is the metaphor of incorporation into Christ, the baptised as 'members' of Christ's mystical body (cf. Eph. 5.30). Hopkins draws on this symbolism in his commentary on the *Exercises*, in the very meditations in which he reflects on man as the 'temple' of God (December 8, 1881). Describing God resting in man as a jewel in a case, Hopkins writes, 'that is / Christ as a solid in his member as a hollow or shell, both things being the image of God; which can only be perfectly when the member is in all things conformed to Christ.'[4] This conformity is also expressed as the 'putting on' of Christ, a metaphorical configuration that lies at the mystical heart of *The Wreck*. In Paul's words, 'as many of you as have been baptized in Christ, have put on Christ.' (Gal. 3.27) As Pusey explains, this putting on of Christ is the means by which men are made sons of God. Pusey urges that Paul's words are meant to emphasise

> that the being clothed with Christ is the gift of God, not any quality in man...for if the having put on Christ, the being clothed with Him, makes us sons of God, then it makes us so, in that we are "made members of Christ:" and "sons of God," because members of His Ever-Blessed Son.[5]

For the human creature, Christ is the garment of immortality. From Galatians 3.27 derives the symbolism of baptism as the 'clothing of incorruptibility' or the 'shining garment' – technical expressions that relate to the ceremony which traditionally concluded the baptismal rite, the clothing in white garments.[6] The removal of old robes symbolises the putting off of the 'old man' (Eph. 4.22) and the new baptismal gowns signify the putting on of the 'new man' (Eph. 4.24). This symbolism relates back to Christ on the cross, who first achieved the death of sin and the stripping off of the old man for the whole of the human race (cf. Rom. 6.6). For the Fathers, the 'garments of skin' of Genesis 3.21 symbolise the mortality and sin put on by Adam in his fall from paradise. It is through Christ the second Adam, that men and women shed these shameful skins and wear again a garment of glory.

Gregory of Nyssa is one of the most prominent of the fourth-century Cappadocian Fathers, whose writing importantly elaborates the distinction between the transcendent nature and immanent energies of God. He applies this distinction to human nature, which he sees as capable of moral and intellectual perfection. For Gregory of Nyssa, the ultimate purpose of human life is to take on the infinite nature of the divine. In a sermon on baptism, he describes the sacrament as signalling a return to paradise. He writes, 'You are outside of Paradise, O catechumen. You share the exile of Adam, our first father. Now the door is opening. Return whence you came forth.'[7] In patristic tradition, baptism is understood to begin a return to the lost paradise of the church. This is reflected in the decoration of baptisteries adorned with trees, flowers and fountains, depicting Christ as a shepherd with his flock in paradise. These decorations often recall Psalm 41, 'As the hart pants for the running waters,' in which the hart or deer represents the catechumen who completes the initiation of baptism and quenches his spiritual thirst at the river of paradise. Another aspect of baptismal symbolism that relates it to eschatological theology is the octagonal formation of baptisteries, based on the belief in ancient Christianity that the number 8 was a symbol of the resurrection. This belief was connected with the ascension of Christ, said to have occurred the day after the Sabbath, on the eighth day.[8] So the seven days of the week represent worldly time, and the eighth day that of eternity; through baptism the Christian enters into this eternal life. In Hopkins's *The Wreck*, baptismal symbolism is fundamentally related to eschatological theology and the text of Psalm 41 is inscribed within the poem's sacramental and mystical subtext.

In patristic writing on baptism, the symbolism of the baptismal seal (Greek *sphragis*) is of particular importance. Frequently spoken of by St Paul and the early church, the word appears in various passages of scripture:

> Now he that...hath anointed us is God: Who also hath sealed us, and given the pledge of the Spirit in our hearts.
>
> (2 Cor. 1.21–22)

> ...you were signed [AV, sealed] with the holy Spirit of promise, Who is the pledge of our inheritance, unto the redemption of acquisition...
>
> (Eph. 1.13–14)

> And grieve not the holy Spirit of God: whereby you are sealed unto the day of redemption.
>
> (Eph. 4.30)

The ritual *act* of 'sealing' or the rite of the *sphragis* (seal) is the imposition of the sign of the cross on the forehead, and this reflects again the idea that the Christian is crucified with Christ in baptism.[9] As Danièlou shows, the term *sphragis* as used in ancient times has various significances, many of which are seen to be reflected in the theological significance of baptism. The word signifies a mark of ownership, used to suggest both the branding of a flock and the *signaculum* borne by soldiers of the Roman army. It is easy to see how both these uses of the term come into Christian application, with the seal of baptism being understood as the sign that marks Christ's flock, and his army. At the same time, another interpretation of the *sphragis* that is connected with Philo of Alexandria links it with the *eikon* (the image). By this interpretation, the seal of baptism imprints within man the image, the likeness to God, which will be restored in the end time. All of these meanings are reflected in Pusey's explication of baptism, in which he emphasises that baptism is not merely an outward sign, but the means for conveying the Holy Spirit:

> a spiritual act, wherein Christ by His Spirit takes the baptized into Himself...being taken out of our state of nature, and marked, guarded, conformed to our Lord...guarded, as His purchased possession and peculiar treasure, whereon He has affixed His seal; conformed, in that it places again upon us the Creator's image,

> renewing us after His likeness, and impressing His cast...His features upon our souls, as a seal gives its stamp to the body, whereon it is impressed.[10]

As the mark or sign of Christian faith, the baptismal seal is also symbolically related to the seal of the Old Covenant. St Paul first establishes this parallel between the seal of the Old Covenant and that of the new: between the rite of circumcision and the rite of baptism.[11] In Paul's words,

> But God forbid that I should glory, save in the Cross of our Lord Jesus Christ; by whom the world is crucified to me, and I to the world. For in Christ Jesus neither circumcision availeth any thing, nor uncircumcision, but a new creature...From henceforth...I bear the marks of the Lord Jesus in my body.
>
> (Gal. 6.14–17)

For Paul, the true sign of his own consecration is the cross received in baptism. What lies behind Paul's text is the juxtaposition of the circumcision of the Old Testament with the baptismal seal in the form of a cross. By contrast, the seal of the new faith is internal, borne within. As Cyril writes, 'After faith, we, like Abraham, receive the spiritual *sphragis*, being circumcised in baptism by the Holy Spirit'.[12] The seal of baptism is a spiritual one; not a mark upon the body, but a transformation worked within the soul by the Spirit. This, as Danièlou points out, is an ambiguity in the symbolism of the baptismal seal – and baptism itself. On the one hand, the seal is an image of the cross and relates to Christ crucified; on the other, it is related by Paul to the Holy Spirit (cf. Eph. 1.13). Accordingly, the seal denotes conformity to the crucifixion and suggests too an outpouring of spirit. This complex symbolism is seen in the words of Ambrose,

> So we were sealed with the Spirit of God. For just as we die in Christ, that we may be born again, so, too, we are signed with the Spirit... truly we are sealed in the heart, that the Holy Spirit may set forth in us the likeness of the heavenly image.[13]

## Typology and Further Types of Baptism

Typology is defined as the science of similitudes between the Old and New Testaments. The *antitypos* stands for the reality in opposition to the *typos*, the figure or type. This is a pattern of shadow and reality, what is realised and what is yet to be realised. The foundation of typology is found in Old Testament prophecies of the end time. This primary typology is fundamentally eschatological, grounded in predictions of a new deluge, a new exodus, a new paradise.[14] The New Testament shows these prophecies as fulfilled in Christ, the new Adam with whom the paradise of the future has already begun. However, the eschatological typology of the Old Testament is realised not only in Christ, but also in the church, specifically in the sacramental typology of the New Testament. Through this sacramental typology the individual imitates and participates in Christ's sacrifice. The flood, the Passion and baptism show the same divine action in three historical phases, each ordered to the end time of judgment. As the central mystery of Christian faith, the death and resurrection of Christ is prefigured in the Old Testament, realised historically in the New Testament, and re-enacted mysteriously through the sacraments.

The theology of baptism is rooted in its Old Testament types. Baptismal theology is at heart dialectic, articulated as a configuration to death and resurrection, a flight from the world and journey into God. This twofold symbolism finds eloquent expression in patristic writings, which explicate the sacrament in the light of its earlier types. The New Testament specifically indicates three important types of baptism: the flood (1 Pt. 3.20–1), the crossing of the Red Sea (1 Cor. 10.1–3) and the rock of Horeb (1 Cor. 10.4). Patristic exegesis connects these three with two further types: the waters of creation described in Genesis 1.2, and the *fons signatus* of the Song 4.12. Tertullian's *De baptismo* is the first major catechetical work to show how various Old Testament types are realised in the sacrament, and the *mystagogic catecheses* of Ambrose are also important here. The theology of baptism as a narrative of re-creation is importantly connected with one particular type, that of the primitive waters of Genesis 1.2: 'And the earth was void and empty, and darkness was upon the face of the deep; and the spirit of God moved over the waters.' This passage is interpreted in exegesis as the brooding of the Holy Spirit on the waters, a prefiguration of the operation of the Spirit and the mystery of baptism.[15] The authority for this interpretation is provided by Pusey in an extensive list of patristic references. It is upheld in Tertullian, Ambrose, Jerome, Cyril of Jerusalem and Hippolytus. Describing the relation between the early waters of creation and the sacramental waters of baptism Hippolytus writes:

> This is the Spirit which from the beginning was borne above the waters, whereby the world is moved, the creation subsists, and all things are quickened; which operated in the prophets, and lighted upon Christ. This David sought, when he said, Create in me a clean heart, O God, and renew a right spirit within me. This is the Spirit the Paraclete sent for thy sake, to show thee to be a Son of God.[16]

The parallel is between the enlightening of the world and of the soul, each restored from darkness. Hippolytus links the presence of the Spirit moving over the waters with the descent of the Spirit upon the Jordan at the baptism of Christ. This is the theological analogy between the first creation and the subsequent redemption or renewal of creation. The Old Testament prophesises a new creation, and in the New Testament this new creation is achieved in the Incarnation and continued in baptism. So is a 'new creature' (2 Cor. 5.17) born, through the regeneration of baptismal waters (cf. Jn. 3.5).

A second major type of baptismal regeneration is the flood, specifically indicated in 1 Peter 3.20–21. This is the baptismal type encountered most frequently in patristic writing. It is not difficult to see how baptism as a configuration to Christ's death and resurrection finds its parallel in the great flood of Genesis. The flood was understood as the divine destruction of a sinful world, in which only the just were saved. So also the descent into baptismal waters is understood as the destruction of the old man and the raising up of a new creation. The waters of baptism are the sacramental antitype of the waters of the flood. The analogy is not merely in the image of water, but in the fundamental theological understanding of each Scriptural phenomenon. In each instance, the waters are symbolic of judgment. This analogy is brought out by St Peter in what is thought to be one of the most obscure passages in the bible:

> Because Christ also died once for our sins, the just for the unjust: that he might offer us to God, being put to death indeed in the flesh, but enlivened in the spirit, In which also coming he preached to those spirits that were in prison: Which had been some time incredulous, when they waited for the patience of God in the days of Noe, when the ark was a building: wherein a few, that is, eight souls, were saved by water. Whereunto baptism being of the like form, now saveth you also ...
>
> (1 Pt. 3.18–21)

This scriptural passage describes Christ's death and descent into the lower world when he proclaimed his victory to the fallen angels. Peter draws a parallel between the deluge, Christ's descent and baptism. Christ's descent is the realisation of the mystery of the deluge. At his death, the whole of sinful humanity is destroyed by the waters of death, until Christ rises again from these waters as the firstborn of the new creation. By relating the flood to Christ's death and descent, Peter shows the baptismal rite to be charged with this very theological meaning. Baptism is an imitation of Christ's descent into hell, and both are foreshadowed by the flood. The connection of baptism with eschatology and judgement is particularly seen in the baptism of John. John's famous words have a primarily eschatological meaning: 'I indeed baptize you with water... he shall baptize you with the Holy Ghost, and with fire' (Lk. 3.16).[17] In John, baptism as a form of immersion is a figure of the end time judgement, which will be a baptism by fire. So, baptism is a configuration to

Christ's death and resurrection, and also a prophecy of eschatological death and resurrection; all these are prefigured in the great flood.

A number of typological analogies are drawn between the antitype of baptism and the figure of the flood. In religious commentary, the ark is frequently seen as a figure of the church. Tertullian in his tract on baptism repeatedly describes the ark as the church.[18] The wood of the ark is also symbolic of the cross and the dove of the ark, which returns to Noe bearing an olive branch, is interpreted as the prefiguration of the Holy Spirit who descended at Christ's baptism. Drawing together these typological parallels, Ambrose asks in *De Mysteriis*, 'You see the water; you see the wood; you perceive the dove – and do you doubt the mystery?'[19] Yet another analogy between the theology of baptism and the flood is seen in the symbolism of the number 8. Eight just souls are saved by Noah's ark, the symbolism of which is connected with the eighth day of Christ's resurrection, the dawning of God's new creation. In the words of Justin,

> Noe the just, with the other men of the Deluge...formed the number 8, and so showed the symbol of the eighth day (*tes ogdoes hemeras*) on which our Christ appeared risen from the dead...For Christ, the first-born of all creation, became in a new sense the head (*arche*) [cf. Col. 1.18] of another race, of that which was regenerated by Him, by the water and the wood which contained the mystery of the Cross, as Noe was saved by the wood of the ark when he was carried on the waters with his family.[20]

In addition to the flood, the baptismal type most frequently encountered in patristic literature is the crossing of the Red Sea. The Exodus narrative as a whole is seen as implicitly sacramental in nature: Egypt is a figure of the sinful world and the exodus of the Israelites is understood as a type of the salvation procured by baptism. The passage through the Red Sea is described by Paul himself as a prophecy of the baptismal sacrament. Both these signify deliverance out of sin and entry into a new life of salvation. Paul's famous words in the First Epistle to the Corinthians are perhaps the strongest evidence for the biblical basis of typological reading. As Paul writes,

> our fathers were all under the cloud, and all passed through the sea, and all in Moses were baptized, in the cloud and in the sea; ...*Haec autem in figura facta sunt nostri...* ['Now these things were done in a figure of us...']
>
> (1 Cor 10.1–6)

Paul clearly asserts this baptismal type, and from the central parallel between baptism and the crossing of the Red Sea other themes are drawn.

The first of these is that of the pillar of cloud that accompanies the Jews in the crossing of the sea, as a visible sign of God's presence. Throughout the Old Testament we find the theme of the cloud as the sign of God's dwelling in the tabernacle. In the New Testament, the cloud is witness to Christ as the new dwelling of God (John 1.14): the cloud is what rests on Mary at the annunciation (Luke 1.35).[21] In other words, the cloud signifies the Spirit or acting presence of God, appearing only at those times when Christ's divinity is manifested: at the annunciation, the transfiguration and the ascension. Paul's own words clearly establish the association between the pillar of cloud and baptism, with the cloud representing the Holy Spirit. The cloud and the waters of the Red Sea together present an image of baptism, prefiguring the union of water and Spirit. The crossing of the Red Sea as a type of baptism is developed by St Ambrose in *De Mysteriis* and *De Sacramentis*. In the latter, Ambrose uses the type to show the greater efficacy of the Christian sacrament:

> What superiority is there over the people of the Jews having passed through the sea...Yet the Jews who passed through, all died in the desert. But he who passes through this font, that is from the earthly to the heavenly...the passage from sin to life...he who passes through this font does not die but rises.[22]

In Ambrose, we see a further line of baptismal typology. In the Exodus narrative, the pillar of cloud appears only by day, at night is seen a pillar of fire. In *De Sacramentis*, Ambrose describes the pillar of cloud as the shadow of the Holy Spirit that follows the Jews through the sea. The pillar of fire, he writes, is Christ.[23] The typological relation of the pillar of light to the Word is a biblical association; as Christ says in John 8.12: 'I am the light of the world. He that followeth me, walketh not in darkness, but shall have the light of life.' Ambrose's exegesis highlights the illuminative aspect of baptism. As Danièlou explains, if the Holy Spirit prefigured by the cloud shows the operation of God in baptism, the Word, prefigured in the pillar of fire, shows that baptism is illumination.[24]

The sacramental and typological character of the Exodus narrative is also reflected in the third baptismal type to be specifically indicated in the New Testament: the rock of Horeb (1 Cor. 10.4). Shortly after describing the baptism of the Jews in the cloud and in the sea (1 Cor. 10.2), Paul in his epistle to the Corinthians writes, 'And all drank the same spiritual drink; (and they drank of the spiritual rock that followed them, and the rock was Christ.)' (1 Cor. 10.4) Here, the rock of Horeb that gave forth water and accompanied the Israelites through the desert is referred to the pre-existent Christ. There is additionally a close material connection between 1 Cor. 10.4 and the call of the saviour in John 7.37.[25] The true meaning of the rock of Horeb is understood only when read against John 7.37 or the companion text of John 4.14:

> And on the last day and great day of the festivity, Jesus stood and cried, saying: If any man thirst, let him come to me, and drink.
>
> He that believeth in me, as the scripture saith, *out of his belly shall flow rivers of living water.*
>
> (Jn. 7.37–38)
>
> ...Whosoever drinketh...of the water that I will give him, shall not thirst for ever: But the water that I will give him, shall become in him a fountain of water, springing up into life everlasting.
>
> (Jn. 4.13–14)

Christ's call in John 7.37 makes use of the idea of the holy rock that grants the waters of life.[26] Christ is understood as the second Moses who repeats the miracle of Horeb; he is the true dispenser of the waters of life, and this living water is the Spirit (cf. Jn. 7.39). In the parallel text of John 4.14, Christ declares that he is the true well and fountain of life. Significantly, this declaration is made just after the Passover, which in part commemorates the crossing of the Red Sea and the rock of Horeb.[27] Christ's words in John 4.14 anticipate the crucifixion, and the blood and water that will flow from his wounded body. But, at the same time, this scriptural text together with John 7.37 emphasises the typological lineage that relates the sacramental waters of the New Testament to the Exodus narrative of deliverance.

Christ as the fountain and well of living waters is also foreshadowed in another Old Testament figure of baptism: the *fons signatus* or sealed fountain of Song 4.12: 'A garden inclosed *is* my sister, *my* spouse; a spring shut up, a fountain sealed.' (AV) The terms 'spring', 'garden' and 'spouse' are generally read synonymously, being typologically interrelated.[28] The imagery of Song 4.12 recalls the fountain in the garden of Eden (Gen. 2.6; AV 'mist,' LXX 'fountain'), and also looks forward to the eschatological pastoral vision of the New Jerusalem. As Christ 'unseals' the fountain in the piercing of his side on the Cross, the figure of the *fons signatus* becomes an important type within the discourse of baptismal typology.

## Reading Baptism

The Old Testament *Song of Songs* is traditionally interpreted in Christian exegesis as a hymn of baptism. But the *Song* itself, together with the typological discourse of baptism, effectively implies also a new semantics – a new method of reading integral to *The Wreck of the Deutschland*. The Old Testament types of baptism emphasise a symbolism of spiritual journey and ascent; baptism begins an incorporation into the mystical body of the church, completed in the end-time of Christ's return. In Hopkins's *The Wreck*, this narrative of mystical encounter is reflected in the body of the text itself. The poem's allegorical language structures a semantic ascent to parallel the sacramental ascent which is the very theme of the poem. This textual ascent moves from the body of the letter to an ultimate spiritual or mystical sense. This is the movement described by Paul when he explains the baptismal seal. Paul describes the seal as both the cross of Christ, borne internally within the body, and the gift of the Holy Spirit. It is the spiritual seal of the New Covenant, representing the law of spirit, which supersedes the letter. As Paul emphasises, the new seal is spiritually received in the heart:

> ...nor *is that* circumcision, which is outwardly in the flesh...circumcision is that of the heart, in the spirit, not in the letter.
>
> (Rom. 2.28–29)

Paul's differentiation between letter and spirit is the basis of centuries of allegorical reading. Meaning is found not in the outward sign, but is contained within an inner, spiritual truth. Paul reiterates this contrast in a famous scriptural passage:

> Being manifested, that you are the epistle of Christ...written not with ink, but with the Spirit of the living God; not in tables of stone, but in the fleshly tables of the heart.
>
> (2 Cor. 3.3)

Paul's words juxtapose the first law given to Moses on Sinai and inscribed in tablets of stone, with the second law of Christ, written in the heart. This inner law is described by Paul as 'the law of God according to the inward man' (Rom 7.22). This formulation recurs in Ephesians 3.16 where Paul writes of the strength of the Spirit in the 'inward man' (AV, 'inner man'). As we have seen, the seal is also interpreted as the image of God given in baptism, the divine likeness restored at the final time of glorification. This double interpretation of the seal as inner script and image finds expression in Paul's formulation of the outward and inward man, the man of the letter and the man of the spirit. In Paul's second epistle to the Corinthians, he offers a more dynamic interpretation of the interrelation between these two images of the human being:

> ...though our outward man is corrupted, yet the inward man is renewed day by day...While we look not at the things which are seen, but at the things which are not seen: for the things which are seen, are temporal; but the things which are not seen, are eternal.
>
> (2 Cor. 4.16–18)

The outward man is a worldly, material being; the inward man, the man of God. Baptism begins a process of sanctification that is continued by a strengthening of the spirit in the inner man, a daily renewal of the covenant. This idea of the two images or natures of man is also developed by Origen in his writings. In his *Homily on Genesis* Origen writes, 'that first heaven indeed, which we said is spiritual, is our mind, which is also itself spirit, that is, our spiritual man which sees and perceives God.'[29] Origen's words emphasise the spiritual man as that part of man capable of seeing God. This mystical meaning is further brought out in the Prologue to his *Commentary* on the Song, where Origen repeatedly turns to Paul's formulation of the outer and inner man. For Origen and the patristic tradition, the *Song of Songs* is the marriage hymn of Christ and church, inaugurated in the Incarnation and continued in the sacraments. This song of marriage is thus the song of the inner man, who, through the sacraments, is joined with Christ the heavenly bridegroom. In Origen's words,

> Moreover, this material man, who also is called the outer, has food and drink of like sort with himself – that is to say, corporeal and earthly; but in the same way the spiritual man, who also is called the inner, has for his proper food that *living Bread which came down from heaven*, and drinks of the water that Jesus promises, saying: *Whosoever shall drink of this water, which I will give to him, shall not thirst for ever.*[30]

It is appropriate that Origen discusses this sacramental and mystical discourse of the inner man in his *Commentary* on the Song, for this Old Testament book is for Origen the heart of Christianity. A proper reading of the *Song of Songs*, Origen suggests, is the culmination of the mystical ascent that is the true function of Scripture and of exegesis. Origen is the first Christian to see scriptural learning as an anagogic exercise, reaching beyond the literal, allegorical and moral senses to an ultimate spiritual or mystical sense. He suggests that the pattern for this ascent is seen in the arrangement of the three books of Solomon: *Proverbs* teaches moral science, *Ecclesiastes* natural science; but the *Song of Songs*, which teaches what Origen calls 'Enoptics'. This is the 'inspective science' taught by Solomon in the Song, through which 'he instils into the soul the love of things divine and heavenly, using for his purpose the figure of the Bride and Bridegroom'.[31] By the teachings of the Song the soul may 'reach out for the things unseen and eternal which, with spiritual meaning verily but under certain secret metaphors of love, are taught in the *Song of Songs*.'[32] The *Song of Songs* is concerned with the unseen that lies behind the seen; the attentive reader of this book of scripture engages in a search for those heavenly realities, which are the realm of the mystical theologian. In other words, the Song exemplifies that method of spiritual or allegorical reading intrinsic to the discourse on baptism and the law of the Spirit.

The following chapters will explore the mystical narrative of *The Wreck,* formed largely through the symbolic vocabulary of baptism. The old and new, the outward and inward man, the law of the letter and spirit, the divine writing in the heart – these formulations are the theological subject of the poem, and the paradigms within which the poem is composed. In effect, they become a set of textual strategies within which *The Wreck* is formed. The spiritual law and theology of baptism suggest in *The Wreck* not only a method of spiritual as opposed to literal reading (seen at the level of theology), but also the metaphorical conception of an inner script, closely allied with a discourse of the heart (seen at a literary or poetic level). Indeed, what is interesting about *The Wreck of the Deutschland* is the way in which it merges a Catholic and Romantic discourse in a mystical narrative that is both abstractly theological and fundamentally solipsistic. Hopkins's mystical narrative of the self is a discourse on the 'inner man' whose spiritual life and ascent to God forms the poem's subtext. Hopkins's imaginative interior narrative draws extensively from scripture and from a rich array of patristic, medieval and baroque religious traditions. Yet it remains, in essence, a discourse of the heart.

*The Wreck of the Deutschland* is a literary and poetic enacting of a scriptural method of allegory; the outward and inward man are paralleled by an outer and inner text. The typology and theology of baptism provide Hopkins with a way of mapping subject and self. If the heart sealed with a spiritual script becomes key to a theological reading of the poem, this heart is also the literary configuration of the poet's own voice. We must read typologically, anagogically, by shadow and spirit and not by the letter, to witness the death and rebirth of a man who is the image of God and the image of the poet himself. *The Wreck* records the mystical journey of Hopkins's 'hidden man of the heart' (1 Peter 3.47). It represents a death in body and letter, and a spiritual resurrection in its own hidden heart, formed in the image of the self, the text and God.

## Notes

1 St Cyril of Jerusalem, *Mystagogic Catecheses,* P. G. XXXIII, Eng. trans., 1081 B, quoted in Danièlou, *Bible and Liturgy,* 43.
2 Cyril of Jerusalem, *Mystagogic Catecheses,* 1082B–1084B, quoted in Danièlou, *Bible and Liturgy,* 45.
3 Edward Pusey, 'Scriptural Views of Holy Baptism,' in *Tracts for the Times,* vol. II for 1834–5, No. 67 (London: J. G. & F. Rivington, 1839), 25.
4 Hopkins, *Sermons and Devotional Writings,* 195.
5 Pusey, 'Scriptural Views of Baptism,' 112.
6 Danièlou, *Bible and Liturgy,* 49. The symbolism of the white baptismal garments is seen as a prefiguration of the soul's future glory and thus relates also to Christ's glorified appearance at His Transfiguration (ibid., 50).

7 Gregory of Nyssa, *Sermon against those who put off their Baptism*, P. G. XLVI, 417 C, quoted in Danièlou, *Bible and Liturgy*, 36.
8 Danièlou, *Bible and Liturgy*, 37.
9 Ibid., 54–55. Like Pusey, Danièlou observes that the significance of the baptismal seal stems from the fact that it often served to denote Baptism as a whole, this being called the *sphragis* (possibly as early as St Paul and in any case the earliest Fathers).
10 Pusey, 'Scriptural Views of Baptism,' 137.
11 Danièlou, *Bible and Liturgy*, 64. As Paul writes in his epistle to the Romans: 'And [Abraham] received the sign of circumcision, a seal of the justice of the faith, which he had, being uncircumcised' (Rom. 4:11).
12 Cyril of Jerusalem, *Mystagogic Catecheses*, 513A, quoted in Danièlou, *Bible and Liturgy*, 63.
13 Ambrose, 'The Holy Spirit' (6.79), Deferrari, 63.
14 Danièlou, *Bible and Liturgy*, 5.
15 As Pusey observes, the two interpretations are complementary in the exegesis of the early Church ('Scriptural Views of Baptism,' 360).
16 St Hippolytus, *Discourse on the Holy Theophany*, 9, quoted in Pusey, 'Scriptural Views of Baptism,' 360.
17 Danièlou, *Bible and Liturgy*, 79. St John however alters this to a sacramental interpretation by which baptism by the Spirit is meant to signify Christian Baptism as against the baptism of John (ibid.).
18 See Tertullian, *On Baptism*, trans. Rev. S. Thelwall (Whitefish, MT: Kessinger Publishing, 2008), 13.
19 Ambrose, 'The Mysteries' (3.10), Deferrari, 8.
20 Justin, *Dialogue*, CXXXVIII, 2–3 (n. p., n. d.) quoted in Danièlou, *Bible and Liturgy*, 78.
21 Danièlou, *Bible and Liturgy*, 91.
22 Ambrose, 'The Sacraments' (I, 4.12), Deferrari, 273.
23 Ibid. (I, 6.22), Deferrari, 276.
24 Danièlou, *Bible and Liturgy*, 93.
25 Kittel, *Theological Dictionary of the New Testament*, Vol. IV, 277.
26 Ibid., 271.
27 Donald R. Dickson, *The Fountain of Living Waters: The Typology of the Waters of Life in Herbert, Vaughan, and Traherne* (Columbia: University of Missouri Press, 1987), 56.
28 Ibid., 55.
29 Origen, 'Homilies on Genesis' (1.2), in *Homilies on Genesis and Exodus*, trans. Ronald E. Heine, *The Fathers of the Church*, Vol. 71 (Washington: The Catholic University of America Press, 1982), 49.
30 Origen, 'Commentary: Prologue,' Lawson, 28.
31 Ibid., Lawson, 41.
32 Ibid., Lawson, 44.

# 5 Sacramental Typology and Second Nature

Our first reading of *The Wreck of the Deutschland* explores the theology and typology of baptism as it runs through the poem. This sacramental symbolism is found at the very opening of Hopkins's ode:

1

THOU mastering me
God! giver of breath and bread;
World's strand, sway of the sea;
Lord of living and dead;
Thou hast bound bones and veins in me, fastened me flesh,
And after it almost unmade, what with dread,
Thy doing: and dost thou touch me afresh?
Over again I feel thy finger and find thee.

Moving between earth and sea, breath and body, the stanza recalls the origin of time and birth of the world. This is juxtaposed with a body's beginning, suggesting the making of man, the first Adam. This is a creation narrative, and Hopkins's portrayal of God as 'giver of breath' and 'sway of the sea' recalls the divine spirit that moved upon the waters at the birth of the world (Gn. 1.2). Certainly, this presence of the spirit is felt in Hopkins's description of the 'finger' of God. As Hopkins writes in a sermon, God's 'finger' signifies the Holy Ghost.[1] At the opening of *The Wreck*, Hopkins portrays the confluence of an external and internal landscape, the creation of a world and a man, set against that unmaking and making 'afresh' that is the realm of the 'inner man'. Hopkins draws on a central parallel of baptismal typology. In the words of Clement of Alexandria, 'The new creation comes about by water and the Spirit, like the creation of the universe: The Spirit of God was borne upon the waters.'[2] What we are witnessing is the baptismal reformation of a man, a man fashioned anew. The 'finger' of God is also associated with the calling of the chosen people out of Egypt[3]; against this allusion, the 'sway of the sea' suggests a further type of baptism, the parting of the Red Sea. Hopkins draws on this dense body of allegory to depict the calling of a soul out of sin, achieved in baptism and renewed daily through the sanctifying work of divine grace in the heart. Reading closely, Hopkins's description of himself bound by bones and veins and touched by God, pointedly prefigures the later description of his heart 'touched' in its bower of bone (stanza 18). The 'finger' of God suggests too the divine writing in the hearts of men (cf. Ex 31.18, 2 Cor. 3.3): the seal of the New Covenant fulfilled in the final outpouring of Spirit. In stanza 18, Hopkins's imaging of the heart is set against a further set of baptismal types:

18

Ah, touched in your bower of bone
Are you! turned for an exquisite smart,
Have you! make words break from me here all alone,
Do you!—mother of being in me, heart.
O unteachably after evil, but uttering truth,
Why, tears! is it? tears; such a melting, a madrigal start!
Never eldering revel and river of youth,
What can it be, this glee? the good yoú have there of your own?

Hopkins's heart weeps a 'river of youth', 'never-eldering', and this description recalls that celebrated 'fountain of water, springing up into life everlasting' (Jn. 4.14) that lies at the centre of New Testament baptismal typology. Origen, in his *Commentary* on the Song, similarly draws on this very passage when he writes, 'For what need is there of showers, when *the river maketh the city of God joyful,* when *a fountain of water springing up into life everlasting is found in every faithful heart*?'[4] This idea of an interior fount or river within every believer is more clearly brought out in John 7.37–38 (the companion text to John 4.14) where Christ says, 'If any man thirst, let him come to me, and drink. He that believeth in me, as the scripture saith, *Out of his belly shall flow rivers of living water.*' To this the Evangelist adds, 'Now this he said of the Spirit which they should receive, who believed in him…' (Jn. 7.39). By a non-literal reading now common in translations of the bible, the 'belly' of John 7.38 is read as the heart: 'as the scripture has said, "Out of his heart shall flow rivers of living water"' (RSV). Scriptural and exegetical writings often use terms such as 'heart', 'womb', 'guts', 'inner being', 'belly' and 'bowel' synonymously. Hopkins, fully aware of the discursive tradition that unites both translations of John 7.38, offers a subtle amalgamation of images. By presenting the heart as 'mother' (whose 'heart-throe' will 'birth' the Word in stanza 30), Hopkins evokes the womb of the heart. This is reiterated in an etymological play: 'madrigal', derived from the Latin *matrix*, 'womb', from *mater*, 'mother'. In this context, the heart in its 'bower' plays on 'bowel', signalling the inner discourse that is at stake here. The spiritual reformation achieved in baptism is achieved in the rebirth and re-creation of the heart.

Stanza 18 of *The Wreck* evokes a further, related baptismal type: the smitten rock. Hopkins's heart in its hardened 'bower of bone' is struck to release 'tears' and 'never-eldering' waters, a poetic rendition of that commonplace Victorian type – the rock of Horeb. George Landow notes that Victorian readers commonly interpreted the type as a prefiguration of the crucifixion, and that poets of the period used this biblical type to depict Christ bringing tears of repentance from the hardened heart. Hopkins's iconography draws from these contexts, while also emphasising a typological interpretation no longer common in the nineteenth century – the more traditional interpretation by which the stricken rock was understood as a type of baptism. The allusion to John 7.37–38 points to this reading; for, as we have seen, John 7.37 makes use of the idea of the holy rock, which dispenses the water of life.[5] Hopkins's merging of the imagery of the heart, the fountain of life and the rock of drinking refers to the discourse of baptismal regeneration central to *The Wreck*. By bringing together the images of 'bower' and 'never-eldering' river or fountain, Hopkins alludes also to the *fons signatus* of Song 4.12: 'A garden enclosed is my sister, my spouse; a spring shut up, a fountain sealed.' Exegetical interpretation relates Song 4.12 to John 4.14; the image of the sealed fountain prefigures the church or soul who has the fountain of life welling up within her. The garden of soul is again a metaphor associated with spiritual regeneration, and Hopkins's complex symbolism incorporates this meaning. The pastoral imagery of 'bower' and 'river' correspondingly looks forward to the tree and river of life of Revelation, the paradisiacal fulfilment of the baptismal promise. A similar pattern of imagery is found in another important passage of *The Wreck*. Here, the sacramental themes of the poem's subtext are retraced to their origin in Christ's Passion; from the side of Christ on the cross, the church is born:

6

Not out of his bliss
Springs the stress felt
Nor first from heaven (and few know this)
Swings the stroke dealt—
Stroke and a stress that stars and storms deliver,
That guilt is hushed by, hearts are flushed by and melt—
But it rides time like riding a river
(And here the faithful waver, the faithless fable and miss).

7

It dates from day
Of his going in Galilee;
Warm-laid grave of a womb-life grey;

Manger, maiden's knee;
The dense and the driven Passion, and frightful sweat;
Thence the discharge of it, there its swelling to be,
Though felt before, though in high flood yet—
What none would have known of it, only the heart, being hard at bay,

8

Is out with it!...

Stanza 6 again merges the imagery of a fluid and melting heart with that of a river whose passage is linked with time – a subtle echo of the 'never-eldering' river of stanza 18. The word 'stroke' is perhaps an intimation of the rock struck by Moses. Typologically, this rock is Christ, who must receive upon the cross the blows that will release the waters of life. It is also, simultaneously, the sinner's heart of stone that is struck by God to undergo a sacramental rebirth. This is precisely the conflation of imagery seen in Hopkins's verse. The 'stroke' that is dealt flushes and melts hearts, overriding time even as it, paradoxically, dates from the day of Christ's Passion. In the New Testament portrayal of Christ as true rock or stone, both Romans 9.33 and 1 Peter 2.4–8 describe Christ as the stone bringing salvation or destruction.[6] Both passages look back to Isaiah: 'And he shall be a sanctification to you. But for a stone of stumbling, and for a rock of offence to the two houses of Israel... And very many of them shall stumble and fall...' (Is. 8.14–15) The concluding line of stanza 6 faintly echoes this portrayal of Christ as stone of salvation or stumbling. Hopkins similarly describes and emphasises a twofold effect, using parentheses to draw the attention of the reader; even the 'faithful' waver, while the 'faithless' seem to stumble as they 'fable and miss'.

The image of the stone or holy rock of waters is continued in the following stanza, where Hopkins ambiguously describes a 'warm-laid grave of a womb-life grey'. The word 'grey' is prominent in its positioning and Hopkins's juxtaposition of 'grave' and 'grey' suggests to the mind's eye a tombstone. In a metaphorical conflation with which we are now familiar, this image is connected with that of the heart. The closing line of stanza 7 describes 'the heart, being hard' – a portrayal that foreshadows the heart in its 'bower of bone' (18), struck to release the sacramental waters. As in the subsequent stanza, Hopkins uses a female vocabulary to suggest baptism as the rebirth of the soul. While the 'bower' of stanza 18 may be read as 'bowel' or 'womb', stanza 7 explicitly describes the 'womb' of the 'maiden'. A further conflation of imagery foregrounds Hopkins's baptismal subtext, for the merging of 'womb' and 'grave' seems an unmistakable evocation of the baptismal font of patristic exegesis. In the words of Cyril of Jerusalem, the waters of baptism are at once 'tomb and mother'.[7] Here in stanza 7, Hopkins's inner, sacramental narrative finds expression through yet another scriptural echo. The 'heart' that is 'hard at bay' is read by John Keating as a paronomasia on 'hart', anticipating the title given to Christ later in the poem where he is described as 'Orion', hunter of souls.[8] However, the paronomasia to which Keating draws attention may be more appropriately related to Psalm 41, 'As the hart pants after the water brooks'. This psalm is integrally linked with the discourse on baptism; in the decoration of early baptisteries, the hart or deer represented the baptised whose spiritual thirst had been quenched. Yet the precise subject of this poetic sequence from stanzas 6 to 8 is, as Hopkins specifies, the origin of sacramental grace. As Keating suggests in his commentary on *The Wreck*, the word 'discharge' (7) relates to the heart, in light of Hopkins's spiritual note of 1884: 'The piercing of Christ's side. The sacred body and the sacred heart seemed waiting for an opportunity of discharging themselves and testifying their total devotion of themselves to the cause of man [.]'[9] The blood and water that flowed from Christ's wounded body at the crucifixion originates in his riven side and heart. The sacrifice of this sacred heart is the central emphasis of this important passage:

7

...only the heart, being hard at bay,

8

Is out with it! Oh,
We lash with the best or worst
Word last! How a lush-kept plush-capped sloe
Will, mouthed to flesh-burst,
Gush!—flush the man, the being with it, sour or sweet,
Brim, in a flash, full!...

The sacramental waters flowing from Christ's heart merge with the eucharistic symbolism of sloe fruit to suggest a fullness of grace that will 'flush' the man and infuse the devout heart. By describing the waters that 'brim' within the believer, Hopkins intimates again the well or fountain of living waters (Jn. 4.14). What we see in this stanza is the fulfillment of Christ's promise, delivered in death: 'He that believeth in me, as the scripture saith, Out of his heart shall flow rivers of living water.' (John 7.38, RSV). In this central passage, Hopkins's sacramental narrative moves easily between Christ as the sacred source of the sacraments and the renewed heart of the believer. Stanza 7 also importantly invokes a further baptismal type: the 'high flood' continued and elaborated in a later section of the poem.

At the opening of *The Wreck*, the refashioning of a man (or heart) is subtly paralleled with the waters of Genesis and the divine spirit that moves over these waters. More precisely, the waters of the heart are imaginatively and typologically connected with the waters of creation; the divine spirit moves and shapes both outer and inner world. In stanza 32, Hopkins evokes a God who is master of the ocean and tides, echoing the deity who presides over the sands and seas of the poem's opening stanza. The setting, however, is no longer the first waters of creation, but instead the 'Yore-flood', the great flood sent upon men by God as described in Genesis:

32

I admire thee, master of the tides,
Of the Yore-flood, of the year's fall;
The recurb and the recovery of the gulf's sides,
The girth of it and the wharf of it and the wall;
Stanching, quenching ocean of a motionable mind;
Ground of being, and granite of it: past all
Grasp God, throned behind
Death with a sovereignty that heeds but hides, bodes but abides;

Once again, Hopkins's words portray a landscape external and internal – a landscape reformed by grace. The ancient waters that destroyed and cleansed the sinful world are simultaneously the waters that comprise the 'ocean of a motionable mind'. 'Mind', 'heart', 'ground (or seat) of the soul', 'conscience' are terms often used synonymously in exegetical and mystical writings, and Hopkins again frames the heart as his hidden referent. In stanza 18, Hopkins addresses that 'mother of being in me, heart', and stanza 32 similarly describes the mind as 'ground of being'. At the same time, the portrayal of God 'throned' in 'a sovereignty that heeds but hides, bodes but abides' reinforces this meaning through a play of image and sound. Hopkins's juxtaposition of bodes/abides suggests God's dwelling or *abode* in man, the heart. The image of a throne draws also on religious heart symbolism and its frequent portrayal of God or Christ enthroned within the human heart. Hopkins's hidden heart is thus set against the waters of the flood that prefigure baptism; at the same time, this heart is connected with the central typological image of the poem: the waters from the rock. For Hopkins, the divine presence in the soul is 'ground of being, and *granite* of it [my italics].' As before, rock and water together form the image of sacramental salvation; the waters of life are the divine spirit in the heart of the believer. A faint echo of St Paul is perhaps Hopkins's clearest cue. In the fourth line of stanza 32, Hopkins describes the vastness of the ocean, and the love of God: 'the girth of it and the wharf of it and the wall'. The passage recalls Ephesians 3.18, which describes the 'breadth', 'length', 'height' and 'depth' of God's love. Indeed, the whole passage from Ephesians 3.16 to 3.19 can be seen as a scriptural accompaniment to stanza 32:

> That he would grant you, according to the riches of his glory, to be strengthened with might by his Spirit in the inner man;
>
> That Christ may dwell in your hearts by faith; that ye, being rooted and grounded in love,
>
> May be able to comprehend with all saints what is the breadth, and length, and depth, and height;
>
> And to know the love of Christ, which passeth knowledge, that ye might be filled with all the fullness of God.
>
> (Eph. 3.16–19 AV)

It is this very image of divine fullness that underwrites stanza 32. Hopkins's evocation of the heart as the abode of God, 'ground' and 'granite' of being, echoes the divine indwelling by which the soul is 'rooted and grounded in love' (Eph. 3.17 AV). Hopkins's imagery suggests a heart flooded by sacramental grace and made vast as an ocean of infinite love. God and man are one in the fullness of 'his Spirit in the inner man' (Eph. 3.16 AV). This working of the Spirit in the inner man is a key passage in patristic writing on the energies and the synergistic operation of grace. Hopkins too evokes this internal union and participation through a merging of mind and heart with the motion and movement of God's Spirit. The baptismal resonances of stanza 32 are continued and developed in stanza 33. Again, it is not only the image of water, but also the idea of judgment connected with these waters, that relates the flood to its sacramental antitype in baptism:

> Because Christ also died once for our sins, the just for the unjust: that he might offer us to God, being put to death indeed in the flesh, but enlivened in the spirit, In which also coming he preached to those spirits that were in prison: Which had been some time incredulous, when they waited for the patience of God in the days of Noe, when the ark was a building: wherein a few, that is, eight souls, were saved by water. Whereunto baptism being of the like form, now saveth you also …
>
> (1 Pt. 3.18–21)

This famous scriptural passage describes Christ's death and descent into the lower world. We hear an almost direct echo of these words in Hopkins's description of the descending love of God, reaching out over the waters to save the souls of the penitent:

33

With a mercy that outrides
The all of water, an ark
For the listener; for the lingerer with a love glides

Lower than death and the dark;
A vein for the visiting of the past-prayer, pent in prison,
The-last-breath penitent spirits—the uttermost mark
Our passion-plungèd giant risen,
The Christ of the Father compassionate, fetched in the storm of his strides.

Hopkins describes Christ descending beneath the flooded surface of the earth, 'lower than death and the dark', to the underworld, to the 'pent in prison…penitent spirits.' The allusion seems clear, and is reinforced by Hopkins's suggestion of a saving 'ark', echoing Noah's ark that is itself a figure of the church and the sacraments by which mankind is saved from sin and death. Typologically, Christ's descent into this lower world realises the mystery of the flood; at his death, the sinful world is destroyed and he rises from these waters as the firstborn of the new creation, the head of a new race. Hopkins goes on to describe this rebirth in the very next stanza:

34

Now burn, new born to the world,
Doubled-naturèd name,
The heaven-flung, heart-fleshed, maiden-furled
Miracle-in-Mary-of-flame,
Mid-numbered He in three of the thunder-throne!
Not a dooms-day dazzle in his coming nor dark as he came;
Kind, but royally reclaiming his own;
A released shower, let flash to the shire, not a lightning of fire hard-hurled.

The 'new born' Hopkins describes here is simultaneously the resurrected Christ and the new creation by baptism. So is the 'name' 'double-natured', for Hopkins suggests the doubling of God-in-man, man remade to the likeness of God. The imagery of stanza 34 echoes that found in the opening stanzas of the poem. The parallel is significant, for it is this opening section of Hopkins's ode that comprises a more directly personal narrative. In both stanzas 34 and 2, Hopkins evokes Christ's spiritual descent into the baptised and believing heart, which is now clearly Hopkins's own:

2

I did say yes
O at lightning and lashed rod;
Thou heardst me truer than tongue confess
Thy terror, O Christ, O God;
Thou knowest the walls, altar and hour and night:

The swoon of a heart that the sweep and the hurl of thee trod
Hard down with a horror of height:
And the midriff astrain with leaning of, laced with fire of stress.

'I did say yes' marks the personal, inner voice of the poet and emphasises the theme of sacramental recapitulation at the heart of the poem. There is a clear overlap in the vocabulary of stanzas 2 and 34. In Hopkins's second stanza, the heart that God will 'hurl', 'hard down' from its height seems unmistakably to parallel the 'heaven-flung', 'hard-hurled' heart of stanza 34. In both stanzas, the subtext is the same: it is Christ who is hurled hard down from heaven and resurrected in the heart of the believer. Both stanzas employ the imagery of fire and flame to suggest the divine *energeia* and the operation of the Spirit. While the 'new born' of stanza 34 suggests the resurrected Christ and the spiritual rebirth of the creature, this is similarly intimated here in Hopkins's description of the 'midriff *astrain* [my italics].' This odd description echoes the 'heart-throe' that Hopkins describes in stanza 30: it is birth of God in the soul, the sacramental regeneration of the heart that is made, at once, womb, bower and inner fountain. The word 'midriff' can be read with reference to John 7.38, 'He that believeth in me, as the scripture saith, *Out of his belly shall flow rivers of living water.*' Here in stanza 2, this living water of the Spirit is described as a 'fire of stress', anticipating that 'stroke' and 'stress' that is described in stanza 6 as the origin of sacramental grace. The divine activity or stress is described in elemental imagery that emphasises the motion or movement that is the principle of all that is created. In the human creature, this divine stress transforms the heart into the spiritual temple of the New Testament (cf. 1 Cor. 3.16). As Hopkins describes in stanza 3, this transformation is the work of the Spirit in the soul:

3

The frown of his face
Before me, the hurtle of hell
Behind, where, where was a, where was a place?
I whirled out wings that spell
And fled with a fling of the heart to the heart of the Host.
My heart, but you were dovewinged, I can tell,
Carrier-witted, I am bold to boast,
To flash from the flame to the flame then, tower from the grace to the grace.

In Hopkins's ode, stanza 3 functions as a powerful nexus of religious and mystical imagery. At one level, Hopkins's 'dovewinged heart' may be understood within the context of liturgical practice. Hopkins's specific mention of the 'Host' in this stanza draws attention to eucharistic devotion. In early churches, the container of the Eucharist took two forms: the tower and the dove. In his evocation of the Host, the dove, and the 'tower[ing]' of the heart in the concluding line of the stanza, Hopkins likely writes with an eye to this liturgical meaning. In the middle ages, the eucharistic case (tower, dove or pyx) was often suspended above the altar wrapped in a veil; in later centuries, the tabernacle became the eucharistic container, covered with a veil and placed at the altar.[10] In stanza 2, Hopkins describes his own conversion, the moment of his assent at the altar of the church. Hopkins's search for a 'place' draws on the symbolism of the tabernacle – for this search leads to the 'heart of the Host'.[11] But what Hopkins actually describes through this ritual symbolism is again the spiritual transformation of his own heart. The winged heart that flies to the place of the tabernacle flies to its own transformation. In the New Testament, the divine 'tabernacle' or 'dwelling place' is the heart itself, housing the Spirit of God. This is the meaning of the scriptural allusion embedded in the stanza. Hopkins's 'dovewinged' heart invokes the dove of the *Song of Songs*, and James Cotter draws attention to Gregory of Nyssa's sermons on the Song. Cotter writes, 'The bride as a dove, according to Gregory, is bid by the Apostle Paul "in the same image to be transformed from glory to glory".'[12] This transformation is made clearer if we look at the full context of Paul's words:

> But even until this day, when Moses is read, the veil is upon their heart.
>
> But when they shall be converted to the Lord, the veil shall be taken away.
>
> Now the Lord is a Spirit. And where the Spirit of the Lord is, there is liberty.
>
> But we all beholding the glory of the Lord with open face, are transformed into the same image from glory to glory, as by the Spirit of the Lord.
>
> (2 Cor. 3.15–18)

This scriptural passage is critical to *The Wreck*, and its full implications will be explored in the next chapter. Here in stanza 3, the heart's movement from 'the grace to the grace' suggests the transition from 'glory to glory' described in 2 Corinthians 3.18. This scriptural passage is again at the centre of patristic thinking about divine *energeia* or glory, and the practice of contemplation as a participation in this divine activity. The veil allegorised by Paul is the one worn by Moses to cover his face as it shone with reflected glory after his encounter with God on Mount Sinai (Exod. 34.33–35). Paul thus describes the transition from the Old Law to the New, and in Hopkins's narrative, the allusion reiterates the poem's sacramental subtext, the transformation of the stony heart into the regenerated heart, which is the spiritual temple of God. The removal of the veil is the transformation begun in baptism. In the words of Gregory of Nyssa,

> The soul, in taking off the tunic of skin with which it was clothed after the fall, opens itself to the Word by taking away the veil from its heart, that is to say, the flesh. And by "flesh" I mean the "old man" who must be taken off...[13]

Gregory's words connect the removal of the veil from the heart with the new creation of baptism, and the regeneration of the 'inner man' of the heart. If the symbolism of the veil and its relation to the 'old man' remains latent in stanza 3, it is reiterated in the very next stanza of *The Wreck*. Here, Hopkins evokes again a fluid baptismal imagery; the 'well' may be understood as the fountain or well of living waters, and is thus intimated by Hopkins as the gift of the 'gospel proffer', 'Christ's gift':

4

I am soft sift
In an hourglass—at the wall
Fast, but mined with a motion, a drift,
And it crowds and it combs to the fall;
I steady as a water in a well, to a poise, to a pane,
But roped with, always, all the way down from the tall
Fells or flanks of the voel, a vein
Of the gospel proffer, a pressure, a principle, Christ's gift.

The stanza enfolds a complex play of word. 'Voel', meaning a bare hill or mountain in Welsh,[14] is an uncommon word, prominent in its choice. Hopkins's true meaning perhaps lies between words. 'Voel' is pronounced 'voil', and the juxtaposition of 'voel' and 'vein' suggests the spectre of a third word: 'veil'. If this seems a case of over-reading it may be seen that Hopkins himself draws out this meaning through careful verbal crafting. Hopkins's deliberate use of 'fells' in conjunction with the corporeal imagery of 'flanks' suggests the etymological derivation of 'fell' from the Old High German *fel*, skin, or Latin *pellis*. It is in fact this very sense of the word that Hopkins draws on in Sonnet 67, 'I wake and feel the fell of dark not day'. Here, 'fell' is read as a pelt, hide or skin. In stanza 4 of *The Wreck*, this metaphor is further drawn out by the word 'pane', which derives from the Middle English *pan* or *pane*, strip of cloth, from the Latin *pannus*, cloth.[15] Two additional verbs reiterate this trope; both 'roped' and 'combs' can be linked with the idea of weaving. These intricate word games move, as always, in the direction of a larger sacramental and theological meaning. The biblical veil evokes Christ's flesh, whose rending or crucifixion grants access to God. Hopkins, through this implied symbolism of the veil, suggests again the movement from glory to glory described in the preceding stanza. Indeed, Hopkins's words '*all the way down from the tall* / fells or flanks of the voel, a vein [my italics]' subtly echo the moment of Christ's death, when the temple veil was rent 'from the top even to the bottom' (Mt. 27.51; cf. Mk. 15.38, Lk. 23.45). The tearing of the veil achieved in Christ's crucifixion signified the transition from the Old to the New Law, from the material temple of the Old Testament to the spiritual temple of the New. This spiritual trajectory is the sacramental and mystical journey of Hopkins's heart as it is transformed from 'the grace to the grace' (3). Casting off the veil of the 'old man', the veil done away within Christ, Hopkins's heart is renewed by the energies of the Spirit. Anticipated in stanzas 3 and 4, this transfiguration is completed in stanzas 28 and 29, where the contemplating heart is truly changed into the divine image, by the Spirit of the Lord (cf. 2 Cor. 3.18):

28

But how shall I ... make me room there:
Reach me a ... Fancy, come faster—
Strike you the sight of it? look at it loom there,
Thing that she ... there then! the Master,
*Ipse,* the only one, Christ, King, Head:
He was to cure the extremity where he had cast her;
Do, deal, lord it with living and dead;
Let him ride, her pride, in his triumph, despatch and have done
with his doom there.

This climactic stanza is a direct counterpart to stanza 3, and must be read in parallel with the earlier passage. Here in stanza 28, Hopkins's search for 'room there' echoes his earlier search for a 'place' (3). Once again it is the divine indwelling that Hopkins describes, understood simultaneously as the temple of Christ's body the church and the temple of the human heart. By evoking Christ as 'Head', Hopkins suggests precisely this metaphor of the mystical body of Christ entered into at baptism. The title can be read with reference to Colossians 1.18 'And he is the head of the body, the church, who is the beginning, the firstborn from the dead; that in all things he may hold the primacy'.[16] In the bible, membership of this body is expressed as a grafting into Christ; the mystical body is 'knit together' in God (cf. Col. 2.19 AV). In stanza 3 of *The Wreck*, the transformation of the soul through baptism and the law of the spirit is suggested through the imagery of the veil. In stanza 28, Hopkins evokes this transformation through the related metaphor of the spiritual clothing of the soul. As we have seen, this symbolism derives from Galatians 3.27: 'as many of you as have been baptized in Christ, have put on Christ.' By drawing on the symbolism of the mystical body and the wearing of spiritual garments, Hopkins describes again the movement from flesh to spirit, from the material to the immaterial and from the temporal to the eternal. In Paul's words,

> For we know, if our earthly house of this habitation be dissolved, that we have a building of God, a house not made with hands, eternal in heaven.
>
> For in this also we groan, desiring to be clothed upon with our habitation that is from heaven. Yet so that we be found clothed, not naked.
>
> For we also, who are in this tabernacle, do groan, being burthened; because we would not be unclothed, but clothed upon, that that which is mortal may be swallowed up by life.
>
> (2 Cor. 5.1–4)

This scriptural passage contrasts the earthly tabernacle that is the physical body with the spiritual body or garment, the heavenly tabernacle. Paul's words express the soul's yearning in its anticipation of the final glorification, when the mortal shall 'put on' immortality (1 Cor. 15.53) and 'in the twinkling of an eye, at the last trumpet…we shall be changed' (1 Cor. 15.52). Hopkins plays with this idea of spiritual clothing through a series of words that can, at one level, be read in metaphorical relation. 'Strike you the sight of it?' Hopkins asks. '…look at it loom there.' The OED lists one of the meanings of strike as 'to card, as wool', a meaning consonant with the reading of 'combs' in stanza 4. 'Loom', read out of syntax, correspondingly suggests an instrument for weaving, while 'cast' can be read to denote a warp, a series of yarns in a loom (OED). At this culminating moment of *The Wreck of the Deutschland*, Hopkins's heart speaks its desire to be clothed with the heavenly raiment or spiritual body. The removal of the veil from the heart is its turning to God (3) and its progressive transformation by the spirit in an anticipation of the eschatological glory of God's promise.

As we saw in the preceding chapter, the symbolism of spiritual garments relates to the theology of the transfiguration and ascension of Christ. Gregory of Nyssa, for example, speaks of the baptised wearing 'the tunic of the Lord, shining li*k*e the sun, which clothed Him with purity and incorruptibility when He went up on the Mount of the Transfiguration'.[17] As Danièlou observes, amongst the traditional names for baptism is the expression 'what carries us to heaven', used by both the Cappadocian fathers, Gregory Nazianzen and Gregory of Nyssa. This symbolism relates to the chariot of Elias and his ascension as a figure of the ascension of Christ (Luke 9.51).[18] Baptism itself is seen as the ascension of the baptised, as a configuration to the ascension of Christ.

As Ambrose writes in *De Mysteriis*, 'Who is this that cometh up made white?'[19] Made white by the vestments put on in baptism, this is the ascent of the baptised made beautiful by the garment of grace. The putting on of Christ or the wearing of the spiritual garments thus signifies configuration to Christ and a prefiguration of future glory. Again, the putting on of incorruption by the creature is the primary way in which the fathers conceive of a participation in the divine *energeiai*. Hopkins's symbolism is both sacramental and eschatological, describing the ascent of the baptised soul and an anticipation of its final glorification. To emphasise this subtext of mystical ascent, Hopkins alludes to the transfiguration of Christ in the very next stanza:

29

Ah! there was a heart right!
There was single eye!
Read the unshapeable shock night
And knew the who and the why;
Wording it how but by him that present and past,
Heaven and earth are word of, worded by?—
The Simon Peter of a soul! to the blast
Tarpeian-fast, but a blown beacon of light.

This stanza holds a number of cues that hint at the mystical phenomenon of Christ's transfiguration; the mention of Peter is one such intimation, for Peter was one of the three witnesses to the transfiguration:

> And after six days Jesus taketh unto him Peter and James, and John his brother, and bringeth them up into a high mountain apart.
>
> And he was transfigured before them. And his face did shine as the sun: and his garments became white as snow.
>
> And behold there appeared to them Moses and Elias talking with him.
>
> And Peter answering, said to Jesus…if thou wilt, let us make three tabernacles, one for thee, and one for Moses, and one for Elias.
>
> And as he was yet speaking, behold a bright cloud overshadowed them. And lo, a voice out of the cloud saying, This is my beloved Son…hear ye him.
>
> (Mt. 17.1–5)

The complex symbolism surrounding the transfiguration subtly permeates stanza 29 of *The Wreck*. Hopkins's description of the 'single eye' has been read with reference to Matthew 6.22. '…lay up to yourselves treasures in heaven…For where thy treasure is, there is thy heart also. The light of thy body is thy eye: If thy eye be single, thy whole body shall be lightsome (Matt. 6.20–22).[20] Hopkins suggests again the soul's ascent and that body or vestment of light, which adorns the ascended soul. This transformation of the soul to a spiritual body of light is symbolically related to Christ's transfiguration, when his garments became 'white as snow' (AV, 'white as the light'). Hopkins's description of the '*unshapeable* shock night [my italics]' may further be seen to relate to the etymology of 'transfigure'; the word derives from the Latin *transfigurare*, from *trans-* + *figurare* to shape or fashion, to give a new and typically exalted or spiritual appearance to. The transfiguration is a mystical 'reshaping', and it is this mystical transformation of the soul in the image of Christ and of God that Hopkins suggests here. The brightness that emanated from Christ's body at his transfiguration is said to have been produced by the interior shining or energies of his divinity.[21] In this context, we may note that the words 'shock' (29) and 'strike' (29) both echo the 'electrical horror' (27) described in the preceding stanza. Hopkins's imagery subtly draws on transfiguration narratives, and the motif of lightning associated with the wearing of spiritual garments (cf. the 'dazzling' garments described in the transfiguration narrative of Luke 9.29 AV; or the 'shining' garments seen at the Resurrection in Luke 24.4).[22] Another cue to the transfiguration symbolism on which Hopkins draws is found in the word 'loom' (28). As a verb, 'loom' suggests 'something that appears on the horizon; loom, as a shadow.'[23] The word perhaps recalls the 'cloud' that 'overshadowed' the disciples at the transfiguration. This cloud itself signifies the spirit and the whole passage suggests again the soul's participation in divinity and the working of the divine energies. St Aquinas in his *Summa Theologica* explains the relation between the putting on of spiritual garments and the cloud that overshadows Christ's disciples at his transfiguration:

> The bright cloud signifies the glory of the Holy Ghost...by which in the glory to come the saints will be covered. Or, again, it may be said fittingly that it signifies the clarity of the world redeemed, which clarity will cover the saints as a tent. Hence when Peter proposed to make tents, 'a bright cloud overshaded' the disciples.[24]

Both cloud and spiritual garment symbolise the transfiguration of the soul. As Aquinas points out there is only one reason for the disciples to witness Christ's transfiguration: to be shown the glory to which Christ will configure his own, as according to Philippians 3.21: '(Who) will reform the body of our lowness, made like to the body of His glory'. He writes:

> The adoption of the sons of God is through a certain conformity of image to the natural Son of God. Now this takes place in two ways: first, by the grace of the wayfarer, which is imperfect conformity;

> secondly, by glory, which is perfect conformity, according to 1 John 3.2: 'We are now the sons of God, and it hath not yet appeared what we shall be: we know that, when He shall appear, we shall be like to Him, because we shall see Him as He is.' Since, therefore, it is in baptism that we acquire grace, while the clarity of the glory to come was foreshadowed in the transfiguration, therefore both in His baptism and in His transfiguration the natural sonship of Christ was fittingly made known by the testimony of the Father...[25]

Aquinas's words make explicit the integral link between the discourse on baptism and the theology of the transfiguration. As a sacramental and mystical narrative, *The Wreck* celebrates man's adopted sonship of God and Hopkins's invocation of the transfiguration is in keeping with his theme of configuration to Christ: 'Know you not that all we who are baptized into Christ Jesus, are baptized into his death?...For if we have been planted together in the likeness of his death, we shall be also in the likeness of his resurrection.' (Rom. 6.3–5) The climax of *The Wreck of the Deutschland* completes the ascent of the baptised soul, drawing on the transfiguration as the model for the soul's eschatological glory, a glimpse of that perfect conformity and glory to come. This is the regeneration of Hopkins's heart, energised and transformed by the Spirit of God (cf. 2 Cor. 3.18).

## Notes

1 Hopkins, *Sermons and Devotional Writings*, 98. Hopkins comments on the variety of spiritual gifts described by St Paul, each a manifestation of the one spirit. 'Therefore he is called the finger of the Father's right hand, that is all the fingers, for the fingers are to the hand or arm as many things are to one' (ibid., 98).
2 Danièlou, *Bible and Liturgy*, 74 n.
3 David Lyle Jeffrey, ed. *A Dictionary of Biblical Tradition in English Literature*. (Grand Rapids, MI: William B. Eerdmans Publishing Co., 1992), 279.
4 Origen, 'Commentary' (3.13), Lawson, 236. Cf. Ps. 45.5 and John 4.14.
5 Kittel, *Dictionary of the New Testament*, vol. IV, 271.
6 Ibid., 271–72.
7 Danièlou, *Bible and Liturgy*, 47.
8 John E. Keating, 'The Wreck of the Deutschland: An Essay and Commentary,' Research Series VI, vol. LI, No. 1 (Kent, OH: Kent State University, 1963), 66.
9 Ibid.
10 *New Advent Catholic Encyclopedia*, ed. Kevin Knight, 2008, 'Tabernacle,' www.newadvent.org/cathen/14424a.htm and 'Pyx,' www.newadvent.org/cathen/12588a.htm.
11 The flight of Hopkins's heart to the Host may also be related to the 'lifting up' of hearts that has since the time of the early church been the congregation's expression of thanks and offering following communion. See Jeffrey, *Dictionary of Biblical Tradition*, 245.

12 James Cotter, 'The *Song of Songs* and "The Wreck of the Deutschland"' in Eugene Hollahan (ed.), *Gerard Manley Hopkins and Critical Discourse* (New York: AMS Press, 1993), 59.
13 Gregory of Nyssa, *Sermon against those who put off their Baptism,* XLIV, 1003 D, quoted in Danièlou, *Bible and Liturgy,* 39.
14 Gardner and MacKenzie, *Poems,* 258 n.
15 'Pane' is further related to 'vane', also akin to Latin *pannus*, cloth. In stanza 4, 'pane' is rhymed with 'vein' and the latter may perhaps be read as a paronomasia on 'vane'.
16 Cotter, *Inscape*, 157–58. Cotter uses the AV.
17 Gregory of Nyssa, *Sermon against those who put off their Baptism,* XLIV, 1005 C, quoted in Danièlou, *Bible and Liturgy,* 50.
18 Danièlou, *Bible and Liturgy,* 108. The typological interpretation of Elias relates first to his crossing of the Jordan, which is seen as a repetition of the crossing of the Red Sea; the ascension of Elias after crossing the Jordan is correspondingly interpreted as a figure of Christ's Ascension.
19 Ambrose, 'The Mysteries' (7.35), Deferrari, 18.
20 Cotter, *Inscape,* 173. Cotter cites the AV.
21 *New Advent Catholic Encyclopedia*, ed. Kevin Knight, 2008. 'Transfiguration,' www.newadvent.org/cathen/15019a.htm.
22 Certain translations of Luke 24.4 describe these garments as 'bright as lightning' (God's Word Translation).
23 The image of the cloud may be seen to be foreshadowed in stanza 26 where Hopkins describes the 'ground-hugged grey', the cloud that 'hovers off' as blue skies appear.
24 St Thomas Aquinas, *Summa Theologica,* translated by the Fathers of the English Dominican Province, 1947. Third Part, Treatise on the Incarnation: Question 45: Of Christ's Transfiguration (Second Article), www.sacred-texts.com/chr/aquinas/summa/sum496.htm.
25 Ibid., Question 45: Of Christ's Transfiguration (Fourth Article).

# 6 Origen and the *Song of Songs*

The *Song of Songs* has been interpreted in three ways in Christian exegesis: while the lover is consistently read as God or Christ, the beloved is read as the church, the individual soul or the Virgin Mary (these readings frequently overlap in religious commentary). While the sensuous imagery of the Song might seem a surprising choice for Hopkins, its patristic application makes it appropriate to Hopkins's narrative of baptism, regeneration and mystical ascent.[1] From the time of the early church, the nuptial imagery of the *Song of Songs* has been understood in relation to the sacraments and the liturgy of initiation. The Song is interpreted in patristic exegesis as the epithalamion of the wedding of Christ and his church, a marriage inaugurated in the Incarnation (cf. Jn. 3.29) and fulfilled in the eschatological marriage (Mt. 25.1–3). Between inauguration and completion, this union is re-enacted in the sacraments. The early catechetical addresses of St Cyril of Jerusalem and St Ambrose, directed to the newly baptised, explicate the baptismal ritual as a 'nuptial bath' and the Eucharist as a wedding banquet.[2] In the New Testament, this sacramental interpretation of nuptial theology finds confirmation in the Epistle to the Ephesians (5.23–32), which presents baptism and the Eucharist as the realisation of the heavenly marriage:

> Because the husband is the head of the wife, as Christ is the head of the church. He is the saviour of his body...Husbands, love your wives, as Christ also loved the Church, and delivered himself up for it: That He might sanctify it, cleansing it by the laver of water in the word of life...that it should be holy and without blemish...For no man ever hated his own flesh; but nourisheth and cherisheth it, as also Christ doth the Church. Because we are members of his body, of his flesh, and of his bones. *For this cause shall a man leave his father and mother, and shall cleave to his wife, and they shall be two in one flesh.* This is a great sacrament, but I speak in Christ and in the Church.
>
> (Eph. 5.23–32)

As St John Chrysostom writes in his *Commentary on the Epistle to the Ephesians*, 'The bath is the purification, the marriage union is itself the complete sanctification, and here the allusion to the Eucharist is clear; it is by this sacrament that Christ and soul are made one flesh, as man and wife.'[3] This important passage from Ephesians demonstrates the doctrine of the mystical body as intimately connected with the metaphor of the spiritual marriage. The nuptial union of the sacraments enjoins the believer to the body of God. Men and women are made members of Christ's body because their nuptial union with him makes them 'one flesh', which in turn is symbolic of being 'one spirit' (e.g. *Sermons* of St Bernard, 71).[4] The sacramental and liturgical application of the Song as seen in catechetical texts makes apparent, at one level, its relevance to Hopkins's baptismal narrative. At another level, the deeper mystical connotations of the Song can be seen from commentaries and exegetical works.

The most influential early writing on the Song is Origen's third-century commentary. Hopkins's great admiration of Origen and sense of kinship with the early Father has already been noted. *The Wreck* suggests that he derived from Origen not only an allegorical method, but also a mystical understanding of the place of the Song in Christian belief. Origen's *Commentary on the Song of Songs* is primarily ecclesiological, but there is a clear parallel in the relationship between the divine Word and the church, and the Word and the soul. In fact, it is Origen's emphasis on the mystical drama of the soul that significantly influences later interpretation of this Old Testament text. For Origen, the Song represents the culmination of the mystical ascent that is the proper end of scriptural study; it teaches 'Enoptics', the third branch of philosophical knowledge. Origen explains, 'The study called inspective is that by which we go beyond things seen and contemplate somewhat of things divine and heavenly, beholding them with the mind alone, for they are beyond the range of bodily sight.'[5] What R. P. Lawson translates as the 'inspective' discipline is known in English as the contemplative or theoretic branch of learning. Lawson, however, asserts that neither of these terms is entirely satisfactory, 'for "contemplative" suggests looking at God (as far as may be without intervening images) and "theoretic"...has lost its original idea of "beholding", and carries an almost wholly intellectual meaning.'[6] Lawson therefore renders 'enoptic' as 'inspective', being the nearest literal equivalent. Nevertheless, it is useful to remember that Enoptics, as understood by Origen, is primarily an activity defined by contemplative paradigms. The experience of contemplation is central to *The Wreck of the Deutschland* and so the vocabulary of the Song becomes an appropriate choice for Hopkins's hidden narrative of mystical ascent. 'Epoptics', as Bernard McGinn describes it, is the science of Jacob who becomes 'Israel', etymologically meaning 'he who sees God.'[7]

Hopkins turns to the Song not only because of its sacramental significance, but also because it represents the heart of mystical Christianity, and demonstrates too the practice of mystical allegory. To understand the Song as the portrayal of the soul's ascent to divine contemplation, the reader must be in some sense incorporated by the text and made privy to its inner heart. By using the Song within the context of an ascent narrative, Hopkins makes a bold promise – read correctly, *The Wreck* offers up its own private *visio Dei*.

Despite a lack of evidence of Hopkins's direct knowledge of Origen's writing on the Song, the poet's unparalleled admiration of the Father makes it doubtful that he was unfamiliar with Origen's most famous works. In his spiritual writings, Hopkins makes direct reference to St Bernard of Clairvaux's sermons on the Song. Though incomplete, Bernard's sermons remain the classic medieval commentary on this book of scripture, and perhaps the most influential example of Christian exegesis of the Song.[8] It is Origen's mystical vision that shapes these medieval readings of the Song. As E. Ann Matter suggests in her book, *The Voice of My Beloved*, Bernard and Origen share an ardent concern for the union of the soul with the divine; the association of the Song with the love between God and soul is present from Origen onwards. Nevertheless, as Matter observes, this reading 'remains a secondary possibility for the [Song] throughout the long tradition of ecclesiological exegesis. As a primary mode of interpretation...this way of reading the *Song of Songs* came into its own in the twelfth century.'[9] Origen's sense of the drama of Christ and the soul prevails in medieval readings, with the writings of Bernard guiding this spiritual understanding. Bernard's 86 homilies reach only four verses beyond Origen's interpretation, and there are clear instances of thematic dependence. Amongst these is the interpretation of the opening verse of the Song, 'let him kiss me with the kiss of his mouth,'[10] alluded to in Hopkins's *The Wreck of the Deutschland*.

Hopkins's reference to Bernard's sermons on the Song is made in the context of his discussion of the devotion to the Sacred Heart. Reflecting on the history of the devotion, Hopkins observes that it is found 'in St. Gertrude's prayers and in St. Bernard's sermons, but little notice was in their days taken of it [.]'[11] These observations suggest Hopkins's knowledge of the theological development of the Sacred Heart devotion, whose emergence in the medieval period is related to the exegetical tradition of the *Song of Songs*. This link between the discourse on the *Song* and the devotion to Christ's Heart is discussed by the Jesuit scholar Peter Milward in a two-part essay on the historical development of the devotion. Milward argues that the devotion develops from a focus on the wound in Christ's side, and he suggests that Augustine's writings on John 19.34 are key to the conceptual development of the devotion. In his *Commentary on John*, Augustine emphasises that it is not a wounding or piercing that is described, but the 'opening' of Christ's side. Milward argues that this conception of the wound in Christ's side as a 'gate' or 'door' first directs attention inward to the sacred heart. This movement from exterior to interior, from the sacraments to their sacred inner source, finds its most persuasive expression in commentaries on the *Song* written after Augustine.[12]

The relation between the discourse on the Song and the devotion to Christ's wounds centres on the image of the bride of Christ as a dove nestling in the clefts of the rock (Song 2.14). These clefts are interpreted as Christ's sacred wounds. The interpretive parallel is between the dove of the Song and Ecclesia, the church and bride of Christ, formed from the wound in his side and the sacred sacraments of blood and water. This connection is first made by Cassiodorus in the sixth century:

> The holes in the rock are the wounds which He received on the cross for our salvation...In these holes, then, the dove – that is, the Church – makes her dwelling; for she places all her hope of salvation in the Passion of her Redeemer.[13]

If these early commentaries on the *Song* show intimations of the devotion to the sacred heart, this theme receives more sustained treatment in the middle ages. Hugh of St Victor's *De Anima* develops these ideas into the medieval devotion to the wounds of Christ, suggesting that

> There is a safe and sure rest...in the wounds of the Saviour. I dwell in them secure; the interior of His heart lies open to me through the wounds...Through the holes in the body appear to me the secrets of the heart; there appears the great mystery of His love, the mercy of our God in which the Orient from on high has visited us.[14]

Significantly, Bernard reproduces these very words of Hugh of St Victor in his *Sermons* on the Song, written in the second half of the same century. Bernard's interpretation is clearly borrowed, but it is his vision of the dove nestling in Christ's wounds that remains within the Christian imagination for centuries. From here on, Song 2.14 denotes the refuge of the soul not simply in the rock of Christ, as Origen portrayed it, but specifically in Christ's wounds. This interest in the sacred wounds is seen throughout the later middle ages. In the thirteenth century, the Franciscan St Bonaventure brings together earlier conceptual developments seen in commentaries on the Song to elaborate a devotion to the heart of Christ. The devotion to the sacred heart is developed through the middle ages as a devotion of the mystical order.

The *Song of Songs* and its related tradition of commentary is thus intimately linked with the mystical and sacramental life of the church. The Song is interpreted in patristic exegesis as a figure of the sacraments as a whole. Its later relation to the devotion to the sacred heart reiterates this significance, as Christ's heart is increasingly emphasised as the source of the sacraments and the gift of redemption bestowed upon the church. Central to both Jesuit and Franciscan spirituality, the devotion to Christ's heart is doubly relevant to *The Wreck of the Deutschland*. Turning now to look at *The Wreck of the Deutschland*, we see how Hopkins draws on varied exegetical, liturgical and catechistical interpretations of the Song to articulate a mystical and allegorical narrative.

## The *Song of Songs* and *The Wreck of the Deutschland*

Although Hopkins's biblical and devotional themes in *The Wreck of the Deutschland* have been extensively examined, there has been little discussion of the central place of the *Song of Songs* and its tradition of commentary. A single article by James Cotter looks at Hopkins's *The Wreck* in relation to the Song, charting a series of thematic and imagistic parallels within the poem. The exegetical tradition associated with the Song formed an important part of nineteenth-century seminary training. Drawing on the work of patristic and later commentators, Cotter suggests Hopkins's ode to be based on the allegory of the *Sponsa Christi*. This reading continues Cotter's analysis, but suggests that Hopkins's allusions to the Song in *The Wreck* are more specific and deliberate in their literary execution, and more rigorously ecclesiological, than has so far been realised. It is the relation of the Song to the waters of baptism (as seen in the union of Christ and Church in the washing of water by the word, Eph. 5.26–32) and its exegetical relation to the devotion to Christ's heart that critically defines Hopkins's application of the Song. To understand the sacramental and mystical paradigms within which Hopkins invokes the Song, we begin with stanzas 2 and 3 of *The Wreck*. Here, Hopkins alludes to that most iconic of images from the Song, the dove in the clefts of the rock (Song 2.14):

2

I did say yes
O at lightning and lashed rod;
Thou heardst me truer than tongue confess
Thy terror, O Christ, O God;
Thou knowest the walls, altar and hour and night:
The swoon of a heart that the sweep and the hurl of thee trod
Hard down with a horror of height:
And the midriff astrain with leaning of, laced with fire of stress.

3

The frown of his face
Before me, the hurtle of hell
Behind, where, where was a, where was a place?
I whirled out wings that spell

And fled with a fling of the heart to the heart of the Host.
My heart, but you were dovewinged, I can tell,
Carrier-witted, I am bold to boast,
To flash from the flame to the flame then, tower from the grace to the grace.

There are a number of important theological strands that run through this key passage. In Chapter 4, we considered the image of the 'midriff' (2) as connected with the belly-heart of John 7.37–38, 'If any man thirst, let him come to me, and drink. He that believeth in me, as the scripture saith, *Out of his belly shall flow rivers of living water.*'[15] John 7.38 describes the receiving of the Spirit in the hearts of the faithful, at the moment of Christ's death. Stanza 2 indeed refers to this very moment in time. The 'swoon of a heart' cleverly and subtly suggests the Passion of Christ and the piercing of Christ's side. We note too that Hopkins traces the consequence of this swooning heart: '*And* the midriff astrain...laced with fire of stress [my italics].' The word 'midriff' evokes a female imagery used to describe the mystical birth of God in the soul; it is the interior being, the belly, gut or heart that becomes the metaphorical dwelling place of the divine. Hopkins's inner narrative describes the birth of the Spirit in the believing heart, the receiving of the Spirit as given in the Passion of Christ. For the speaker at the altar, it is the moment of rebirth, the moment of acquiescence and a heart that will forever be bound to the sacred heart sacrificed by God.

In stanza 3, Hopkins goes on to describe his own 'dovewinged heart'. This allusion to Song 2.14 must be placed in the context of Hopkins's portrayal of the gift of sacramental salvation given in Christ's Passion. Hopkins uses the classic image of the dove nestling in the clefts of the rock to portray the sacred heart and the sacraments that flowed at the piercing of Christ's side. The flight of Hopkins's dovewinged heart ends in the 'heart of the Host' (3). The relation of the host or eucharistic wafer to Christ's sacred heart is well known. Hopkins draws on this association to emphasise his meaning, depicting the flight of his own heart to the sacred heart of Christ. Stanzas 2 and 3 together present a poetic imaging of the Sacred Heart devotion as it emerged from commentaries on the Song. St Bonaventure's *Lignum Vitae*, for example, reflects:

> In order that the Church might be formed from the side of Christ sleeping on the cross...it was ordained by divine providence that one of the soldiers should pierce with his lance and open that sacred side; so that in the blood flowing out with the water, the price of our salvation might be poured forth – thereby from the very source (namely the secret of the Heart) imparting abundant power to the sacraments of the Church for conferring the life of grace, and for

> bestowing on those who already live in Christ a cup of living water springing up into eternal life. Behold the lance has now made a hole in the rock and a hollow in the wall, as it were a dwelling for doves. Arise, then, beloved of Christ, be like a dove nestling in the opening of the hole...there place your mouth to drink water from the sources of the Saviour.[16]

Hopkins too portrays the sacramental gift of eternal life bestowed by Christ upon his dove-bride, both the church and the individual soul. Drawing on the devotional link between the dove of the Song and the heart of Christ, Hopkins's narrative incorporates a further level of symbolic meaning. This is the exegetical link between Song 2.14 and the 'hole of the rock' (Ex. 33.22, AV 'cleft of the rock') of Moses's vision, found in Origen's *Commentary* on the Song. As God says to Moses, 'And when my glory shall pass, I will set thee in a hole of the rock...and thou shalt see my back parts: but my face thou canst not see' (Ex. 33.22–23). God's promise to Moses famously describes the partial vision of the divine glory, as seen in the Old Testament. In the New Testament, it is the Word made flesh who himself becomes this cleft in the rock, and through whom alone the soul comes to a vision of God.

Importantly, Exodus 33.22–23 is of particular importance to the fourth-century Cappadocian Fathers when writing on the energies. The key distinction here is between God as he knows himself, and as he is known by mortal beings through his energies – the manifestation of his glory in the created world. Gregory of Nazianzen, for example, describes himself 'sheltered by the rock' and beholding the 'back parts of God'. He writes, 'I saw, not the first and unmingled nature, known to itself – to the Trinity, I mean; not that which abides within the first veil...but only that nature which at last even reaches to us. And that is, so far as I can tell, the majesty, or as holy David calls it, the glory which is manifested among the creatures, which it has produced and governs. For these [i.e., majesty and glory] are the back parts of God, which He leaves behind Him, as tokens of Himself like the shadows and reflections of the sun in the water..."[17] Here in *The Wreck*, Hopkins's allusion to the dove of Song 2.14 carries with it precisely this intimation of a *vision* that is a *participation* in divinity. 'Bold to boast' Hopkins's heart traces a contemplative journey even to the 'face' of God described at the opening of the stanza. This is the passage from 'grace to grace' (3), when 'we all beholding the glory of the Lord with open face, are transformed into the same image from glory to glory, as by the Spirit of the Lord. (2 Cor. 3.18).[18]

Hopkins continues these themes of sacramental and mystical union in stanza 5. This delicately allusive stanza evokes two of the most critical verses of the *Song of Songs* as elaborated in early and medieval commentaries:

5

I kiss my hand
To the stars, lovely-asunder
Starlight, wafting him out of it; and
Glow, glory in thunder;
Kiss my hand to the dappled-with-damson west:
Since, tho' he is under the world's splendour and wonder,
His mystery must be instressed, stressed;
For I greet him the days I meet him, and bless when I understand.

Hopkins's twice-repeated 'kiss' subtly suggests the first verse of the Song: 'let him kiss me with the kiss of his mouth' (Song 1.1). This text is interpreted in exegesis to suggest the nuptial union of the soul and Christ achieved in Eucharist. Ambrose writes, 'You have come to the altar; the Lord Jesus calls you – both your soul and the Church – and He says: "Let him kiss me with the kiss of his mouth;"' Ambrose suggests that the altar is itself a figure of Christ's body and the 'kiss' the eucharistic communion in which the lips receive the body of Christ.[19] Stanza 5 implicitly continues the image of the speaker at the altar in stanza 2. It also echoes the sacramental and nuptial metaphors suggested by Hopkins in his portrayal of the flight of his heart to Christ's sacred heart. While Hopkins's evocation of the host (stanza 3) draws on the traditional relation between the Eucharist and the sacred heart to suggest a spiritual union of hearts, we find a similar inscape of meaning here. Hopkins's use of the word 'kiss' as suggesting eucharistic communion is reiterated in his portrayal of the 'damson' in line 5, an image of eucharistic fruit. Nevertheless, it is above all Hopkins's unusual description of Christ's 'wafting' that acts as a key signifier to his sacramental and soteriological subtext. Commentaries on the Song have particularly emphasised Song 1.2: 'Smelling sweet of the best ointments. Thy name is as oil poured out…' Interpretations of the Song understand this verse to refer to Christ's spiritual descent and Incarnation. The Bridegroom's name is likened to a fragrance, and this 'fragrance-wafting' is a key motif in early Christian soteriology, signifying the divine presence in the world.[20] The opening of the 'Procatechesis' of Cyril of Jerusalem serves as an example here.

> Already the perfume of blessedness is wafted to you, O catechumens. Already you gather spiritual flowers to weave heavenly crowns. Already the sweet perfume of the Holy Spirit is poured out. You are in the vestibule of the royal dwelling. May you be led into it by the king. From henceforth, indeed, the flowers have appeared on the trees. Now the fruit must ripen.[21]

BOOK IV. EMBLEMS. 163

Emblem 8.

CANTICLES I. 3, 4.

*Draw me; we will run after thee because of the savour of thy good ointments.*

THUS, like a lump of the corrupted mass,
I lie secure, long lost before I was:
And like a block, beneath whose burthen lies
That undiscover'd worm that never dies,
I have no will to rouse, I have no power to rise.

Can stinking Lazarus compound or strive
With death's entangling fetters, and revive?
Or can the water-buried axe implore
A hand to raise it, or itself restore,
And from her sandy deeps approach the dry-foot shore?

*Figure 6.1* 'Fragrance of thy ointments'. From Francis Quarles, *Emblems, divine and moral: The school of the heart; and Hieroglyphics of the life of man* (London: William Tegg, 1866), p. 163. Original from University of Illinois at Urbana-Champaign; digitised by Internet Archive.

The allusions to the Song here are numerous: 'the flowers have appeared' (cf. Song 2.12); the 'perfume is poured out' (cf. Song 1.2); 'the king leads into His dwelling' (cf. Song 1.4). In the Song, the likening of the bridegroom's name to a perfume is understood as the scent of the Spirit, the grace by which God draws souls to paradise. As Origen writes in his commentary on the Song, the material oil represents the ointment of the Holy Spirit with which Christ was anointed at his Incarnation; the likening of Christ's name to the pouring out of oil symbolises Christ's emptying of himself, by which the world received 'the fullness of the Divine Spirit'.[22] This is the soteriological subtext in Hopkins's evocation of Christ's 'wafting' presence. As in stanzas 2 and 3, this gift of salvation is given in Christ's Passion, which endows human souls with the divine spirit. Hopkins perhaps follows Origen's exegesis of the Song, which specifically relates the pouring forth of fragrance to the charity of God poured forth in human hearts by the Holy Ghost (Rom 5.5).[23] This is the trajectory Hopkins charts in *The Wreck*, for the wafting starlight of Christ's spiritual presence in stanza 5 is precipitated within the human heart in stanza 6:

6

Not out of his bliss
Springs the stress felt
Nor first from heaven (and few know this)
Swings the stroke dealt—
Stroke and a stress that stars and storms deliver,
That guilt is hushed by, hearts are flushed by and melt—
But it rides time like riding a river
(And here the faithful waver, the faithless fable and miss).

Stanzas 6–8 may be read as a sequence congruent with verses 2 and 3, similarly portraying the church born from the side of Christ upon the cross. Tracing the trajectory that begins with Christ's 'wafting' descent, we see that the 'starlight' of stanza 5 now becomes the 'stars and storms' that deliver a 'stroke and a stress'. This 'stress', riding and overriding time, is received in the 'flushed' and flowing heart. In stanza 5, Hopkins suggests that '[Christ's] mystery must be instressed, stressed,' and the mystery he describes is that of the Incarnation, by which divinity as spirit is received in human hearts. With characteristic precision, Hopkins asserts that the origin of this (in) stress lies not in bliss nor in heaven; rather, this inflow of spirit relates to Christ's Passion, for the Holy Spirit comes at Christ's departure (cf. Jn 16.7):

7

It dates from day
Of his going in Galilee;
Warm-laid grave of a womb-life grey;
Manger, maiden's knee;
The dense and the driven Passion, and frightful sweat;
Thence the discharge of it, there its swelling to be,
Though felt before, though in high flood yet—
What none would have known of it, only the heart, being hard at bay,

8

Is out with it! Oh,
We lash with the best or worst
Word last! How a lush-kept plush-capped sloe
Will, mouthed to flesh-burst,
Gush!—flush the man, the being with it, sour or sweet,
Brim, in a flash, full!—Hither then, last or first,
To hero of Calvary, Christ's feet—
Never ask if meaning it, wanting it, warned of it—men go.

In the second and third stanzas of the poem, Hopkins draws on Song 2.14 to suggest the sacred heart and the sacraments that flowed from Christ's side. Here, once again, Hopkins presents a composite image of birth, death and the beginning of time: the church formed from Christ's sacrifice upon the cross. As Cotter points out, in the seventh stanza Hopkins 'follows the commentators on the Song by having this stream of grace pour forth from Christ's side on Calvary "in high flood yet".'[24] The heart that is now 'out with it!' (8) evokes not only Christ's wounded heart, but also the human heart that conceives the divine Word. Hopkins suggests a doubling of hearts. Relating the stress and flush of men's hearts (6) to the 'high flood' of Christ's Passion (7), he describes the inflow of spirit at Christ's death. Men and women are made children of God by the Incarnation and this rebirth occurs at the moment when God 'sent the Spirit of his Son into [their] hearts' (Gal. 4.6; cf. Rom. 5.5, 2 Cor. 1.22). It was then that 'we received the spirit of adoption of sons, whereby we cry: Abba, Father.' (Rom. 8.15) In the heart that is 'out with it', Hopkins's doubling of hearts suggests again the sacramental re-enactment of Christ's Passion, the continuation of that nuptial union of Christ and church achieved first on the cross. As Jean Danièlou explains, the Passion is the carrying-out of the eschatological marriage and it is because the sacraments of baptism and the Eucharist re-enact the Passion that they are in turn a nuptial mystery.[25] In stanza 3, Hopkins's 'heart of the Host' emphasises the relation between the Eucharist and the sacred heart. In stanza 8, the 'sloe' repeats the implied eucharistic imagery of the 'damson'. Now, the 'flesh-burst' continues the violence of the Passion portrayed in the previous stanza and the (sacred) heart that 'is out with it!' The suggestion of taste, of a fruit that is 'mouthed' and found 'sour or sweet' suggests again a eucharistic reading. The second chapter of the *Song of Songs* depicts Christ as an apple tree among the trees of the wood, of whom the bride says: 'his fruit was sweet to my palate' (Song 2.3). Commentaries on the Song interpret this fruit with reference to the Eucharist, and a similar reading applies in Hopkins's text.

The nuptial theology of the *Song of Songs* that underwrites *The Wreck of the Deutschland* is perhaps best seen in stanza 28. We have already explored some of the ways in which the stanza inscribes an experience of mystical union. Reading the passage again, we find a delicate incorporation of images from the Song, which further bears out this mystical meaning:

28

But how shall I ... make me room there:
Reach me a ... Fancy, come faster—
Strike you the sight of it? look at it loom there,
Thing that she ... there then! the Master,
*Ipse,* the only one, Christ, King, Head:
He was to cure the extremity where he had cast her;
Do, deal, lord it with living and dead;
Let him ride, her pride, in his triumph, despatch and have done with his doom there.

Hopkins's description of Christ as 'Head' is usually read with reference to Colossians 1.18: 'And he is the head of the body, the church; who is the beginning, the firstborn from the dead...' This allusion continues the baptismal theme that runs through *The Wreck*. Christ who is firstborn shares this divine sonship with men and women, adopted as joint heirs. Yet this adopted sonship is given only through membership of Christ's body, and it is this theme of incorporation into Christ that is suggested here in stanza 28. Hopkins deals out his inner meaning through a number of interconnected metaphors. To begin, the title 'Head' importantly relates to Ephesians 5.23–32, in which Paul elaborates the nuptial metaphor that is the basis of the doctrine of the mystical body. This scriptural passage helps to explicate the nuptial symbolism at work here. In Ephesians, Paul describes Christ as the head of his church, who is his body and bride. Men and women are made 'members' of this body of Christ through the eschatological marriage, realised in the sacraments of baptism and the Eucharist. Sanctified by the 'laver of water in the word of life' (Eph. 5.26) Christ and church become 'one flesh' (Eph. 5.31), which is symbolic of being 'one spirit' (cf. 1 Cor. 6.17). If stanza 3 of *The Wreck* suggests divine union by alluding to 2 Corinthians 3.18 – the soul remade in the image of God – stanza 28 repeats this union in the metaphor of the mystical body. By suggesting a grafting into Christ's mystical body, Hopkins suggests again that union of hearts described in the third stanza of the poem.

Here at the climax of the poem, Hopkins draws on the nuptial vocabulary of the Song to reiterate his theme of sacramental and mystical union. Hopkins suggests what may at one level be read with reference to an important passage of the Song used in baptismal catecheses. This is Song 1.3, 'Draw me: we will run after thee to the odour of thy ointments. *The king has brought me into his store-rooms...* [my italics].' Earlier in the poem, Hopkins alludes to the fragrance of Christ, which draws souls to God. Stanza 28 evokes the latter part of this scriptural image: the storerooms into which the bride is led by Christ the king. In exegetical commentary, Song 1.3 is read allegorically, suggesting entry into the marriage chamber, the place where the mysteries of baptism occur. Turning again to the opening passage of Cyril of Jerusalem's 'Procatechesis', we see that the writer describes this chamber as signifying entrance into the baptistery and so into the soul's sacramental marriage to Christ. 'Already the perfume of blessedness is wafted to you, O catechumens...You are in the vestibule of the royal dwelling. May you be led into it by the king.'[26] Further on in the 'Procatechesis' this symbolism is made even clearer. Cyril writes, 'Until now you have been standing outside the door. May it come about that you will be able to say: 'The king has brought me into his store-rooms'.[27] This theme is also found in other important patristic texts. In *De Sacramentis*, Ambrose applies this passage from the Song to describe the entry into the place of the eucharistic banquet; elsewhere he reads this bridal chamber as the place of baptism.[28] In the climax of stanza 28 of *The Wreck of the Deutschland*, Hopkins's hope of 'room there' subtly recalls these very 'store-rooms' of Song 1.3. This allusion is supported by Hopkins's description of Christ as 'King' in the fifth line of the stanza. Similarly, Hopkins's otherwise surprising use of the verb 'ride' in the stanza's penultimate line may be linked with descriptions of the bride as mare in the Song (1.9).

In an important passage that precedes the climax of stanza 28, Hopkins again draws on the discourse of baptism and the Song to articulate his central theme of the sacramental re-enactment of Christ's Passion. Stanza 22 is *The Wreck*'s clearest, most dramatic invocation to Christ's five sacred wounds, and the stanza's delicate wordplay relates these wounds of Christ to the seal of faith spiritually worn by the believer upon the soul:

22

Five! the finding and sake
And cipher of suffering Christ.
Mark, the mark is of man's make
And the word of it Sacrificed.
But he scores it in scarlet himself on his own bespoken,
Before-time-taken, dearest prizèd and priced—
Stigma, signal, cinquefoil token
For lettering of the lamb's fleece, ruddying of the rose-flake.

As J. Hillis Miller suggests, a chain of metaphors operating within the stanza suggest a kind of verbal process, a marking, scoring, or lettering. Hopkins's description of the 'cipher' of Christ and his suffering suggests more specifically a process of inscription; for 'cipher', according to the *Oxford English Dictionary*, may mean 'an intertexture of letters, especially the initials of a name, engraved or stamped.' Hopkins implicitly draws on Paul's famous description of the heart inscribed with the divine Word: 'you are the epistle of Christ...written not with ink, but with the Spirit of the living God; not in tables of stone, but in the fleshly tables of the heart' (2 Cor. 3.3). This idea is found also in Ephesians 1.13: 'signed with the holy Spirit of promise' the believer obtains through Christ the divine name inscribed upon his soul. Paul's meaning is spiritual and sacramental, as is Hopkins's. Stanza 22 describes the spiritual 'mark' or inscription upon the soul that is the seal of baptism. This is the seal of Christ that the bride of the Song receives upon the heart as the mark of her spiritual betrothal (cf. Song 8.6). Hopkins draws out this sacramental subtext through a further metaphor. We have already noted that patristic exegesis frequently compares the baptismal seal or mark upon the soul with the mark placed by shepherds upon sheep. Hopkins's lines enfold this further symbolism in their description of the 'token / for lettering of the lamb's fleece.'[29]

The heart sealed with the divine spirit is the central metaphor and silent referent of stanza 22. This heart is inscribed with the cipher of Christ's sacrifice: this is the word scored in scarlet, the ruddied rose, the 'cinquefoil token'. Embedded in this last phrase is a visual emblem of the heart. At one level 'cinquefoil' suggests simply as a reference to the *cinque* or five wounds of Christ. But seen in conjunction with the 'rose-flake' described in the stanza's last line, the word shapes a visual image of the heart. 'Cinquefoil' in fact refers to any of the *Potentilla* genus, the rose family with five-lobed leaves and five-petaled flowers – seen to have five heart-shaped petals. If this seems tenuous, we may note that Hopkins draws out this meaning in the very next stanza, describing the nuns as Christ's 'five-livèd and *leavèd* favour and pride...sisterly sealed in wild waters [my italics].'

23

Joy fall to thee, father Francis,
Drawn to the Life that died;
With the gnarls of the nails in thee, niche of the lance, his
Lovescape crucified
And seal of his seraph-arrival! and these thy daughters
And five-livèd and leavèd favour and pride,
Are sisterly sealed in wild waters,
To bathe in his fall-gold mercies, to breathe in his all-fire glances.

The 'five...leaved favour' described here in stanza 23 replicates Hopkins's earlier description of the 'cinquefoil token', both in the continued botanic symbolism and in another semantic parallel: the word 'favour' may be read as a 'token' or 'emblem' (OED). The twice repeated 'seal' and 'sealed' reiterates this meaning and continues the metaphor of inscription; the word 'seal' now more clearly evokes the baptismal seal worn upon the heart. As the Christ says to his bride in the *Song of Songs*, 'Put me as a seal upon thy heart, as a seal upon thy arm' (Song 8.6).[30] Here in stanza 23, Hopkins carefully presents the word 'Lovescape' as a synonym for 'seal'. A love*scape* seems naturally to evoke an image of the heart even as it emphasises a process of engraving or inscribing (repeated too in the description of 'gnarls', 'nails' and 'niche'). What is at work here is a delicate theological and typological symbolism. The seal that the bride of the Song puts on her heart is the Old Testament prefiguration of the spiritual seal (the Latin *signaculum spiritale* or Greek *sphragis*), ritually expressed as the marking of the cross on the foreheads of the baptised. As discussed, the rite of the *sphragis* denotes both conformity to the crucifixion and the anointing or outpouring of Spirit. Ambrose's explication of Song 8.6 in *De Sacramentis* demonstrates the complexity of the religious symbolism of the seal, and his exegesis throws light on the sacramental symbolism at work in stanza 23 of *The Wreck*:

> God, who anointed you, and the Lord sealed you, and placed the Holy Spirit in your heart [Cf. 2 Cor. 1.21, 22]...as the Holy Spirit is in the heart, so also is Christ in the heart...you were sealed unto the form of the cross itself, unto His passion. You have received the seal unto His likeness, that you may rise again unto His form, may live unto His figure...[31]

Hopkins's portrayal of the nuns 'sealed in wild waters' (23) reminds us, through the image of immersion, that the 'seal' often served to denote baptism as a whole. Nevertheless, Hopkins's descriptions of the 'Lovescape' and the 'five...leaved favour' trace an image of the heart itself, and the spiritual seal received in the heart. Hopkins suggests this seal as both the anointing of the spirit, and the imprinting of the cross of Christ. In the final line of the stanza, the images of 'fire' and 'breath[e]' evoke the activity or energy of the spirit, and the bathing of the nuns in gold and fire perhaps looks forward to that baptism by fire and spirit described by John (cf. Lk. 3.16). Hopkins emphasises too the underlying sacramental theology, the idea that the believer is crucified with Christ in baptism. To this end, Hopkins draws on the example of St Francis of Assisi. The saint was known for his miraculous vision of a seraph carrying the image of Christ on the cross; following this vision, wounds are said to have appeared in the saint's hands and feet, and in his right side a wound like that made by a lance.[32] Emphasising these instruments of pain, 'nails' and 'lance', Hopkins retraces the wounds upon the body of St Francis. Hopkins cleverly uses this replication of Christ's wounds to suggest the image of the crucified Christ imprinted upon the heart of every believer. This is the seal of the cross in the hearts of the baptised. This is 'his / 'Lovescape crucified', the spiritual sealing of the heart that is crucified with Christ.

In stanza 21, Hopkins again evokes the image of Christ within the heart, using imagery similarly reminiscent of the *Song of Songs*. Through the sacramental discourse of the Song, Hopkins traces his inscape of meaning:

21

...but thou art above, thou Orion of light;
Thy unchancelling poising palms were weighing the worth,
Thou martyr-master: in thy sight
Storm flakes were scroll-leaved flowers, lily showers—sweet heaven was astrew in them.

Hopkins's floral imagery in this passage foreshadows the imagery of the rose-heart in stanza 22 and simultaneously echoes the language of the Song. Both 'lily' and 'rose' are used in Song 1.9 to describe the beauty of the bride. The appearance here of 'flakes' (21) prefigures too the later 'rose-flake' (22), while the description of 'scroll-leaved flowers, lily showers' (21) intimates that process of inscribing emphasised in the following stanza. The leaves described here are a pun on the pages or leaves of a book, suggesting the divine writing in the heart. The word 'leaved' may also be connected with the 'five...leaved favour' (23), the heart-like form of the cinquefoil rose. The interior image of stanza 21 is once again the heart, and it is against this silent referent that we may read one of the most important allusions to the Song seen in *The Wreck*. As James Cotter has observed, Hopkins's use of the word 'unchancelling' (21) suggests the Latin *cancelli* or 'lattices' as it appears in Song 2.9: 'Behold he standeth behind our wall, looking through the windows, looking through the lattices'.[33] The allusion is correct, but its interpretive significance is greater than has been realised. Cotter observes that Bernard understands Song 2.9 to depict Christ's Incarnation and indwelling, but he understands Hopkins's allusion to this passage primarily in connection with the poet's description of Christ as 'Orion' (21). Hopkins, Cotter suggests, portrays Christ as hunter and judge of souls. His allusion to the lattices of the Song follows Bernard, who 'sees the lattices as the soul's compunction for its sins.'[34]

Rereading Bernard's sermon, his explication of the lattices of the Song can be seen to have a rather different emphasis. Bernard writes:

> Our flesh is the wall, and the Bridegroom's approach is the incarnation of the Word...The windows and lattices through which he is said to gaze can be understood, I think, as the bodily senses and human feelings by which he began to experience all our human needs.[35]

In other words, these windows are an analogy for the human senses through which Christ opened himself to mortal suffering. Further on in his sermon, Bernard suggests that the confession of sin 'accompanied by anguish of heart' opens only a narrow window; the celebration of God's gifts by which 'the heart expands in love' opens up to the bridegroom 'not a narrow lattice but a wide-open window'.[36] The underlying analogy is that which exists between the figure of the window and that of the heart. Critically, it is this lattice of the heart that Hopkins evokes, and his description of 'Orion' subtly echoes that 'starlight / wafting' (5), which is Christ's spiritual descent into the heart, the outpouring of divine spirit described in Romans 5.5.

Hopkins's juxtaposition of 'Orion' and 'unchancelling' offers a further cue to this reading. In his commentary on *The Wreck*, John Keating suggests that 'Orion' can be read as a possible paronomasia on Oriens, 'an epithet for Christ derived from the song of Zachary: "the Orient (AV, 'dayspring') from on high hath visited us" (Lk 1.78).'[37] It is the full context of the scriptural reference that proves fundamental to understanding the allusion. Luke 1.78 reads: 'Through the bowels of the mercy of our God, in which the Orient from on high hath visited us.' Bowels, as used in the plural, denote the seat of pity, tenderness or courage; it is, in essence, the heart. By bringing together the implied images of the Orient and the *cancelli* of the Song, Hopkins suggests Christ not only as dayspring or morning star, but also more specifically as the rising light of the divine-human heart. Hopkins's subtle evocation of the imagery of Luke 1.78 follows Bernard's allusion to this scriptural passage in his sermons on the Song. In Sermon 61, Bernard writes:

> The secret of his heart is laid open through the clefts of his body... laid open too the tender mercies of our God, in which the morning sun from on high has risen upon us
>
> (cf. Lk. 1.78)[38]

These are the very words reproduced by Bernard from the writings of Hugh of St Victor; by alluding to this passage here in stanza 21, Hopkins draws again on the discourse on the Song as applied to the devotion to the sacred heart. This famous passage is part of a sermon in which Bernard reflects at length on the interpretation of Song 2.14, the dove in the clefts of the rock. By alluding to this image of the light of Christ or God in the sacred heart (and implicitly in the heart of the believer), Hopkins effectively returns to the central image of the dove seen at the opening of *The Wreck* (3). In stanza 21, as in stanza 3, Hopkins's allusion to the Song functions as an invocation to Christ's heart. Here, again, Hopkins intimates a union of hearts and the soul's spiritual union with Christ. In the closing stanza of *The Wreck of the Deutschland*, Hopkins presents a final vision of Christ within human hearts:

35

Dame, at our door
Drowned, and among our shoals,
Remember us in the roads, the heaven-haven of the reward:
Our King back, oh, upon English souls!
Let him easter in us, be a dayspring to the dimness of us, be a crimson-cresseted east,
More brightening her, rare-dear Britain, as his reign rolls,
Pride, rose, prince, hero of us, high-priest,
Our hearts' charity's hearth's fire, our thoughts' chivalry's throng's Lord.

In the concluding stanza of *The Wreck*, Hopkins uses the titles of 'King' and 'Dame' to suggest a nuptial relationship between the Christ and the nun. The title of 'King', used here as in stanza 28, relates to Song 1.3: 'the King has brought me into his store-rooms'. This room or chamber, as seen, is interpreted in exegesis as the place of baptism, the marriage chamber of Christ and soul. In this final stanza, Hopkins's evocation of Christ as the light of the east may be read against Psalm 19 (AV), which famously compares the rising of the sun in the east to a bridegroom emerging joyfully from the bridechamber (Ps. 19.4–5 AV).[39] This image cannot be far from Hopkins's mind. The twice repeated 'east' and 'easter' hints at a sunrise while Hopkins's description of the 'brightening' and 'roll[ing]' light suggests again the sun's rising over the landscape of Britain. The symbolism of the east is significant in baptismal discourse. By turning towards the east, Ambrose writes, the man 'turns himself to Christ. He sees Him face to face.'[40]

Critically, Hopkins's vision of Christ as sun of the east is connected with stanza 21 through a powerful image. As Keating notes, 'dayspring' is a synonym for Oriens,[41] and Hopkins's evocation of Christ as 'east' and 'dayspring' in this closing stanza reinforces the paronomasia on 'Oriens' suggested by Keating in stanza 21. Yet again, this image is vitally framed by an image of the heart. Here, as in the earlier section of the poem, Hopkins invokes Christ not only as rising light, but as rising light of the heart. If Hopkins's earlier description is of Christ as 'Orion', seen through the window of the heart, this light of Christ is now seen through the heart's 'door'. Stanza 35 opens with the image of a door, which may be read with reference to the Song, signifying Christ's in-dwelling in the soul. The hand coming through the door hole (Song 5.4) is interpreted by Christian commentators to symbolise the dwelling of the Word, with the house representing human life.[42] The biblical image of the door is also an eschatological image, as seen in the Revelation 3.20 text: 'Behold, I stand at the door, and knock (AV).' This scriptural text has constantly given rise to the mystical idea of Christ knocking at the heart's door;[43] in Victorian times, this is an allegory made common-place by the popularity of William Holman Hunt's (1853) 'The Light of the World', a painting that portrayed Christ at a door, based on the Revelation text.

At the close of *The Wreck,* it is this vision of Christ's visitation that is the central image of Hopkins's final stanza. Christ's descent is his emptying of himself whereby men's hearts receive the divine spirit. This in-dwelling of the Spirit in turn foreshadows that final outpouring of God's Spirit in the end time (Acts 2.17). At the close of the poem, Hopkins's evocation of Christ's indwelling is also a plea for his return. Both 'door' and 'east' carry an eschatological symbolism. This is seen in the Gospel of Matthew: 'As the lightning comes from the East, so shall the Son of Man appear' (Mt. 24.27 AV). This eschatological meaning is also seen in the antiphon of the Roman liturgy: *O Oriens, splendor lucis aeternae et sol iustitiae, veni ad illuminandos sedentes in tenebris et umbra mortis* ('O dayspring, splendour of eternal light and sun of justice, come and illumine those who sit in darkness and in the shadow of death.')[44] This is Hopkins's vision of Christ as rising light of the heart – a heart that will ultimately be joined with God. Hopkins in a sermon describes the Holy Ghost as 'a spirit of multitude,'[45] and it is this Spirit who presides in the concluding line of *The Wreck*. 'Throng's Lord' and 'heart's charity' it is the Spirit poured forth in men's hearts in a prefiguration of the outpouring of divine Spirit in the end time.

The *Song of Songs* and its tradition of patristic commentary offer Hopkins a store of powerful imagery to articulate his narrative of mystical ascent and union. With its baptismal significance and connection with the Incarnation and gifts of the spirit, the Song naturally reflects and expresses a soteriological mysticism of the spirit. The nuptial metaphors of the Song are easily read in conjunction with that co-operation of human and divine activity suggested by Paul and developed by the Greek fathers in their writings on the energies. Following Origen's commentary, the Song is understood under two complementary aspects; as presenting, at the level of the text, the marriage of Christ and bride, and as simultaneously unveiling the true spirit of scripture, with all its power to make the reader 'one spirit' with God.[46] Through the *Song of Songs*, mysticism becomes itself the 'depth meaning' of texts and life, the movement from letter to spirit, glory to glory, by the working and energy of the divine spirit.

## Notes

1 A large part of the content of this chapter first appeared in an article titled 'Gerard Manley Hopkins and the *Song of Songs*,' *Victorian Poetry* 45.2 (Summer 2007): 195–208. This is reproduced here by the permission of John Lamb, editor of *Victorian Poetry*.
2 Jeffrey, *Dictionary of Biblical Tradition*, 108. Although Ambrose wrote no commentary on the Song, he frequently cited the text in his writings. His comments on the Song were later compiled by a twelfth-century Cistercian William of Saint-Thierry, E. Ann Matter, *The Voice of My Beloved: The Song of Songs in Western Medieval Christianity* (Philadelphia: University of Pennsylvania Press, 1990), 36.
3 Danièlou, *Bible and Liturgy*, 206.
4 Jeffrey, *Dictionary of Biblical Tradition*, 107.
5 Origen, 'Commentary: Prologue,' Lawson, 40.
6 Lawson, notes to *Song of Songs Commentary and Homilies* by Origen, 318 n.
7 McGinn, *Foundations of Mysticism*, 117.
8 Bernard had commented on the Song only to the beginning of Chapter 3 when he died; Sermon 86 remains incomplete.
9 Matter, *Voice of My Beloved*, 123.
10 Ibid., 39.
11 Hopkins, *Sermons and Devotional Writings*, 100.
12 Peter Milward, 'Devotion to the Sacred Heart' (Part II), in *The American Ecclesiastical Review* 148 (1960):40–48.
13 Cassiodorus, *In Cantica*, II, 14: PL 70, 1066, quoted in Milward, 'Devotion to the Sacred Heart,' 43.
14 Hugh of St Victor, *De Anima*, Lib. IV, XXI: PL 177, 181, quoted in Milward, 'Devotion to the Sacred Heart,' 45.
15 This passage, as we have seen, is the companion text to John 4.14, which describes the fountain of water springing up into life everlasting.
16 Milward, 'Sacred Heart,' 47, quoting St Bonaventure, *Lignum Vitae*, Fr. VIII, 30 (n. p., n. d.).
17 Gregory of Nazianzen, *Orations* 28.3 (*PG* 36 29A-B; *NPNF* 7, 289), quoted in Bradshaw, *Aristotle East and West*, 168. Bradshaw points to the frequent appearance of the divine glory through the OT, e.g. Ex. 16.10, 24.16–17, 40.34–35, Num. 14.21, Deut. 5.24, 1 Kings 8.11, II Chron. 5.14, 7.1–3, Ps 19.1, 63.2, 72.19.
18 See Chapter 5 which also discusses the symbolism of the veil in stanzas 3 and 4 of *The Wreck;* this symbolism is consonant with the current reading.
19 Ambrose, 'The Sacraments' (V, 5–7), Deferrari, 311.
20 Mark Elliott, *The Song of Songs and Christology in the Early Church, 381–451* (Tubingen: Mohr Siebeck, 2000), 53.
21 Cyril of Jerusalem, *Mystagogic Catecheses*, XXXIII, 333 A, quoted in Danièlou, *Bible and Liturgy*, 193.
22 Origen, 'Commentary' (1.4), Lawson, 83. Origen writes, '"Thy name is as ointment poured out"...For, if He had not emptied out the ointment – that is, the fullness of the Divine Spirit – and humbled Himself even to a

servant's form, no one would have been able to receive Him in that plenitude of Godhead…'

23 Origen, 'First Homily' (5), Lawson, 274.
24 Cotter, 'The *Song of Songs* and "The Wreck",' 60.
25 Danièlou, *Bible and Liturgy,* 207.
26 Cyril of Jerusalem, *Mystagogic Catecheses,* XXXIII, 333 A, quoted in Danièlou, *Bible and Liturgy,* 193.
27 Ibid. XXXIII, 428 A, Danièlou, *Bible and Liturgy,* 194.
28 Danièlou, *Bible and Liturgy,* 194.
29 Hopkins's words 'on his own bespoken' (22) suggest also that ownership and protection signified by the baptismal seal (see Chapter 3).
30 Hopkins's intimation of the bride of the Song is perhaps also suggested in the female vocabulary of 'daughters' and 'sister[s]' (23).
31 Ambrose, 'The Sacraments' (VI, 6–7), Deferrari, 320–21.
32 Keating, 'The Wreck: Essay and Commentary,' 87.
33 Cotter, 'The *Song of Songs* and "The Wreck",' 62.
34 Ibid.
35 Bernard of Clairvaux, *On the Song of Songs* III, trans. Kilian Walsh and Irene Edmonds, *Cistercian Fathers Series: Number Thirty-One* (Kalamazoo, MI: Cistercian Publications Inc., 1979), 87–88.
36 Ibid., 93–94.
37 Keating, 'The Wreck: Essay and Commentary,' 83.
38 Bernard, *Song of Songs* III, 144. Cotter suggests that Hopkins refers specifically to this passage from Bernard in his own Sermon on the Sacred Heart. See Cotter, 'The *Song of Songs* and "The Wreck",' 63. However, I cannot find evidence of this.
39 Jeffrey, *Dictionary of Biblical Tradition*, 106.
40 Ambrose, *De mysteriis* (7), trans. B. Botte; Sources chrétiennes, Les éditions du Cerf, 1949, 109, quoted in Danièlou, *Bible and Liturgy,* 30.
41 Keating, 'The Wreck: Essay and Commentary,' 109.
42 Elliot, *Song of Songs in the Early Church*, 89.
43 Kittel, *Dictionary of the New Testament,* Volume III, 178. Kittel also notes that in Rev. 3.8 the image of the opened door seems to be used in terms of access to eschatological glory. He suggests that the idea is that of access to the eschatological palace of God, as seen from the quotation of Is. 22.22 in Rev. 3.7.
44 Danièlou, *Bible and Liturgy,* 32. This passage is also quoted by Keating, though he does not relate it specifically to the operation of Christ and the Spirit in the heart.
45 Hopkins, *Sermons and Devotional Writings*, 98.
46 See J. Christopher King, *Origen on the Song of Songs as the Spirit of Scripture: The Bridegroom's Perfect Marriage-Song* (Oxford: OUP, 2005).

# 7 The Visible and Invisible in Augustine's *Confessions*

In a letter to A. W. M. Baillie written in 1879 Hopkins reflects: 'I think Boswell is with the exception of St Austin's Confessions, and some other spiritual works the most interesting book I ever read.'[1] In a later letter to Bridges, dated 1884, Hopkins describes St Patrick's 'Confession' as 'a work worthy to rank (except for length) with St Austin's Confessions and the Imitation and more like St Paul and the Catholic Epistles than anything else I know...'[2] Hopkins's correspondence shows that his admiration of Augustine's *Confessions* is close to unparalleled. In his 1881 notes on the *Spiritual Exercises*, Hopkins quotes from memory from the *Confessions* in Latin, recording Augustine's observation that God is "*interior intimo meo*" ("interior to my innermost being").[3] As Augustine's testament to God acting within the soul, the *Confessions* seems in some ways a natural model for Hopkins's narrative of conversion and personal spiritual renewal in *The Wreck of the Deutschland*. Yet, despite some critical interest in the general relationship between Augustine and Hopkins, only one essay addresses the influence of Augustine in the context of Hopkins's commemorative ode.[4] This is James Cotter's 1994 article, 'Augustine's *Confessions* and *The Wreck of the Deutschland*.'[5] In his article, Cotter suggests Augustine's text as a model for Hopkins's 'confession' of faith, noting imagery shared by both works and examining their common themes of time and memory. What is left unremarked by Cotter is the mystical and contemplative theology centrally expressed in the *Confessions* and embedded at the heart of Hopkins's masterwork.

Of course, Augustine cannot be described as a mystic in the traditional sense understood by Catholic neo-scholastic theology. But this does not preclude for Augustine a founding role in the history of Western mysticism. His writings give substantial attention to the mystical element in Christianity and nearly all later Western mystics invoke his work. Nowhere does Augustine's mysticism become more apparent than in his conception of *contemplatio*, the seventh grade of the soul that anticipates the final stage of the medieval mystical progression of purgation, illumination and union. *Contemplatio* for Augustine is closely akin to what he describes as *visio Dei*, each denoting the act of recognition by which God's presence is known; indeed, one may be identified with the other.[6] Both *contemplatio* and *visio Dei* imply a form of vision that is beyond sight; a vision that is also the beatification of the soul. As Augustine writes in *The Trinity,*

> That vision of God whereby we shall contemplate the unchangeable and to human eyes invisible Substance of God, alone is our *summum bonum...*
>
> (*de Trin.* i. 31)[7]
>
> The contemplation of God "face to face" is promised to us as the end of all our actions and the perfection of all our joys.
>
> (*de Trin.* i. 17)[8]

Although Augustine's views on contemplation are discussed in his theoretical works, it is the *Confessions* that best exemplify his contemplative theology. Here, Augustine famously describes the act of contemplation in three key autobiographical passages that portray his ascent to mystical vision; these are the famous Milan and Ostia accounts found at 7.10.16 and 7.17.23, and 9.10.24, respectively.[9] The interior narrative of *The Wreck* is in part modelled on these mystical experiences as recorded by Augustine in his *Confessions*. Hopkins's ode portrays the heart's journey to God in an interior narrative deliberately interlaced with these "ascent narratives". By turning to the church Fathers, Hopkins suggests a return to the old tradition of Christianity, which saw contemplation as the attainable goal of serious spiritual life.

In Augustinian theology, perfect vision or contemplation properly belongs to the next life, when the beatified soul gazes for eternity upon God. But, critically, Augustine's writings teach that the soul may also be afforded glimpses or intuitions of the divine during its earthly life. Augustine's thinking in this respect hinges upon his interpretation of 2 Corinthians 12.2–4.[10] Paul's famous description of a man 'caught up to the third heaven' is understood by Augustine to mean that Paul himself, in his rapture, saw the very essence of God. Paul's rapture becomes the grounds on which Augustine develops his theory of knowledge and contemplative vision.[11] Interpreting the 'third heaven', Augustine postulates three heavens to be understood as representing three kinds of vision: corporeal, spiritual, intellectual. The first two types of vision involve the senses either directly or indirectly; the third, however, is contemplation proper – the direct intuition of the divine, *facie ad faciem* (cf. 1 Cor. 13.12). Augustine writes:

> In this kind of vision is seen the brightness (claritas) of God, not by some corporeally or spiritually figured signification, as through a glass in an enigma, but face to face... that is, by the "species" [essence] by which God is what He is... ... [St Paul] was rapt unto this

> transcendent vision, wherein we may believe that God vouchsafed to show him that life wherein, after this life, we are to live for ever.[12]

Implicit in Augustine's three kinds of vision is the progress of knowledge by which the soul ascends to contemplative vision. Augustine's debt to Platonism (and in particular to the *Enneads* of Plotinus) has often been noted, and the Platonic influence is evident here, for it was Plato who originally conceived of contemplation as the fruit of the soul's ascent. For Plato, the human subject is seen in restless pursuit of the Absolute Good; the soul achieves its desire by returning to God through an ascending purification of love and knowledge, followed by contemplative vision (*theōria*), by which the soul is assimilated to its divine source. For Augustine like Plato, only love and knowledge can together attain to contemplative vision. In the *Confessions,* Augustine explicitly claims Platonism as an ally of Christianity, with specific reference to contemplation. The mystical experiences of Book 7 are connected by Augustine with the 'books of the Platonists' (7.9.13) and the contemplative accounts in Books 7 and 9 represent a clear synthesis of Platonism and Christianity. In 7.10.16 Augustine employs a Plotinian triple pattern of mystical progression: a withdrawal from the sensory world is followed by a movement into the inner depths of the soul and finally a movement above the soul to the contemplation of God.[13] Again, much as Platonic contemplation mediates between the world of appearances and the world of eternal Forms or Ideas, contemplation for Augustine implies the soul's rise above the temporal world to an apprehension of unchanging immortality. For Augustine, contemplation, 'wisdom', 'lies in cognition and love of That Which always is and unchangeably abides, namely God.'[14] Augustine's contemplative discourses repeatedly describe his vision of the unchangeable Truth or the 'Light unchangeable' (*Conf.* 7.10.16). As Cuthbert Butler notes, Augustine's mystic experiences are expressed in terms of this idea of the unchangeable; it is this 'fundamental idea' that is common to many of his accounts of contemplation.[15]

Perhaps because of the equal role of love and knowledge in the soul's ascent (the Milan account in the *Confessions* 7.10.16 notes that *caritas* knows the vision) and perhaps because of that necessary withdrawal into the depths of the heart or soul that precedes mystical vision, contemplation for Augustine is critically mediated by another of his classic tropes: that of the 'eyes of the heart'. This trope derives from Augustine's favourite beatitude, 'Blessed are the pure of heart, for they shall see God' (Matt. 5.8). In his sermon on Matthew, Augustine explains that the *visio Dei* may only be seen through the 'eyes of the heart'; he writes:

> When we come to the "pure in heart," there is the vision of God promised. And not without good cause; for there, in the heart, are

> the eyes, by which God is seen. Speaking of these eyes, the Apostle Paul says, "The eyes of your heart being enlightened."[16]

The enlightening of the *oculi cordis* becomes an important part of Augustine's contemplative thought and is related by him to that very vision "face to face" by which he defines the act of contemplation (cf. 1 Corinthians 13.12).[17] The illumination of the heart relates also to that other key image that Augustine powerfully associates with mystical experience: the flash of light by which God is seen in contemplation. In the *Confessions* as elsewhere in Augustine's writings we find the recurring image of the soul's ascent to a brief vision of the divine Light.[18] In the mystical account of 7.10.16 Augustine writes, 'And I entered and beheld with the eye of my soul, (such as it was), above the same eye of my soul, above my mind, the Light Unchangeable...' Augustine frequently writes interchangeably of the 'eye of the heart', the 'eye of my soul' and the 'eye of the mind'; what is key is the central place of this trope in his contemplative discourses. If contemplation for Augustine is, in some instances, the vision of a divine Light, this light is one that may only be seen through the eyes of the heart. The *oculi cordis* become for Augustine a central representation of transformed sense experience, of that third and highest form of vision, which is contemplation itself.

In *The Wreck of the Deutschland*, Hopkins's contemplative narrative is developed through a complex imagery of the heart. The word 'heart' appears eighteen times in the poem, delineating the soul's ascent in an interior narrative that culminates in a central depiction of contemplation. This contemplative experience is portrayed by Hopkins, after Augustine, as the heart's vision of the Light Unchangeable. In Hopkins's ode, stanza 3 marks the beginning of the soul's spiritual ascent. Here, Hopkins's searching heart is reminiscent of what Cuthbert Butler calls the 'Great Mystic Postulate' of Augustine's theology: the famous declaration at the opening of Augustine's *Confessions*: 'for Thou madest us for Thyself, and our heart is restless, until it repose in Thee' (1.1.1).[19]

3

The frown of his face
Before me, the hurtle of hell
Behind, where, where was a, where was a place?
I whirled out wings that spell
And fled with a fling of the heart to the heart of the Host.
My heart, but you were dovewinged, I can tell,
Carrier-witted, I am bold to boast,
To flash from the flame to the flame then, tower from the grace to the grace.

What Hopkins describes in stanza 3 is the beginning of the soul's journey to God; 'carrier-witted', Hopkins's heart searches for its heavenly home. As discussed, there is embedded here a primitive symbolism of the Eucharistic container in the form of a dove or tower. Hopkins's description of the 'Host' emphasises this aspect of eucharistic devotion and, in this respect, the 'place' searched for is understood as the tabernacle or 'dwelling place' of divinity. Yet, the passage reaches towards a further symbolism. In the New Testament, the tabernacle is the body of Christ, the mystical union of the church and its members. For Augustine, membership of this mystical body is the beginning of the soul's contemplative ascent, and he frequently emphasises the unity of this body. In *The Wreck*, spiritual assent and acceptance as depicted in stanza 2 is likewise followed by a union of hearts, an incorporation into the tabernacle that is, at this level, Christ's church ('I...fled with a fling of the heart to the heart of the Host.').[20] The spiritual, mystical journey of the heart suggested by Hopkins is in keeping with that central paradigm of Augustine's contemplative theology: the contrast between the vision of God possible through the earthly tabernacle of the church (*tabernaculum* or *templum domini*) and that perfect contemplation of God possible only in the heavenly home (*domus Domini*). Hopkins treats this theme across two key stanzas (stanzas 3 and 28), whose parallel development articulates the poem's contemplative narrative. In stanza 3, this journey is merely foreshadowed. But, 'bold to boast', Hopkins's heart envisages its return to God, from glory to glory, earthly to heavenly tabernacle. This transformation of the heart or soul as achieved in contemplation is the very meaning of the scriptural allusion noted in stanza 3. In his article on *The Wreck* and the *Song of Songs*, Cotter suggests that Hopkins's 'dovewinged' heart may be read with reference to the transformation of the dove-Bride according to 2 Corinthians 3.15–18 'But we all beholding the glory of the Lord with open face, are transformed into the same image from glory to glory, as by the Spirit of the Lord.[21] Cotter, however, fails to unpack the full significance of this allusion and in his article on Hopkins and the *Confessions* he omits this point altogether. 2 Corinthians 3.18 is, vitally, the complementary passage to that found at 1 Corinthians 13.12; together these are amongst the most important scriptural texts in the history of Christian mysticism.[22] The relation between the two may be understood from Augustine's *The Trinity*. Describing the final and perfect contemplation of God achieved through perfect conformity to his son, Augustine writes:

> "We see now through a mirror in an enigma, but then face to face." [cf. 1 Cor. 13.12]...nothing else is seen in a mirror except an image. We have, therefore, tried to do this in order that through this image which we are, we might see Him by whom we have been made...

> Such is also the meaning of the words spoken by the same Apostle: "But we, with face unveiled, beholding the glory of God, are transformed into the same image, from glory to glory, as through the Spirit of the Lord." [2 Cor. 3.18] ... it is quite clear that the Apostle was referring to a mirror...when he said "beholding the glory of the Lord"; but when he says: "we are transformed into the same image," he undoubtedly means the image of God...
>
> (15.8.14)[23]

Augustine's exegesis helps elucidate the delicate and complex set of meanings at work in stanza 3 of *The Wreck*. Hopkins's description of the 'face' of God at the start of the stanza signifies the contemplative meaning inscribed here. These two Pauline texts in fact underwrite the entire stanza. Hopkins's doubling of 'flame' / 'flame' and 'grace' / 'grace' can be read as the linguistic enactment of that mirror image implicit in both scriptural texts. Hopkins's description of the heart that flashes from flame to flame also evokes 2 Corinthians 3.18 in a further sense; for the passage may be alternatively translated as 'we... grow brighter and brighter as we are turned into the image that we reflect'.[24] 2 Corinthians 3.18 emphatically portrays that contemplation of Christ by which the soul is transformed into the very image of God. This transformation, alluded to yet incipient in stanza 3 of *The Wreck*, is enacted in the culmination of stanza 28. Here, Hopkins follows Augustine in emphasising the central role of Christ and the mystical body in the soul's ascent. For Augustine, the contemplative soul may achieve union with God only through the 'one heart' that is Christ's church.[25] Hopkins similarly frames the experience of stanza 28 in the terms of this mystical body.

28

But how shall I... make me room there:
Reach me a... Fancy, come faster –
Strike you the sight of it? look at it loom there,
Thing that she... There then! the Master,
*Ipse,* the only one, Christ, King, Head:

In Hopkins's careful interlinking of stanzas 3 and 28, the 'room' of 28 is congruent with the 'place' of 3 – that is, the tabernacle that is both earthly church and heavenly abode; both mystical union of hearts and the single heart of the individual believer. Hopkins's use of the title 'Head' in fact further emphasises this trope of the mystical body; the title is linked with Colossians 1.18, which describes Christ as 'the head of his body, the Church'.[26] This reference to the spiritual body of Christ is reiterated in Hopkins's description of Christ as 'the only one'.

In his book *Inscape,* Cotter links the phrase to the twice repeated '*primogenitus*' in Colossians 1.15–20 (in the authorised Douay translation of 1846 the word is annotated: 'The first born...*the only begotten* of his Father').[27] Cotter does not, however, draw attention to that interlinking of scriptural texts which reveals the development of Hopkins's mystical narrative. Crucially, Colossians 1.15–20 is specifically related to 2 Corinthians 3.18.[28] Colossians 1.15–20 similarly describes Christ as the image of the invisible God, the firstborn through whom all things are conformed to the very image of God. This scriptural parallel supports the argument that together stanzas 3 and 28 suggest the soul's ascent to contemplation. In stanza 28, Hopkins suggests the final action of contemplation that fulfils the transformation of the heart begun in stanza 3.

28

...Strike you the sight of it? look at it loom there,
Thing that she... There then! the Master,
*Ipse,* the only one, Christ, King, Head:

Here at the enigmatic climax of Hopkins's ode, the idea of contemplation is suggested first and foremost in Hopkins's emphasis on the act of looking. At the same time, Hopkins's direct question to the reader draws added attention to the visual nature of this experience: 'Strike you the sight of it?' The word that is key, however, is the one that links Hopkins's poem directly to the mystical accounts of the *Confessions* – the Latin 'ipse'. Meaning 'himself, very, it, the very thing', the italicised appearance of '*Ipse*' is given undoubted prominence by Hopkins who uses it as an epithet for Christ. It is an unusual choice of word for Hopkins who rarely uses foreign words in his English poetry and the word can be seen to deliberately allude to the 'Self-same': the singular, unchangeable and eternal God invoked by Augustine in the *Confessions.* In Book 11.13.16 Augustine writes '*tu autem idem ipse es*' ('thou art always the selfsame')[29] and this formulation of God as the 'Self-same' notably appears in his famous accounts of mystical contemplation. In the Ostia vision of Book 9, Augustine uses the related term *idipsum* to describe his experience of the divine; the term is also used in the ascent narrative of Book 7. As James O'Donnell notes in his commentary on the Latin text of the *Confessions*, '*idipsum*' is 'for [Augustine] a mystical name for God, equated with Exodus 3.14, *ego sum qui sum.* Notably so at Ostia (9.10.24) and cf. 7.17.23 (*id quod est*)'.[30] God's words to Moses in Exodus 3.14 may be translated as 'I am that I am' and, as we have seen, it is this perception of the unchangeable that is intrinsic to Augustine's conception of contemplation. In the vision at Ostia Augustine writes:

> And when our discourse was brought to that point, that the very highest delight of the earthly senses...was, in respect of the sweetness of that life, not only not worthy of comparison, but not even of mention; we raising up ourselves with a more glowing affection towards the "Self-same," did by degrees pass through all things bodily, even the very heaven, whence sun and moon, and stars shine upon the earth; yea, we were soaring higher yet, by inward musing, and discourse, and admiring of Thy works; and we came to our own minds, and went beyond them, that we might arrive at that region... where life is the Wisdom by whom all these things are made, and what have been, and what shall be, and she is not made, but is, as she hath been, and so shall she be ever... And while we were discoursing and panting after her, we slightly touched on her [i.e. Wisdom] with the whole effort of our heart; and we sighed, and there we leave bound *the first fruits of the Spirit...*
>
> (9.10.24–25)[31]

In this seminal passage Augustine describes the elevation of his soul 'raising up' towards an experience of the "Self-same", passing through sun, moon and stars, and 'soaring higher yet, by inward musing'. This is the soul's contemplative ascent where 'earthly senses' are left behind and the mind turns inwards, first finding itself before coming to the knowledge of that which is unchangeable. Augustine alludes here to Romans 8.23, 'ourselves also, who have the first fruits of the Spirit, even we ourselves grone within ourselves, waiting for the adoption of the sons of God, the redemption of our body.' Here as elsewhere in Augustine's writings the phrase is used in a mystical sense to suggest the higher part of human nature, 'anticipating but not compromising the full vision of God'.[32] For Augustine the touch of divine Wisdom is an effort of the heart: '*ictus cordis*';[33] love and knowledge are inextricably intertwined in Augustine's contemplative accounts. Turning to *The Wreck* we see that the contemplative experience intimated in stanza 28 is shortly preceded by Hopkins's subtle portrayal of the soul's ascent in a verse that is again reminiscent of Augustine's vision at Ostia.

26

For how to the heart's cheering
The down-dugged ground-hugged grey
Hovers off, the jay-blue heavens appearing
Of pied and peeled May!
Blue-beating and hoary-glow height; or night, still higher,
With belled fire and the moth-soft Milky Way,
What by your measure is the heaven of desire,
The treasure never eyesight got, nor was ever guessed what for the hearing?

The stanza begins with the heart, whose buoyant emotion is presented in parallel with a series of ascending images. Hopkins moves the mind's eye first from a low cloudy sky to the higher 'heavens'; then appears the night sky 'still higher' in its vision of the stars. The reiteration of 'height' and 'higher' emphasises an upward ascent and the stanza echoes that ascent described by Augustine at Ostia, where he feels himself to 'pass through all things bodily, even the very heaven whence sun and moon and stars shine upon the earth...soaring higher yet' (9.10.24). At the end of stanza 26, Hopkins's words allude to 1 Corinthians 2.9, 'Eye hath not seen, nor ear heard, neither have entered into the heart of man, the things which God hath prepared for them that love him.' What is highest, Hopkins implies, above both skies and stars, is that 'heaven of desire' in which the soul sees or knows what has never been known before. Critically, it is this very scriptural passage to which Augustine also refers while narrating his contemplative experience at Ostia. In 9.10.23 Augustine writes:

> We were discoursing then together, alone, very sweetly; and forgetting those things which are behind, and reaching forth unto those things which are before, we were enquiring between ourselves in the presence of the Truth, which Thou art, of what sort the eternal life of the saints was to be, which *eye hath not seen, nor ear heard, nor hath it entered into the heart of man.*
>
> (1 Cor 2.9)[34]

Augustine draws on 1 Corinthians 2.9 to describe the contemplation by which the saints in heaven gaze upon God. This allusion vitally frames his own ascent to contemplation as described in 9.10.23–25. In like manner, Hopkins's allusion to this Corinthian text shortly before his invocation of the Self-same God in stanza 28 reiterates the poem's contemplative subtext in relation to the *Confessions*. Hopkins's reference to this scriptural text is also significant in view of its association with the rapture of Paul, which lies at the foundation of Augustine's contemplative theology. Augustine's interpretation of Paul's rapture is vastly influcntial in the middle ages and this is a subject considered by St Aquinas in his *Summa Theologica*. Addressing the question 'Whether Paul, when in rapture, saw the essence of God?' Aquinas answers in the affirmative, avowedly following Augustine's arguments as recorded in *De Videndo Deo* and *De Genesi ad. lit.* xii, 28. Aquinas writes:

> Indeed the words themselves of the Apostle [Paul] indicate this. For he says that "he heard secret words, which it is not granted unto man to utter": and such would seem to be words pertaining to the vision of the blessed, which transcends the state of the wayfarer,

> according to Is.64.4, "Eye hath not seen, O God, besides Thee, what things Thou hast prepared for them that love [Vulg.: 'wait for'] Thee" [*1 Cor.2.9]. Therefore it is more becoming to hold that he saw God in His essence.[35]

In stanza 26 of *The Wreck*, Hopkins's hierarchy of heavens, read in conjunction with his allusion to 1 Corinthians 2.9, works as a double allusion – not only to the Ostia vision of the *Confessions*, but also to the rapture of Paul on which Augustine's contemplative accounts are themselves founded. Hopkins's heavens above heavens subtly call up that 'third heaven' to which Paul was rapt (2 Cor. 12.2). In this third heaven Paul heard 'unspeakable words, which it is not lawful for a man to utter' (2 Cor. 12.4) and, according to Augustine's interpretation, see the very substance of God. Indeed, Hopkins's own mystical experience as recorded at the climax of *The Wreck* mimes through its breakdown of language those 'unspeakable words' heard by Paul, implicitly communicating that direct mediation outside of the senses (and outside of language), which is the contemplation of God, *facie ad faciem*.

28

But how shall I... make me room there:
Reach me a... Fancy, come faster –
Strike you the sight of it? look at it loom there,
Thing that she... There then! the Master,
*Ipse*, the only one, Christ, King, Head:

We have already seen that Hopkins's allusion to Colossians 1.15–20 in stanza 28 must be read in conjunction with 2 Corinthians 3.18 as invoked in stanza 3. 'Fancy' – which can at one level be read as an intimation of Coleridge's discussion of the imagination – perhaps also hints at the word '*facie*' as used at the counterpart to 2 Corinthians 3.18 – *facie ad faciem* (1 Cor 13.12). If this seems to be a case of over reading it may be seen that immediately following this climactic passage, stanza 29 suggests that very enlightening of the eyes of the heart, which Augustine relates to the contemplation of God, 'face to face'.

29

Ah! there was a heart right!
There was single eye!
Read the unshapeable shock night
And knew the who and the why;
Wording it how but by him that present and past,

Heaven and earth are word of, worded by?
The Simon Peter of a soul! to the blast
Tarpeian-fast, but a blown beacon of light.

'Single eye' is commonly read with reference to Luke 11.34, 'The light of the body is the eye; therefore, when thine eye is single, thy whole body also is full of light'.[36] Hopkins effectively suggests an experience of illumination, and the alignment of 'heart' and 'eye' subtly evokes Augustine's *oculi cordis*. As discussed, Augustine's paradigm derives from Matthew 5.8 and Hopkins's description of a 'heart right' likely echoes this purity or rightness of heart described in scripture, 'Blessed are the pure of heart, for they shall see God' (Matt. 5.8). Hopkins further reiterates this imagery of light and enlightening – not only implied in the 'single eye' of line 2, but also made explicit in the 'blown beacon of light' that closes the stanza. By evoking Augustine's paradigm of the eyes of the heart and simultaneously describing an experience of illumination, Hopkins draws on an Augustinian understanding of contemplation as the enlightening of the heart through divine vision. Hopkins's reference to Simon Peter may in fact be read as an allusion to the transfiguration, and to the mystical vision and contemplation of Christ. We may read more fully the mystical account in the *Confessions* 7.10.16 where Augustine describes the soul's ascent to a vision of the divine Light, describing the 'eye of [his] soul' in its contemplation of the Light Unchangeable:

> And being thence admonished to return to myself, I entered even into my inward self...And I entered and beheld with the eye of my soul, (such as it was), above the same eye of my soul, above my mind, the Light Unchangeable... he that knows It, knows eternity... ...And Thou criedst to me from afar; "Yea verily, *I AM that I AM*." And I heard, as the heart heareth...
>
> (7.10.16)[37]

As seen, the words 'I am that I am' spoken by God to Moses in Exodus 3.14 are equated with the Self-same God encountered in 9.10.24 and 7.10.23. In this latter passage, the counterpart to 7.10.16, Augustine describes his contemplation of the Unchangeable in a 'flash' of light. Ascending from his own changeable mind Augustine glimpses the unchangeable truth, *id quod est* ('that which is', as related to *idipsum*).[38] He describes how his soul raises itself up

> ...so it might find what that light was, whereby it was bedewed, when, without all doubting, it cried out, "That the unchangeable was to be preferred to the changeable;" ... And thus with the flash

> of one trembling glance it arrived at THAT WHICH IS. And then I saw Thy *invisible things understood by the things which are made.* [Rom 1.20][39]

In stanza 29 of *The Wreck*, the enlightened heart is shown to 'read' the world anew, 'Wording it how but by him that present and past, / Heaven and earth are word of, worded by?' Hopkins's meaning is similar to that suggested by Augustine's use of Romans 1.20 in his account of mystical contemplation; the illuminated soul comprehends the 'invisible things' of God, understood through his created world. Hopkins's interior narrative is, in this way, delicately developed in deliberate relation to all three of Augustine's autobiographical accounts of contemplation in the *Confessions.*

A final reading of stanza 28 reveals that this climactic passage alludes not only to the 'Self-same' God of the *Confessions*, but also intimates that flash of light by which Augustine describes the experience of mystical contemplation. Reading again, the word 'strike' (28) can be seen to anticipate the enlightening of the heart seen in 29. Looking back to stanza 3 we see that Hopkins's dovewinged heart is similarly described to 'flash' from flame to flame; 'flash' may be equated with 'strike', suggesting that the latter too relates to the heart. Both words suggest an image of lightning, and this conjunction of metaphor is seen in stanza 7 where Hopkins describes the 'discharge of the heart'. The word 'discharge' has clear 'electrical associations.'[40] It is this metaphor of illumination that forms an integral part of the delicate allegorical formation of stanza 28. The flash of light intimated here is the interior and unchangeable Light, portrayed as in the *Confessions* both within and simultaneously above the soul. Turning back to Part I, we read the only direct allusion to St Austin, or St Augustine, found within the poem.

9

...Thou art lightning and love, I found it, a winter and warm;
Father and fondler of heart thou hast wrung:
Hast thy dark descending and most art merciful then.

10

With an anvil-ding
And with fire in him forge thy will
Or rather, rather then, stealing as Spring
Through him, melt him but master him still:
Whether at once, as once at a crash Paul,
Or as Austin, a lingering-out swéet skíll

Make mercy in all of us, out of us all
Mastery, but be adored, but be adored King.

In the next chapter, we will see that these stanzas draw also on baroque emblems of the heart to suggest God acting within the soul. Within this interior space of the heart or soul Hopkins suggests again the contemplative vision central to the poem – now presented in conjunction with Augustine himself. Comparing Augustine's conversion to Christianity with that of Paul, Hopkins asks God to change and master men's hearts, 'Whether at once, as once at a crash Paul, / Or as Austin, a lingering-out sweet skill'. '[O]nce at a crash' is understood to refer to Paul's sudden illumination and blinding on the road to Damascus, the miraculous event that brings about his conversion to Christianity. What is vital to our reading, however, is the knowledge that this biblical episode served as a model for Augustine's portrayal of the contemplation of God in a flash of light. Hopkins's double allusion to Paul and Augustine effectively foregrounds the contemplative subtext within the poem. Once again, Hopkins's wording of 'lightning' (9) and 'crash' (10) stresses an imagery of light and illumination that is linked, explicitly or implicitly, with the heart. Here at the emphatic close of Part I, Hopkins describes the heart that is changed and turned to God. But more subtly, Hopkins anticipates the soul's contemplative ascent and divine illumination; foreshadowed here is the poem's enigmatic culmination where Hopkins's heart, in its rapture, contemplates the Light Unchangeable.

## A Note on Hopkins, Augustine and Prayer

The term 'ejaculatory prayer', deriving from the Latin '*jaculum*' ('to throw a javelin'), originates from a remark of St Augustine in his 'Letter to Proba' in which he describes the prayer style of the Desert Fathers as *jaculatas*, 'darted'.[41] In his *Introduction to the Devout Life,* the seventeenth-century French writer St François de Sales draws on Augustine's comments, relating 'ejaculatory prayer' to 'aspirations' – short prayers that he suggests as a method of bringing the believer into the presence of the divine.[42] The mystical uses of ejaculatory prayer are intimated in its objectives; such prayer enables 'the practice of the presence of God'.[43] From Augustine, Hopkins derives not only a mysticism centred on Christ's mystical body and the soul's contemplative ascent, but also a method of mystical prayer whose rhythms charge his verse. In stanzas 2 and 3, in particular, Hopkins evokes and exercises this method of 'ejaculatory prayer' inaugurated by Augustine. By utilising this Augustinian form of prayer, Hopkins reiterates his central theme of divine union.

The term 'ejaculations' is frequently used by devotional writers of the seventeenth century. George Herbert uses the term as the subtitle for his collection of poems *The Temple: Sacred Poems and Private Ejaculations*, which develops the religious metaphor of the temple of the heart. Hopkins read and admired this collection of Herbert's poetry, and his admiration of Herbert links him with the devotional and meditative influences of the seventeenth century, including the writings of François de Sales. A major figure in Counter-Reformation spirituality, the influence of Sales was widely felt in England. In *The Poetry of Meditation*, Martz connects the subtitle of Herbert's *The Temple* with the 'iaculatorie prayer' described in Sales's *An Introduction to the Devout Life*. In his treatise, Sales explicitly ascribes this form of prayer to Augustine and suggests this to be a spiritual discourse central to the contemplative life.[44]

Hopkins's admiration of St François de Sales has been noted by Justus Lawler,[45] if in passing, and the example of Herbert serves as an additional avenue of influence between the French writer and Hopkins himself. Sales's *Introduction to the Devout Life* is itself written as a compilation of the numerous translations that were the focus of Catholic and Protestant spirituality in the sixteenth century, and serves as a useful starting point in understanding the seventeenth-century development of ejaculatory prayer. Describing the practice of the 'aspirations, ejaculatory prayer, and holy thoughts' that occupy the soul in 'spiritual retreat' François de Sales writes:

> We retire with God, because we aspire to him, and we aspire in order to retire with him; so that aspiration after God and spiritual retreat excite one another, while both spring from the one Source of all holy thoughts. Do you then, my daughter, aspire continually to God, by brief, ardent upliftings of heart; ...Such is ejaculatory prayer, as it was so earnestly inculcated by S. Augustine upon the devout Proba...
>
> (Part II, chapter XIII)[46]

As Martz points out, 'the practice of the presence of God' that is the essence of spiritual life in the seventeenth century is summed up in François de Sales's treatise.[47] Ejaculatory prayer is a means to achieving this 'presence' of God. In the opening stanzas of *The Wreck of the Deutschland*, Hopkins perhaps alludes to François de Sales in evoking an Augustinian method of ejaculatory prayer.

2

I did say yes
O at lightning and lashed rod;
Thou heardst me truer than tongue confess

Thy terror, O Christ, O God;
Thou knowest the walls, altar and hour and night:
The swoon of a heart that the sweep and the hurl of thee trod
Hard down with a horror of height:
And the midriff astrain with leaning of, laced with fire of stress.

3

...where, where was a, where was a place?
I whirled out wings that spell
And fled with a fling of the heart to the heart of the Host...

The strong presence of Augustine in these stanzas has already been discussed and Hopkins's evocation of a heart that is 'hurl[ed]' (2) may be read as a deliberate transcription of the Latin *ejaculari*, 'to toss or hurl quickly'. No doubt the heart's direction here is downward, descending from God, but this direction is soon reversed in stanza 3. The passage conveys too that sense of emergency, immediacy and intensity suggested by this form of prayer. If we look to the *Oxford English Dictionary* definition of 'ejaculation' one sense of the term is: 'the putting up of short earnest prayers in moments of emergency; the hasty utterance of words expressing emotion'. In stanza 3, Hopkins's search for the presence and 'place' of God becomes an upward flight, to the 'heart of the Host'. In this movement from heart to heart we hear an echo of the words of François de Sales. The words in question are those taken up by Newman as his motto as Cardinal and undoubtedly known to Hopkins. Hopkins's description of his flight as a 'fling of the heart to the heart of the Host' seemingly echoes François de Sales's well-known expression, 'heart speaks to heart'. Hopkins's use of the word 'fling' is perhaps an additional cue, suggesting the same movement as the word 'hurl' used earlier in the passage. The overall sense of stanza 3 is that of ejaculatory prayer as described by de Sales, the 'inward upliftings of the heart' to God.[48]

Ian Ker in *The Revival of Catholicism in English Literature* also suggests that Hopkins's language in stanzas 2 and 3 of *The Wreck* may be linked with the practice of ejaculatory prayer, but he discusses this within the contemporary context of Victorian Catholic devotion. Ker points out that the raising up of the host during a Catholic mass is typically accompanied by the adoration of the host in the form of ejaculatory prayer.[49] This is the ceremonial backdrop against which Ker reads Hopkins's ejaculatory exclamations in stanza 2: 'O Christ', 'O God'. In addition to the ritual contexts suggest by Ker, Hopkins's etymological cues intimate the mystical context of such devotion, not merely the form of contemporary Catholic worship. Hopkins's use of language is nearer to that suggested by Geoffrey Hill, whose views in this respect are contested by Ker. Hill suggests that Hopkins's propensity for the monosyllabic words of demotic speech 'could be reconciled' with 'the mystic discipline of "short prayer".'[50] Ker writes:

> Hill's apparent reference to the repetition of the brief prayer formula (or "mantra") in contemplative prayer would hardly have played any part in Hopkins's spiritual life – because the *Spiritual Exercises* would have provided an exclusive meditative framework of prayer for Hopkins as a Jesuit and because the twentieth-century revival of contemplative prayer in the Catholic church had not begun...

Ker suggests that Hopkins's brevity of language may be related instead to the recitation of litanies and to the common language of Catholic piety, which includes standard ejaculatory devotions. However, it is in fact more likely that Hill is correct in relating Hopkins's language to the mystic discipline of short prayer. The sixteenth and seventeenth centuries did not often differentiate between meditation and contemplation and Hopkins's links to this period, as will be further examined in the following chapter, suggest that like many of these writers Hopkins is likely to have understood ejaculatory prayer within the context of mystical, individual experience of God.[51] At the opening of *The Wreck*, Hopkins deliberately intimates a knowledge of the mystical, ejaculatory prayer seen in the writing of François de Sales. Hopkins's use of devotional ejaculations can be connected with the heart-mysticism that underwrites the narrative of *The Wreck*. The conception of ejaculatory prayer in fact relates to the very scriptural text found at the centre of stanza 28 (the counterpart to stanza 3). As Elizabeth Clarke observes, the most effective ejaculations described by Augustine are those that are entirely silent:

> there is a hidden groaning which is not heard by man...there is another way of praying, interior and unbroken, and that is the way of desire...love's glowing ardour is the clamour of the heart.[52]

The text that inspired Augustine in formulating his concept of prayer language as silent groans is none other than Romans 8.26, which describes the unutterable groanings of the Spirit who searches hearts, interceding on behalf of men to God.[53] It is this scriptural text that is integral to Hopkins's contemplative methods of prayer. It lies at the centre of his heart-centred mysticism and his narrative of ascent; by this sighing of the Spirit in the heart is man raised into the presence of God. These themes will be further explored in chapter eight in relation to a number of Hopkins's sonnets. But here in *The Wreck*, Hopkins's invocation of ejaculatory prayer is only one component of the mystical, contemplative subtext of this imposing composition.

94 EMBLEMS. BOOK III.

BOOK THE THIRD.

PSALM XXXVIII. 9.

*Lord, all my desire is before thee: and my groaning is not hid from thee.*

The Entertainment.

ALL you whose better thoughts are newly born,
And (rebaptiz'd with holy fire) can scorn
The world's base trash, whose necks disdain to bear
Th' imperious yoke of Satan; whose chaste ear
No wanton songs of Sirens can surprise
With false delight; whose more than eagle-eyes

*Figure 7.1* Psalm 38 'my groaning is not hid from thee'. From Francis Quarles, *Emblems, divine and moral: The school of the heart; and Hieroglyphics of the life of man* (London: William Tegg, 1866), p. 94. Original from University of Illinois at Urbana-Champaign; digitised by Internet Archive.

## Notes

1 Hopkins, *Collected Works* vol. 1, *Correspondence*, 379. The content of this chapter was first published as the article, 'The Light Unchangeable: Hopkins and Augustinian Contemplation', *Literature and Theology* 27, no. 1 (2013): 65–80. Reproduced by permission of OUP journals.
2 Hopkins, *Collected Works* vol. 2, *Correspondence*, 678.
3 Hopkins, *Sermons and Devotional Writings*, 128, 285 n.
4 For a comprehensive summary of recent criticism on the relationship between Hopkins and Augustine, see Emily Taylor Merriman, '"Words, Those Precious Cups of Meaning" Augustine's Influence on the Thought and Poetry of Gerard Manley Hopkins, S.J.,' in *Augustine and Literature*, eds.

Robert Kennedy, Kim Paffenroth, John Doody (Lanham, MD: Lexington Books, 2006), 233–54.

5 James Cotter, 'Augustine's Confessions and The Wreck of the Deutschland,' in *Saving Beauty: Further Studies in Hopkins*, eds. Michael E. Allsopp and David A. Downes (New York: Garland Publishing Inc., 1994), 313–25. Outside of Cotter's work, the discussion perhaps most relevant to this present chapter is found in Catherine Phillips's recent book *Gerard Manley Hopkins and the Victorian Visual World* (Oxford: OUP, 2007), 253–55. In a chapter on Hopkins's theories of vision, Phillips suggests Hopkins's visual imagination to be influenced by Augustine's optical theories and his perception of God as expressed through images of physical vision. While Phillips' discussion touches on ideas central to this article, she examines these themes in a number of Hopkins's sonnets, and not in *The Wreck of the Deutschland*. Moreover, Phillips is not ultimately concerned with the mystical and contemplative theology to which Augustine's model of vision pertains.

6 This is argued by Augustine scholar Fulbert Cayré in his book *La contemplation augustinienne: Principes de spiritualité et de théologie*, 2nd ed. (Paris: Desclée, 1954), 133. Contemplation is further defined by Cayre as the recognition of God in the gift of *sapientia* or wisdom. In addition to *visio Dei* this is the Augustinian term most closely related to *contemplatio*. *Sapientia* is both human and divine; it points towards the most superior intelligence, by which the mind contemplates God and divine truths.

7 Butler, Dom Cuthbert, *Western Mysticism: Augustine, Gregory and Bernard on Contemplation and the Contemplative Life*, repr. of 2nd ed. 1926 (New York: Dover Publications, 2003), 27.

8 Ibid., 26.

9 7.10.16 is commonly read as a failed vision but the mystical nature of this experience and its relevance to the discussion here cannot be in doubt. James O'Donnell writes

> This paragraph (7.10.16) presents A. seeking the ecstasy that Plotinus taught comes from the ascent of mind to union with highest being; this attempt ends in failure. The following paragraphs (7.11.17–7.16.22) represent further intellectual ruminations at the time, which makes possible a renewed attempt at union, which is described in 7.17.23. This second attempt is successful – *on Plotinian terms as A. understood them.*

James J. O'Donnell, *The Confessions of Augustine: An Electronic Edition*, ed. J. J. O'Donnell, http://ccat.sas.upenn.edu/jod/conf, Commentary on 7.10.16.

10 Also key is Augustine's reading of Moses in Numbers 12.8; for a more detailed discussion of the place of both scriptural accounts in Augustine's contemplative thought, see 'The Vision of God' in Butler, *Augustine, Gregory and Bernard,* 55–62.

11 Indeed the two cannot be separated in Augustine as shown by Gerald Bonner in 'The Spirituality of St Augustine and its influence on Western mysticism,' *Sobornost* 4 (1982), 148, quoted in McGinn, *Foundations of Mysticism*, 234.

12 *De Genesi ad litteram*, xii. 28, 56, quoted in Butler, *Augustine, Gregory and Bernard*, 57. Butler suggests, however, that Augustine's translation of 'species' as 'essence' is in fact a misinterpretation, ibid., lxvii–viii.

13 McGinn, *Foundations of Mysticism,* 233.

14 Augustine, *Exposition on Psalm Cxxxv,* quoted in Butler, *Augustine, Gregory and Bernard*, 34–35. For the relation between contemplation and *sapientia* (wisdom), see above, n 9.

15 Ibid., 35.
16 Augustine, 'Sermon 3 on the New Testament (On the words of the Gospel, Matthew 5.3–8)' *New Advent*, www.newadvent.org/fathers/160303.htm, Paragraph 6.
17 Ibid.
18 This motif in Augustine is discussed by John Burnaby in *Amor Dei: A Study of the Religion of St Augustine* (London: Hodder & Stoughton, 1938), 33.
19 Butler, *Augustine, Gregory and Bernard*, 27.
20 As we have seen Hopkins in his sermon on the Gospel of John 16.5–14 refers to Augustine in his description of the community of hearts that is the Christian church and mystical body of Christ. Hopkins writes,

> "the Holy Ghost makes Christ known by living in his Church, he makes his temple in Christian hearts and dwells within us...the Holy Ghost ... passes like a restless breath from heart to heart and is the spirit and life of all the Church: what the soul is to the human body that, St. Austin says, the Holy Ghost is to the Church Catholic, Christ's body mystical."
> (*Sermons and Devotional Writings*, 99–100)

21 Cotter, 'The *Song of Songs* and "The Wreck",' 59.
22 McGinn, *Foundations of Mysticism*, 71.
23 Augustine, *The Trinity*, trans. Stephen McKenna, The Fathers of the Church, ed. Roy J. Deferrari (Washington, DC: The Catholic University of America Press Inc., 1963), 469–70.
24 Ibid.
25 McGinn, *Foundations of Mysticism*, 249. See Augustine, Sermon 103.4, PL 38.615. Here Augustine reflects on the Mary-Martha episode of Lk. 10.38–42, which represents the difference between the active and contemplative life.
26 Cotter, *Inscape*, 158.
27 Ibid.
28 McGinn, *Foundations of Mysticism*, 71.
29 O'Donnell notes that Augustine's formulation is taken from Psalm 101.28, *The Confessions*, Commentary on 11.13.16. I give the quotation in full,

> In the beginning, O Lord, thou foundest the earth: and the heavens are the works of thy hands. / They shall perish but thou remainest: and all of them shall grow old like a garment: And as a vesture thou shalt change them, and they shall be changed. / But thou art always the selfsame, and thy years shall not fail.
> (Psalm 101.26–29)

30 Augustine, *The Confessions*, ed. J. J. O'Donnell, Commentary on 9.4.11.
31 Augustine, *Confessions of S. Augustine*, rev. from a trans. by Rev. E. B. Pusey (Oxford: J. H. Parker, London: F. and J. Rivington, 1853), 173–74.
32 Augustine, *The Confessions*, ed. J. J. O'Donnell. Commentary on 9.10.24.
33 McGinn, *Foundations of Mysticism*, 235, 411.
34 Augustine, *Confessions*, trans. E. B. Pusey, 173.
35 St Aquinas, Question 175 Article 3 'Whether Paul, when in rapture, saw the essence of God?' in *Summa Theologica*, www.ccel.org/a/aquinas/summa/SS/SS175.html#SSQ175A3THEP1.
36 Gardner and MacKenzie, *Poems*, 261.
37 Augustine, *Confessions*, trans. E. B. Pusey, 120–21.
38 Augustine, *The Confessions*, ed. J. J. O'Donnell, Commentary on 9.4.11.
39 Augustine, *Confessions*, trans. E. B. Pusey, 125–26.
40 This is Michael Wheeler's reading in *Death and the Future Life in Victorian Literature and Theology* (Cambridge: CUP, 1990), 353.

41 Augustine, *Opera* (Paris, 1688), ii. 389 ff, quoted in Elisabeth Clarke, *Theory and Theology in George Herbert's Poetry* (Oxford: Clarendon Press, 1997), 100.
42 Martz, *Poetry of Meditation,* 252.
43 Ibid., 250.
44 In chapter 13 of his *Introduction* Sales writes, 'without [iaculatorie prayer], we cannot well lead a contemplative life, and but badly perform the active life,' quoted in Clarke, *Theory and Theology,* 100.
45 Lawler, *Hopkins Re-constructed*, 190. Lawler describes Hopkins as 'devoted' to St François de Sales.
46 François de Sales, Chapter XIII: 'Aspirations, Ejaculatory Prayer and Holy Thoughts' in *Introduction to the Devout Life*, www.ccel.org/ccel/desales/devout_life.iv.xiii.html, Paragraph 91.
47 Martz, *Poetry of Meditation,* 250.
48 François de Sales, *Introduction to the Devout Life,* Part II, Chapter XIII, Paragraph 91.
49 Ian Ker, 'From Oxford to Liverpool: The Conversion and Poetry of Gerard Manley Hopkins,' in *The Catholic Revival in English Literature, 1845–1961: Newman, Hopkins, Belloc, Chesterton, Greene, Waugh* (Notre Dame, IN: University of Notre Dame Press, 2003), 41.
50 Ibid., 35.
51 Clarke observes that for the French author Louis de Blois, whose treatment of ejaculatory prayer most recently precedes that of François de Sales, such prayer is seen as the foundation of mystical theology, *Theory and Theology,* 104–105.
52 Augustine, *Enarrationes in Psalmos* xxxvii. 13–14, *Corpus Christianorum Series Latina* (Turnhout, Belgium, 1956), xxxviii. 391, translated and quoted in Clarke, *Theory and Theology,* 112.
53 Clarke, *Theory and Theology,* 165.

# 8 Emblems of the Heart

We have considered the ways in which *The Wreck of the Deutschland* fundamentally reflects the meditative and contemplative theology of Augustine. This chapter will show that the contemplative subtext of *The Wreck* is further articulated with specific reference to a religious tradition closely connected with the art of meditation, and one that owes much to Augustine.[1] This is the tradition of the meditative emblem, which developed during the seventeenth century when emblematic practice was being turned from its moral and humanist ends to the expression of Christian doctrine. The tradition of the religious or meditative emblem is implicitly founded on Augustine's theory of signs as elaborated in *De Doctrina Christiana*.[2] Augustine's argument that God instituted not only words, but also things, as signs meant that both scripture and nature could be understood allegorically. These are the grounds for what Michael Bath points out as the conformity of meditation and emblem in the seventeenth-century redefinition of allegory as divine emblematics. By this new understanding, the created world or the Book of creatures could be contemplated to arrive at divinely inscribed meanings and at the knowledge of God himself; as it is written in Romans 1.20: 'For the invisible things of him...are clearly seen, being understood by the things that are made'. This spiritual sight, however, is once again related to the eye of the soul, mind or heart, which we have seen to derive from Augustine; this is a favourite trope of meditative and emblematic discourse, for it is only through the eye of the soul that the world may be understood as impress and sign of God.

In *The Wreck of the Deutschland,* Hopkins's evocation of Augustine's 'eye of the heart' intimates not only the contemplative ascent that is the subject of Hopkins's narrative, but also the emblematic discourse through which this narrative is partly structured. The seventeenth-century religious emblem is closely related to the practice of biblical exegesis, and Hopkins's choice of an emblem-inspired imagery is consonant with the exegetical and allegorical methods central to the poem. Baroque religious emblems were often specified precisely as 'allegorical' or even 'typological' emblems (in the sixteenth and seventeenth centuries these terms were not generally differentiated and were often used as synonyms).[3] In their unique formulation of allegorical image and religious teaching, both Catholic and Protestant emblem books drew extensively on scriptural and patristic sources, redirecting allegory to its religious and doctrinal purposes. The seventeenth-century devotional emblem shows close ties with the Ignatian method of meditation prescribed in the *Spiritual Exercises* and to other important Counter Reformation treatises of the time. Yet this important aspect of Hopkins's work has been overlooked in meditative studies that have focussed only on Hopkins's relation to Ignatian meditation itself. If both Martz and Downes have described Hopkins as a 'meditative' writer, it is a label that is understood as specifically Ignatian. Nevertheless, a proper understanding of the meditative emblem helps us to see how Hopkins, once again, moves beyond a narrowly Ignatian method to the contemplative, mystical progression that finds its origins in Augustine.

Hopkins's connections to the seventeenth-century emblem tradition are several. Outside of Hopkins's Jesuit training, an important link back to this tradition is the poetry of Herbert. Throughout his life Hopkins admired Herbert, whose verse has long been linked with the meditative tradition of the period. In her important study *English Emblem Books* (1948) Rosemary Freeman demonstrates the emblematic influence pervasive in the devotional poetry of Herbert, and to varying degrees in that of Vaughan, Donne and Crashaw. These writers were also of interest to the leaders of the Oxford Movement. Tractarian exploration of seventeenth-century High Church theology led to the publication of *The Anglo-Catholic Library*, a series edited by Pusey. Unsurprisingly, the Victorian emblematic revival shows clear and direct connections with the Oxford Movement.[4] The Tractarian poet Isaac Williams, also a devoted disciple of Herbert, published in 1842 a translation of the Jesuit Antoine Sucquet's (1620) *Via vitae aeternae* or *Way of Eternal Life* using the very plates found in Hugo's *Pia Desideria*. Hopkins himself was obviously aware of the connection between Herbert and the emblematic tradition, as evidenced by a letter of 1881 in which he refers to the emblems of Herbert's 'school'.[5]

The poetry of Herbert and his contemporaries reflects a specific development of the devotional emblem, and it is to this tradition that much of the emblematic content of *The Wreck* may be traced. Towards the end of the sixteenth century the Dutch engraver Anton Wiericx developed for the first time a full series of cardiomorphic emblems entitled *Cor Iesu amanti sacrum*. Wiericx's emblematic sequence reflected and promoted the cult of the Sacred Heart as developed in the late Middle Ages; with the revival of this cult by Jean Eude and Marguerite Alacoque in the seventeenth century the heart became the favourite emblem of the time and a likely influence on the poetry of Herbert, Vaughan and Donne.[6] Taken up by the Jesuits, the Wiericx emblems formed the basis of a long tradition of devotional books across the Continent, in French, Latin, Dutch, German and Italian, down to the nineteenth century. These engravings are reproduced in *Le Coeur Devot* by the Jesuit Fathers Luzvic and Binet (Douai, 1627). Translated by Henry Hawkins in *The Devout Heart* (1634), this became one of the only two known English Recusant emblem books, and an important example of the fusion of emblem and meditation.[7] While the Wiericx heart-emblems show Christ entering and acting in a large human heart they are complemented by the equally popular seventeenth-century emblem books of Daniel Cramer (Frankfurt, 1624) and Benedictus van Haeften (Antwerp, 1629), in which a small heart undergoes physical and mechanical manipulations. Haeften's *Schola Cordis* was the source for Christopher Harvey's *The School of the Heart* (1647). The Anglican counterpart of Hawkins's heart book, Harvey's work underwent numerous reprints down to the nineteenth century, when frequently ascribed to Quarles and published together with Quarles's *Emblems* (cf. the reprints of 1808, 1812, 1823, 1866).

The renewal of interest in emblems in nineteenth-century England was seen not only in the continued production of devotional works and the efforts of Tractarian authors, but also in the search for a new symbolic language by artists of the Pre-Raphaelite brotherhood. Perhaps the most dramatic example of the revival of a Wiericx motif in Victorian England is William Holman Hunt's (1851) *The Light of the World*, whose possible relevance to *The Wreck* has already been noted. Depicting Christ knocking at the door of the heart, Hunt's painting led to a Protestant re-evaluation of the role of allegorical art and was finally accepted as an Anglican icon by the entire nation.[8] Hopkins's interest in Pre-Raphaelite art would have served as an additional source of emblematic influence. Like the poetry of Herbert and his contemporaries, Hopkins's verse is deeply imbued with seventeenth-century emblematics. Hopkins perhaps goes even further than his Anglican predecessors, using the concept of the emblem as both artistic and theological principle. The *Ratio Studiorum* (1599), the official Order and Method of Studies for the Society of Jesus, lists emblems as a topic for scholarly enquiry and suggests 'emblematic compositions and poems' as appropriate for the commemoration of feast days.[9] *The Wreck of the Deutschland*, written in the 'happy memory' of the nuns, is conceived as just such an emblematic composition. The imagery of Hopkins's great ode may be seen to be shaped by the heart-emblems of the seventeenth century; particularly the Wiericx emblems of Hawkins's Catholic work,[10] and additionally the 'School of the Heart' emblems that appear in Quarles's book.

*Figure 8.1* 'The most amorous Jesus knocks at the door of the heart'.
Source: From Stephanus Luzvic, *The Devout Hart or Royal Throne of the Pacifical Salomon*, trans. into English by Henry Hawkins (Rouen: John Cousturier, 1634), 45. Reproduced from a copy in the library of Eton College, by permission of the Provost and Fellows.

In utilising an emblematic system of imagery in *The Wreck*, Hopkins does so within the distinctly mystical paradigms that frame this combination of emblem and meditation. In both the Wiericx emblems and the more physical trials of the heart seen in the emblems of Cramer and van Haeften, the progress of the heart is interpreted spiritually and mystically. Van Haeften's book is based on St Bonaventure's *Itinerarium Mentis in Deum* or *The Journey of the Mind to God*; the three-part structure of van Haeften's work embodies the three stages of traditional meditative ascent of the soul to union with God (purgation, illumination, union). The Wiericx plates similarly represent this progress of the mystical life and so merge easily with the Ignatian program of meditation, which is itself partly derived from this *scala mystica*. The structure of Hawkins's *The Devout Heart* closely follows that of the St Ignatius' *Spiritual Exercises*. As Karl Höltgen observes,

> The *pictura* of the devotional or meditative emblem represents the *composition loci*, where the application of the senses takes place. The explanatory poem of the emblem stands for the *analysis*, and the final epigram for the *colloquium* (the second and third parts of the Ignatian meditation).[11]

Hopkins's *The Wreck of the Deutschland* may thus be shown to map a broader spiritual and meditative project. The emblematic inscape of the poem portrays the mystical journey of the soul; not surprisingly the poem begins with a classic image of the soul imprisoned within the body of flesh.

1

THOU mastering me
God! giver of breath and bread;
World's strand, sway of the sea;
Lord of living and dead;
Thou hast bound bones and veins in me, fastened me flesh,
And after it almost unmade, what with dread,
Thy doing: and dost thou touch me afresh?
Over again I feel thy finger and find thee.

In earlier readings, we saw that Hopkins's opening stanza intimates the presence of the Spirit in the baptised heart. We see now that this spiritual heart is presented in opposition to the body of 'flesh' that is 'bound' and 'fastened'. Hopkins's opening stanza may be linked with a well-known emblem found in Quarles's *Emblems* (V, 8),[12] and derived from St Ignatius's *Spiritual Exercises*. The emblem is a gruesome image of the soul or Anima imprisoned in the ribcage of a skeleton, with the motto after Romans 7.24, 'O wretched man that I am! who shall deliver me from the body of this Death?' (AV) This is an emblematic version of a conceit from the *Spiritual Exercises*, taken from the First Preamble of the First Exercise for the First Week (No. 47). Here St Ignatius Loyola recommends the first part of a meditation to be the 'composition of place'; he writes:

> ...the composition consists in seeing with the eye of imagination the corporeal place where the subject you wish to contemplate is found. If you want to meditate on something invisible, like sin, look with the eye of imagination how your soul is incarcerated in this corrupt body.[13]

Hopkins subtly evokes Quarles's emblem, contrasting the bound body of flesh with the fresh and free touch of God's finger, the Holy Spirit. The 'finger' of God is also commonly associated with the divine writing in the heart (cf. Ex. 31.18, 2 Cor. 3.3) and points to a subtext whose meaning will gradually be made clear. Delicately drawing on the very emblem that exemplifies Ignatius's conceit for the composition of place, Hopkins not only follows this prescribed meditative format, but also simultaneously reflects on the idea of meditation, and the poem itself as meditative exercise.

Hopkins continues to chart the heart's progress through an inscape of emblematic imagery embedded in the text. The first stanza of *The Wreck* suggests a *locus*, the soul or heart fastened in flesh and awaiting its release. This is the start of a meditation on mystical union via the *scala mystica*. Almost immediately following this, we see that famous emblematic image of the soul's ascent, the winged heart.

3

The frown of his face
Before me, the hurtle of hell
Behind, where, where was a, where was a place?
I whirled out wings that spell
And fled with a fling of the heart to the heart of the Host.
My heart, but you were dovewinged, I can tell,
Carrier-witted, I am bold to boast,
To flash from the flame to the flame then, tower from the grace to the grace.

The winged heart is a trope familiar from emblematic tradition. Quarles's 'The Flying of the Heart' shows a heart flying up to heaven, with the accompanying Epigram 'Oh that mine heart had wings like to a Dove, / That I might quickly hasten hence and move...towards the celestial spheres...'[14] Hopkins's flashing and flaming heart also subtly intimates that Augustinian ejaculatory prayer popular in the sixteenth and seventeenth centuries.[15] Hawkins's *Devout Heart* addresses the stony heart with the reprisal: 'Sigh therefore and groan the while, and privily shoot forth the fiery shafts of vehement love'.[16] An emblem from Quarles similarly shows the soul or Anima in a garden with arrows shooting up from her breast to the ear of God hovering above. In attempting to understand Hopkins's emblematic inheritance, it is of less importance to isolate specific references to specific emblems in Hopkins's stanzas; it is rather more valuable to understand how this emblematic imagery permeates the poem, performing the formal and imaginative function of transforming text into meditation. Hopkins's use of eucharistic theology in stanza 3 further emphasises the heart's centrality; his linking of heart and host echoes a medieval sacramental theology that viewed the host as food of the heart. Hopkins develops this sacramental mysticism through varied emblematic tropes.

6

Not out of his bliss
Springs the stress felt...
...That guilt is hushed by, hearts are flushed by
and melt—
But it rides time like riding a river...

7

It dates from day
Of his going in Galilee;...
...The dense and the driven Passion, and frightful sweat;
Thence the discharge of it, there its swelling to be,
Though felt before, though in high flood yet—
What none would have known of it, only the heart, being hard at
bay,

8

Is out with it! Oh,
We lash with the best or worst
Word last! How a lush-kept plush-capped sloe
Will, mouthed to flesh-burst,
Gush!—flush the man,...

I have already suggested that this important passage evokes the river or fountain of life, and this is an image frequently encountered in emblem books. Hawkins's *Devout Heart* depicts Christ as a fountain in the heart,[17] and it is this image that is suggested by Hopkins. The fluid and 'flushed' heart is merged with a 'river' that rides time, a reflection of the highly emblematic river or fountain of life. As seen, John Keating reads 'heart' as a paronomasia on 'hart';[18] the allusion is to Psalm 41.2: 'As the hart panteth after the fountains of water; so my soul panteth after thee, O God.' Psalm 41 is in fact frequently quoted in emblem books. Following Augustine's commentary on the psalm, the hart or stag is seen to symbolise the soul's swift progress to the waters of salvation,[19] and quotations of the psalm in emblem books often accompany pictures of Christ as a flowing fountain.[20] Hawkins similarly describes the 'grace' that comes from the Son of God, 'derived by certain pipes or aqueducts as from the rock or head of these living waters'; in his colloquy to the sacred wounds Hawkins writes, 'the streams of thy side, hands, and feet...flow with a copious channel into my heart...'[21] By locating the origin of this river in Christ's Passion Hopkins suggests that first flow of the sacred blood and water; it is a sacramental reformation, a change and exchange of hearts that is the merging of sacred and human. The flesh-burst of fruit (8) suggests again an image of the Passion and of eucharistic fruit, and this opens onto a further emblematic trope. The eucharist is often seen as a door or gate, and so Hopkins is brought to the best-known Wiericx engraving, Christ knocking at the door of the heart as painted by Holman Hunt.

*Figure 8.2* 'Jesus the living fountain in the heart'.

Source: From Stephanus Luzvic, *The Devout Hart or Royal Throne of the Pacifical Salomon*, trans. into English by Henry Hawkins (Rouen: John Cousturier, 1634), 83. Reproduced from a copy in the library of Eton College, by permission of the Provost and Fellows.

9

Be adored among men,
God, three-numberèd form;
Wring thy rebel, dogged in den,
Man's malice, with wrecking and storm.
Beyond saying sweet, past telling of tongue,
Thou art lightning and love, I found it, a winter and warm;
Father and fondler of heart thou hast wrung:
Hast thy dark descending and most art merciful then.

10

With an anvil-ding
And with fire in him forge thy will
Or rather, rather then, stealing as Spring
Through him, melt him but master him still:
Whether at once, as once at a crash Paul,
Or as Austin, a lingering-out sweet skill,
Make mercy in all of us, out of us all
Mastery, but be adored, but be adored King.

Hopkins often emphasised that his poetry was to be read not merely by sight but by sound. It is this principle that is in operation in this passage; a series of puns make a typically emblematic riddle, to be read and then re-read by rhyme. In stanza 9 the repetition of 'wring thy rebel' and 'heart thou hast wrung' alerts us to a play on 'rebel'. Later in the poem Hopkins describes the 'breast / of the Maiden a bell to, ring of it' (31). Breast and heart are often used synonymously and here too Hopkins plays on the rebel or (re) *bell* heart. This is an image that is found in another poem, unfinished, where Hopkins describes 'these heart-song powerful peals'.[22] Here, the suggestion of a sounding of a bell is intimated too in Hopkins's use of the word 'ding'. Meaning 'to sound as metal when struck' (1819), 'ding' is possibly abstracted from ding-dong (1659), of imitative origin. Through an instrumentality of language is suggested an instrumentality of the heart, an emblematic heart that is musical and mechanical apparatus.

*The Devout Heart* depicts a heart formed as a harp and Hawkins describes Jesus as the musician who plays on this harp of the heart. So struck, the heart releases its melody and there is made 'a triple music... the first...heard in Heaven, the second in earth, the third in the heart of man, devout to God'; in Hawkins's words, a 'symphony is held in the Temple of man's heart'.[23] Hopkins too draws on this emblematic portrayal of the heart as musical instrument. For Hopkins, the sounding of the heart is the striking of a bell, and perhaps the metallic imagery is suggested by yet another emblematic conceit. Quarles's emblems depict

*Figure 8.3* 'Jesus sings in the choir of the heart'.

Source: From Stephanus Luzvic, *The Devout Hart or Royal Throne of the Pacifical Salomon*, trans. into English by Henry Hawkins (Rouen: John Cousturier, 1634), 185. Reproduced from a copy in the library of Eton College, by permission of the Provost and Fellows.

the heart being hammered upon an anvil and melted within a furnace,[24] and this is similarly Hopkins's subtextual narrative. By 'anvil', 'forge' and 'fire' will Christ 'melt' the unyielding man. Though used in verb form, 'forge' naturally evokes a furnace, and 'ding' may also be taken to mean 'to deal heavy blows', probably from the Old Norse *dengja* 'to hammer'. Hopkins's plea that God '*make* mercy *in* all of us' (my italics) points by way of its oddness to a substratum of meaning: 'mercy' as from *misericordia*, 'benevolence, mildness or tenderness of heart'. The making of mercy in man is the forging of a new heart, and by this heart is Christ 'adored'. Now alert to Hopkins's play of word we read again, finding the word 'adored' repeated thrice between stanzas 9 and 10. It is the 'door' of the heart Hopkins suggests, the door at which Christ knocks. In stanza 21, this door becomes a window or 'lattice'.

21

...but thou art above, thou Orion of light;
Thy unchancelling poising palms were weighing the worth,
Thou martyr-master: in thy sight
Storm flakes were scroll-leaved flowers, lily showers—sweet
heaven was astrew in them.

22

Five! the finding and sake
And cipher of suffering Christ.
Mark, the mark is of man's make
And the word of it Sacrificed.
But he scores it in scarlet himself on his own bespoken,
Before-time-taken, dearest prizèd and priced—
Stigma, signal, cinquefoil token
For lettering of the lamb's fleece, ruddying of the rose-flake.

As discussed in Chapter 5, Hopkins's use of the word 'unchancelling' may be linked with the '*cancelli*' or 'lattices' of Song 2.9. In the final meditation of *The Devout Hart,* Hawkins too invokes this very image of Christ who stands at the grate (cf. Song 2.9).[25] Found in Hawkins's 'Incentive' to the meditation, this scriptural text is significant precisely because it is used to contrast the image of Christ standing at the grate – an image similar to Christ knocking at the door of the heart – with Christ who fully enters the soul to manifest himself in the heart. (Hopkins's suggested paronomasia on 'Oriens,'[26] read in conjunction with his subtle allusion to the Song, suggests a similar image of Christ who lights the heart with his presence.) The image of Song 2.9 is thus integrally linked with the contemplative progression of the heart. Unsurprisingly, Hawkins in his 'Incentive' similarly suggests the consideration of other-worldly delights – 'such as here, neither eye hath seen, nor ear hath heard, nor hath ascended into mans hart'.[27] Hopkins, in *The Wreck of the Deutschland,* alludes to both this well-known Pauline text (cf. 1 Cor. 2.9), and to Song 2.9 in his narrative progression to the contemplative experience of stanza 28.

In stanzas 21 and 22, Hopkins's hidden inscape of the heart finds expression in yet another set of emblematic images deriving from the Song. Emblem books often portrayed the virtuous heart as a flowering garden,[28] and visual representations depicted the heart adorned with the roses and lilies of the Song (cf. Song. 2.1). Describing 'storm-flakes', 'lily showers' and 'rose-flake(s)', Hopkins evokes this same floral imagery and draws out his emblematic image of the heart through a delicate play of word. The word 'token' denotes an emblem; 'flake' may also be read as a synonym for 'token'. Hopkins's 'cinquefoil token' shapes a floral heart, and this play is continued in Hopkins's description of the nuns as Christ's 'five-lived and leaved favour and pride'; the word 'favour' echoes again the semantics of 'flake' and 'token', for the word may be taken to signify a badge. So we are returned again to that unspoken inscape: the self-emblem of the poet; the heart that speaks itself in emblematic metaphor: flower, favour, love-token, sign and cinquefoil form. Hopkins's dramatic invocation of the 'five' wounds of Christ (23) is consonant too with the emblematic lineage on which he draws, for devotional emblems promoting the cult of the heart were developed from images of the wound in Christ's side and the shield of the Five Wounds.[29] Yet Hopkins's semantic cues suggest that his thematic emphasis remains very specifically the wounded heart, a heart that is at once Christ's sacred heart and the human heart that is sealed with his name.

THE HEART. 315

**The Law-Table of the Heart.**

Leave the stone tables for thy Saviour's part;
Keep thou the law that's written in thy heart.

JER. XXXI. 33.

*I will put my law in their inward parts, and write it in their hearts.*

EPIG. 26.

IN the soft table of thine heart I'll write
A new law, which I will newly indite.
Hard stony tables did contain the old:
But tender leaves of flesh shall this infold.

*Figure 8.4* 'The Law table of the heart'.

Source: From Francis Quarles, *Emblems, divine and moral: The school of the heart; and Hieroglyphics of the life of man* (London: William Tegg, 1866), 315. Original from University of Illinois at Urbana-Champaign; digitised by Internet Archive. [The school of the heart is erroneously ascribed to Quarles; it is adapted from Benedictus von Haeften's Schola cordis.]

While intimating its devotional and emblematic inheritance, stanza 22 suggests a familiarity too with the theoretical thinking that surrounded the emblem tradition. Hopkins's string of synonyms (cipher, mark, scores, stigma, signal, token) form something of an emblematic riddle. The words are thrown into sudden relief when read against the writings of the practitioner-theorists of sixteenth and seventeenth-century emblem books: the distinctions made among 'emblemata', 'imprese', 'devices', 'enseigns', 'hieroglyphs', 'blazons' and other such terms.[30] This play on ideas of inscription, representation and emblematics is also an extension of a powerful and key biblical metaphor, the divine writing in the heart (cf. 2 Cor. 3.3). It is this metaphor that gave rise to the idea of the inner scroll or book of the heart common in the middle ages,[31] and writers of emblem books played on this conception of the heart-book. The opening of the heart is the opening of a book, the pages or leaves of the heart receive the Word of God. Hawkins advises his reader: 'confidently open both the leaves of thy heart unto (Christ), receive him...in thy bosom, in thy bowels with thy whole heart.'[32] Hopkins's 'scroll-leaved flower' is thus a triple play; the floral form of the heart suggests not only the five-leaved cinquefoil rose, but also the leaves of this inner scroll or book of the heart. The metaphor of course cuts both ways; like Herbert, whose page shapes the altar that is his own heart,[33] Hopkins's *The Wreck of the Deutschland* is in many ways the poet's heart on the page.

Merging sign and sacrifice the next stanza continues this metaphor of the scripted heart, and suggests a further stage in its spiritual and meditative ascent.

23

Joy fall to thee, father Francis,
Drawn to the Life that died;
With the gnarls of the nails in thee, niche of the lance, his
Lovescape crucified
And seal of his seraph-arrival! and these thy daughters
And five-livèd and leavèd favour and pride,
Are sisterly sealed in wild waters,
To bathe in his fall-gold mercies, to breathe in his all-fire glances.

Here, once again, the imagery of Hopkins's hidden heart may be seen to have emblematic precedent. The word 'Lovescape' seems naturally to signify the heart and perhaps echoes those scapulars of the sacred heart, which became popular in the latter half of the nineteenth century.[34] The imagined subjection of the heart to the instruments of Christ's Passion is an important part of the meditative process described by emblem writers, and this meaning is inscribed in Hopkins's subtext. Hawkins

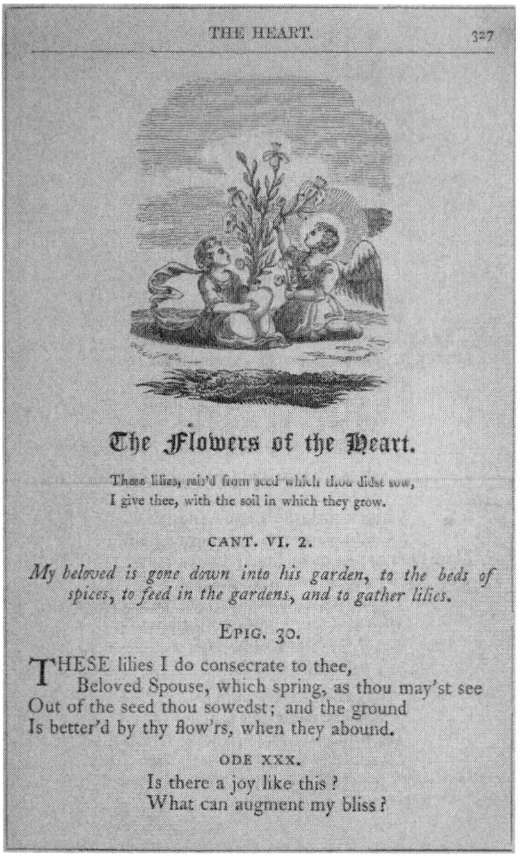

THE HEART. 327

**The Flowers of the Heart.**

These lilies, rais'd from seed which thou didst sow,
I give thee, with the soil in which they grow.

CANT. VI. 2.

*My beloved is gone down into his garden, to the beds of spices, to feed in the gardens, and to gather lilies.*

EPIG. 30.

THESE lilies I do consecrate to thee,
Beloved Spouse, which spring, as thou may'st see
Out of the seed thou sowedst; and the ground
Is better'd by thy flow'rs, when they abound.

ODE XXX.

Is there a joy like this ?
What can augment my bliss ?

*Figure 8.5* 'Flowers of the heart'.

Source: From Francis Quarles, *Emblems, divine and moral: The school of the heart; and Hieroglyphics of the life of man* (London: William Tegg, 1866), 327. Original from University of Illinois at Urbana-Champaign; digitised by Internet Archive. [The school of the heart is erroneously ascribed to Quarles; it is adapted from Benedictus von Haeften's Schola cordis.]

describes Christ who 'brings in the Cross into the heart, and easily imprints it in the lover'; Hawkins urges, 'Go in lovely Cross enter lance, sponge, nails, scourge, bloody, thorns, get you in to the Closet of the heart.'[35] Hopkins's gnarls and nails, niche and lance, repeat that scoring or engraving intimated in preceding stanzas, even as the 'Lovescape crucified' embodies this very imprinting of the Cross in the heart. Hopkins's twice repeated 'seal' and 'sealed' may also be seen to suggest the baptismal seal received in the heart and prefigured in the *Song of Songs*. Hawkins's own meditation on the imprinting of the Cross in the heart explicitly invokes these famous words of the Song, 'Put me as a seal upon thy heart' (Song 8.6).[36]

The reformation of the heart finds further form in stanza 18, where Hopkins draws on the classic seventeenth-century image of Christ wringing tears of repentance from the hardened heart.

18

Ah, touched in your bower of bone
Are you! turned for an exquisite smart,
Have you! make words break from me here all alone,
Do you!—mother of being in me, heart.
O unteachably after evil, but uttering truth,
Why, tears! is it? tears; such a melting, a madrigal start!
Never-eldering revel and river of youth,
What can it be, this glee? the good you have there of your own?

The stanza abounds in emblematic tropes. The 'exquisite smart' and 'melting' of the heart echo the wounding, softening and dissolving of the heart common in emblematic discourse.[37] Hopkins also suggests again the sacramental river of stanza 6, but even more clearly than before, he locates this river in the heart. 'Never-eldering' in its course this 'river of youth' flows from the bower of the heart, a 'fountain of water, springing up into life everlasting' (John 4.14). We may look again to Hawkins's emblem of Christ as a fountain in the heart. Here Hawkins writes, 'O miraculous things behold here from the bottom of the heart, an endless spring to arise'.[38] Once again, Hopkins's play of word enfolds multiple meanings. 'Madrigal', as song, echoes that musical heart already inscribed. Here, the speaking and singing heart perhaps takes inspiration from the chorus of the heart described by Hawkins. Hawkins exhorts his reader to 'sing from the inmost bowels', and Hopkins's description of the heart in its 'bower' may at one level be read as a paronomasia on 'bowel', a word frequently used in emblem books to describe the inner seat of the soul. Hopkins's use of both 'madrigal' and 'mother' reinforces such a reading; as seen, 'madrigal' derives from the Latin *matrix*, or 'womb', a word again used synonymously with 'bowel' by emblem writers. For Hawkins, the heart is the 'bower of the immortals', a room or bedchamber, indeed 'the Bedchamber of the Spouse Jesus himself'.[39] This is one of the central metaphors of emblematic books on the heart: the heart as room, chamber and chapel of the Godhead. Hopkins draws on this metaphor in stanza 28.

28

But how shall I ... make me room there:
Reach me a ... Fancy, come faster—

Strike you the sight of it? look at it loom there,
Thing that she … there then! the Master,
*Ipse,* the only one, Christ, King, Head:…

The stanza communicates an immediate sense of mystical rapture, a rapture beyond the reach of language. As seen, this stanza implicitly conveys the culmination of the soul's ecstatic ascent to the place of God. This is the mystical union of hearts, the transformation of the devout heart into the tabernacle and house of God. This is the heart's chamber, the place wherein soul and spouse are united in heavenly nuptials. By calling upon Christ as Head Hopkins signals both the mystical body of the church of which Christ is Head (cf. Col. 1.18), and also the nuptial nature of this metaphor, the Church as both bride and body (cf. Eph. 5.23). As Hawkins writes,

> Here now Jesus stands not behind the wall, peeping at this Spouse through a grate; but…shows her his face, the divine Essence, the three divine Persons, so clearly and manifestly…in the Crystal of the heart. O Paradise! O delights! O joys![40]

This is the final emblem of the Wiericx series, the culmination of the soul's meditative ascent that is Christ's manifestation in the heart. For Hopkins, as for Hawkins, this is an unspeakable encounter. It is described by Hawkins in the terms of St Paul's rapture, when he was 'ravished into the third heaven' to hear 'mysterious words, as man might not utter' (cf. 2 Cor. 12.2–4).[41] Drawing on Psalm 41 and the soul's desire to appear before the 'face' of God, Hawkins's meditation describes the soul's delight to behold the divine Trinity eternally, in the mirror of the heart. For Hopkins too the 'thing' (28) evoked here is the 'one thing' described earlier in the poem (19): the union with the Holy Trinity in the heaven of the ascended heart. This is the divine essence, reflected in the enlightened heart. This is the heart's vision, and so Hopkins continues:

29

Ah! there was a heart right!
There was single eye!
Read the unshapeable shock night
And knew the who and the why;
Wording it how but by him that present and past,
Heaven and earth are word of, worded by?—
The Simon Peter of a soul! to the blast
Tarpeian-fast, but a blown beacon of light.

30

Jesu, heart's light,...

Aligning heart and eye, Hopkins conjures that classic emblematic representation: the eye of the heart. This is Augustine's 'eye of the soul' or 'eye of faith', and Hopkins implicitly reiterates the spiritual and meditative paradigm within which we are to read. The inscribed image of the stanza is that of the heart's illumination. As seen, the 'single eye' may be read with reference to Matthew 6.22 or Luke 11.34, both of which suggest an experience of illumination; this is echoed in Hopkins's description of the Word of God as 'beacon of light' and 'heart's light'. In Quarles's *Emblems* we find an emblem entitled 'The Watching of the Heart'; the engraving displays a heart that contains a wide-open eye, with the accompanying quote: 'I sleep, but my heart waketh.' (Song 5.2).[42] As Bath notes, this emblem belongs to the *via illuminativa* section of van Haeften's original work. Harvey writes, 'Sleep must refresh my senses, but my mind's / A sparkle of heav'nly fire, that...needs / No time of rest'.[43] Harvey's explicatory ode continues to contrast bodily senses with the operation of the eye of the mind or soul. Speaking of the soul he writes, 'But that the more she looks, the more she longs;' and finally concludes, 'If not thy face, Lord, let mine heart / Behold with Moses thy back part.'[44] While Bath observes that Harvey's ending risks banality, we may instead note that Harvey's allusion to Moses's vision of God reiterates the contemplative nature of this emblem, and the Augustinian paradigm on which it draws. For Hopkins too, the emblematic imagery of the heart reiterates his mystical subtext; this is the eye of the heart by which God is seen.

35

Dame, at our door
Drowned, and among our shoals,
Remember us in the roads, the heaven-haven of the Reward:
Our King back, oh, upon English souls!
Let him easter in us, be a dayspring to the dimness of us, be a crimson-cresseted east,
More brightening her, rare-dear Britain, as his reign rolls,
Pride, rose, prince, hero of us, high-priest,
Our hearts' charity's hearth's fire, our thoughts' chivalry's throng's Lord.

In Hopkins's final stanza, emblematic inscapes inscribed earlier in the poem bring his subtextual narrative to its completion. Here, for the first and only time, Hopkins makes explicit the image of a door. Suggested in the closing stanza of Part I of the poem, the image evokes a personal conversion, Christ at the door of the heart, melting and mastering man's soul (10). Here, at the close of Part II of the poem, the image signals a change in the heart of a nation, the broader body of Hopkins's Britain. Hopkins's evocation of Christ as 'rose' repeats his earlier emblematic representation of the heart. Christ who was earlier 'Orion of light' (21) is here a new dawn, a dayspring rising within human hearts, a 'crimson-cresseted east'. Christ as cresset, or beacon, continues Hopkins's description of that 'beacon of light...heart's light' (29, 30). This is a portrayal common in emblem books: the heart lit up by a lamp carried by or symbolic of Christ. Hopkins's description of the 'heart's charity's hearth's fire' also echoes emblematic portrayals of the heart enflamed with love. In Hawkins's words, 'This is the fire which encloses the heart so... Of this lamp mercy is the oil...as flowing from an inexhaustible channel, the very bowels of God.'[45] For Hopkins as well, it is this mercy of God that fuels the heart's fire and lights the last line of the poem's dramatic close. This is the charity of God poured forth in the heart (Rom. 5.5). We are reminded of Augustine, as quoted by Hawkins: 'Thou hast shot our heart, my God, with thy charity (Note: Cant. 4).'[46]

For Augustine and Hawkins, Christ is a divine archer who shoots through the heart with fiery arrows; and we may ask if there is not a suggestion of this archetypal image at the conclusion of *The Wreck*. Hopkins's evocation of 'charity' and 'chivalry' (cognate of chevalier) may be seen to subtly suggest that medieval ideal of Christ as lover-knight.[47] In *The Windhover* Hopkins writes, 'Buckle! AND the fire that breaks from thee then, a billion / Times told lovelier, more dangerous, O my chevalier!'[48] 'Thee' is suggested to address the heart itself, from which issues this breaking fire.[49] Here too, in the final stanza of *The Wreck,* Hopkins calls on Christ as chivalric 'prince', to wound the heart with his redeeming love. We have come full circle, the heart that shoots forth fiery shafts (3) now receives this fire into itself. This is Hopkins's mystical vision of the heart infused with the energies of God: morning sun, cresset, rose, hearth and door. In this final conflagration, in this strange emblematic alchemy of images, *The Wreck of the Deutschland* does, in Hopkins's words, '*explode*'.[50] As Hawkins writes:

> Burn therefore my heart, o Jesus, the dearling of my soul, and let not the oil of the lamp be ever wanting: be this fire...as a sun... that I burn and be consumed with this flame: Yea, and be reduced into ashes...and presently become a new heart. O Metamorphosis of love![51]

*Figure 8.6* 'The heart enflamed with the love of Jesus shines all with light and flames'.

Source: From Stephanus Luzvic, *The Devout Hart or Royal Throne of the Pacifical Salomon*, trans. into English by Henry Hawkins (Rouen: John Cousturier, 1634), 226. Reproduced from a copy in the library of Eton College, by permission of the Provost and Fellows.

## Notes

1 The content of this chapter appears in the article, 'The Heart's Bower: Emblematics in *The Wreck of the Deutschland*,' *Literature and Theology* 22.1 (2008): 32–47. Reprinted by permission of Oxford University Press Journals.

2 Michael Bath, *Speaking Pictures: English Emblem Books and Renaissance Culture* (London: Longman, 1994), 222. In Book IV of his *On Christian Doctrine,* Augustine establishes the conventional distinction between *res* and *verba,* arguing that words are both things and signs, but that things are also sometimes used as signs; this Augustinian theory of signs is implicit in Renaissance emblem theory even before the development of the specifically religious and meditative emblem (ibid).

3 Ibid., 172.
4 Ibid., 277.
5 Hopkins, *Collected Works* vol. 1, *Correspondence,* 503. Hopkins writes,

> I remember, by the by, once taking up a little book of the life of St Stanislaus told or commented on under emblems; it was much in the style of Herbert and his school and about that date; it was by some Polish Jesuit. I was astonished at their beauty and brilliancy, but the author is quite obscure.
>
> (Ibid.)

6 K. J. Höltgen, Introduction to *Henry Hawkins: The Devout Hart 1634* (London: The Scolar Press, 1975), 16–17.
7 The other Recusant emblem book is Hawkins's *Partheneia Sacra* (Rouen, 1633). *Ashrea: or the Grove of Beatitudes* by E. M. is the third English Catholic emblem book, though not classed as Recusant; it lies however somewhat outside the emblematic and meditative tradition.
8 K. J. Höltgen, 'Henry Hawkins: A Jesuit Writer and Emblemist in Stuart England' in J. W. O'Malley, S.J., et al. (eds), *The Jesuits: Cultures, Sciences, and the Arts 1540–1773* (Toronto, ON: University of Toronto Press, 1999), 621.
9 'Rules of the Prefect of Lower Studies.' *The Jesuit Ratio Studiorum of 1599*. Trans. A. P. Farrell, S. J. (Washington, 1970). Boston College Libraries, Digital Library Projects. www.bc.edu/bc_org/avp/ulib/digi/ratio/ratio_web.html.
10 Published in 1634, the first edition of Hawkins's translation has only blank pages for the missing Wiericx plates; the engravings are however found in a reissue dated 1638. The plates additionally appear in Luzvic's own Latin translation of 1722, and it is equally likely that Hopkins encountered the French or Latin versions of the book. This study however will refer to the English text of Hawkins's translation.
11 Höltgen, 'Hawkins: A Jesuit Writer and Emblemist,' 605.
12 Quarles, *Emblems,* 208.
13 Höltgen, 'Hawkins: A Jesuit Writer and Emblemist,' 604.
14 Quarles, *Emblems,* 351.
15 Clarke, *Theory and Theology*, 106, 112.
16 Luzvic, Stephanus, 'The most amorous Jesus knocks at the door of the heart, the Preamble to the Meditation.' *The devout hart or Royal throne of the pacifical Salomon. Composed by F. St. Luzuic S. I. Translated out of Latin into English. Enlarged with incentive by F. St Binet of the same S. and now enriched with hymnes by a new hand* (1634). Early English Books Online. http://eebo.chadwyck.com. The title of the work suggests Christ as a second Solomon who makes a throne for himself in the devout heart of the Christian.
17 Luzvic, 'Jesus the living fountain in the heart.' *The Devout Hart.*
18 Keating, *The Wreck of the Deutschland: An Essay and Commentary* (Research Series 6, Kent, OH: Kent State University, 1963), 66.
19 Bath, *Speaking Pictures,* 206. In his commentary on Psalm 41 Augustine writes, 'For we find in the stag a symbol of swiftness' (ibid.).
20 Quarles, *Emblems*, 217.
21 Luzvic, 'Jesus purges the heart with expiatory blood, the Colloquy to the wounds of our Saviour.' *The Devout Hart.*
22 Hopkins, *Poems*, 'What being in rank-old nature...,' 179.
23 Luzvic, 'Jesus sings in the choir of the heart, to the Angels playing on musical instruments, the First Point of the Meditation.' *The Devout Hart.*

24 Quarles, *Emblems,* 261, 300.
25 Luzvic, 'Jesus manifests himself and the most holy Trinity in the mirror of the heart, the Incentive.' *The Devout Hart.*
26 This suggestion is made by Keating. See chapter 5, 35 n.
27 Luzvic, 'Jesus manifests himself and the most holy Trinity in the mirror of the heart, the Incentive.' *The Devout Hart.*
28 Luzvic, 'The heart consecrated to the love of Jesus is a flourishing garden.' *The Devout Hart.* Cf. Quarles, *Emblems,* 327.
29 Höltgen, Introduction to *Henry Hawkins: The Devout Hart 1634* (London: The Scolar Press, 1975), 11.
30 Mario Praz, *Studies in Seventeenth-Century Imagery*, 2nd. ed. (Rome: Edizioni di Storia e Litteratura, 1964).
31 This is discussed at length by Eric Jager in *The Book of the Heart* (Chicago, IL: University of Chicago Press, 2000).
32 Luzvic, 'The most amorous Jesus knocks at the door of the heart, the Preamble to the Meditation.' *The Devout Hart.*
33 George Herbert, 'The Altar', in *The Temple 1633: A Scolar Press Facsimile* (London: The Scolar Press Ltd., 1968), 18.
34 Jean Bainvel, S.J., *Devotion to the Sacred Heart: The Doctrine and Its History* (London: Burns, Oates and Washbourne Ltd., 1924), 314.
35 Luzvic, 'Jesus brings in the cross into the heart, and easily imprints it in the lover, the Incentive.' *The Devout Hart.*
36 Luzvic, Jesus brings in the cross into the heart, and easily imprints it in the lover, the Prelude.' *The Devout Hart.* Hawkins transcribes this as 'a sign upon thy heart'.
37 Cf. Quarles, *Emblems,* 285. The emblem is entitled 'The Softening of the Heart' and Quarles describes a heart of marble ice, to be melted by divine love.
38 Luzvic, 'Jesus the living fountain in the heart, the Preamble to the Meditation.' *The Devout Hart.*
39 Luzvic, 'Jesus celebrates the heavenly nuptials in the heart, the Incentive.' *The Devout Hart.*
40 Luzvic, 'Jesus manifests himself and the most holy Trinity in the mirror of the heart, the Incentive.' *The Devout Hart.*
41 Luzvic, 'Jesus manifests himself and the most holy Trinity in the mirror of the heart, the Preamble to the Meditation.' *The Devout Hart.*
42 Quarles, *Emblems,* 333.
43 Ibid., 334. See Bath, *Speaking Pictures,* 181.
44 Quarles, *Emblems,* 335.
45 Luzvic, 'The heart enflamed with the love of Jesus shines all with light and flames, the Preamble to the Meditation.' *The Devout Hart.*
46 Luzvic, 'Jesus wounds and pierces the heart with the shafts of love, the Prelude.' *The Devout Hart.*
47 This is discussed by Rosemary Woolf in 'The Theme of Christ the Lover-Knight in Medieval English Literature,' *The Review of English Studies* 13.49 (1962): 1–16.
48 Hopkins, *Poems,* 69.
49 Lawler, *Hopkins Re-Constructed,* 203.
50 Hopkins, *Collected Works* vol. 1, *Correspondence,* 367.
51 Luzvic, 'The heart enflamed with the love of Jesus shines all with light and flames, the Preamble to the Meditation.' *The Devout Hart.*

# 9 Love, Spirit, Breath, Fire

For now we see through a glass darkly, but then face to face
...Now abideth faith, hope, charity, but the greatest of these is charity
(1 Cor 13.12–13)

Many of the themes of Hopkins's *The Wreck of the Deutschland* can be seen to recur in the 1877 poems written in its aftermath. A mystical understanding of the sacraments, an emphasis on the doctrine of the mystical body, the deification of the soul, the indwelling of the Spirit and the soul's contemplative ascent to divine vision – these are some of the themes continued in poems that follow *The Wreck*. Several of these poems similarly employ emblematic and typological methods. It becomes possible to speak of a number of 'agglomerations' that are central to understanding Hopkins's heart-mysticism.[1] This imagery, heavily influenced by baroque emblem tradition, becomes inextricably linked with the soul's ascent. In Hopkins's poetry, what is at stake is not merely a visual and poetic vocabulary of the heart, but a deeply inscribed imagining of a personal union with the divine, achieved in and by the spirit.

Hopkins's nature sonnets of 1877 express an exuberant recognition of the divine in nature. Written during his final year at St Beuno's, these are some of Hopkins's best-known poems: 'God's Grandeur', 'The Starlight Night', 'Spring', 'In the Valley of the Elwy', 'The Sea and the Skylark', 'The Windhover', 'Pied Beauty', 'Hurrahing in Harvest', 'The Caged Skylark'. Perhaps the most famous is 'The Windhover', describing the flight of a falcon at dawn. The subtitle of the poem '*To Christ our Lord*' prompts questions about the falcon as a symbol of Christ and the poem seems to suggest a moment of contemplative apprehension. One reading of 'The Windhover' is that the poem is developed through visual metaphors deriving from the 'School of the Heart' emblem tradition. The poem's conception is itself perhaps emblematic: the falcon is the heart-bird of emblematic discourse. This is the central metaphor of the sonnet and one that is easily related to Christopher Harvey's *Schola Cordis*. As we have seen, Harvey's anonymously published engravings were regularly assigned to Quarles and printed together with Quarles's *Emblems*, which appeared in at least thirty nineteenth-century editions.[2] Chapter 8 looked closely Hopkins's emblematic inheritance, and his general acquaintance with Quarles and the emblem-literature of 'Herbert's school'.[3] Interestingly, the 1844 edition of Herbert's *The Temple* includes Harvey's 'The Synagogue' and suggests Harvey as the probable author of the *Schola Cordis*.[4] Whether or not Hopkins knew of the true authorship of the *Schola Cordis*, he was clearly aware of the relation between emblematic tradition and Herbert's poetry. The emblematic and Continental heart-imagery of 'The Windhover' shows some parallels with the ways in which Herbert himself drew on and influenced emblematic imagery of the seventeenth century.[5]

Critics writing on 'The Windhover' have heard in the penultimate line of the poem an echo of Herbert's 'Love' (III).[6] Yet Herbert's influence on the poem has not so far been connected with baroque emblem literature. The dovewinged heart of *The Wreck of the Deutschland* shows striking similarities to Emblem 38 of the 'School of the Heart': 'The Flying of the Heart.'[7] 'The Windhover' suggests the continued influence of this heart-bird emblem on Hopkins's poetic imagination, and further suggests a knowledge of the emblem as it relates to Herbert. In the *Schola Cordis*, the emblem of the winged heart is accompanied by an ode that draws on Herbert's 'Easter Wings'. As in Herbert's poem, the lines of verse are shaped as wings, and Harvey points this out to his readers.

This one desire
methinks hath imp'd it so,
That it already flies like fire
And ev'n my verses into wings doe grow.[8]

Harvey alludes here to the closing lines of Herbert's 'Easter Wings': 'For, if I imp my wing on thine, / Affliction shall advance the flight in me.' The theme of Herbert's 'Easter Wings' is that of death and resurrection: only by 'imping' its wings to those of the saviour can the creature leave behind the earth; this is the soul's engrafting into Christ. Harvey's engraving, with its accompanying text, effectively links the emblematic image of the heart-bird with Herbert's famous portrayal of the soul's winged flight. Harvey's emblem and Herbert's verse may be seen to form an abiding imaginative amalgam in Hopkins's mind, from which springs 'The Windhover'.

...how he rung upon the rein of a wimpling wing
In his ecstasy! then off, off forth on swing,
As a skate's heel s weeps smooth on a bow-bend: the hurl and gliding
Rebuffed the big wind. My heart in hiding
Stirred for a bird, - the achieve of, the mastery of the thing![9]

Hopkins's description of 'a wimpling wing' echoes, through half-rhyme, the imping of wing to wing described by Herbert. The direct meaning of 'wimple' as a nun's habit perhaps has some visual bearing on the poem. But the semantic interpretation of the line perhaps lies in a play of sound. Though such a reading may seem fanciful, 'imp' is in fact entirely appropriate to the subject of Hopkins's sonnet. 'Imp', as a noun means 'graft;' as a transitive verb, 1: to graft or repair (a wing, tail, or feather) with a feather to improve a falcon's flying capacity 2: to equip with wings. The founding metaphor of *The Temple* is God's spiritual abode in the soul, and Herbert's 'Easter Wings' is implicitly linked with the religious and poetic trope of the heart. In the *Schola Cordis,* this link is made explicit in Harvey's emblematic application of the poem. I am suggesting that for Hopkins the emblematic image of the bird-heart becomes inextricably linked with a particular religious theme: the 'imping' of human and divine, figured by and in the heart. This is the 'ecstasy' Hopkins describes in the first stanza of 'The Windhover': the ecstasy of divine union. A later poem perhaps provides proof of the persistence of this Herbertian imagery in Hopkins's imagination. In 'Brothers', a little-known poem, Hopkins describes the relationship between two siblings; the poem opens with the exclamation 'How lovely the elder brother's / Life all laced in the other's, / Love-laced!' Hopkins goes on to describe this elder who

> ...Smiled, blushed, and bit his lip;
> Or drove, with a diver's dip,
> Clutched hands through clasped knees;
> And many a mark like these,
> Told tales with what heart's stress
> He hung on the imp's success...[10]

The 'imp's success' here is the success of the younger brother. But this imagery perhaps also draws on that of 'The Windhover'. As in Hopkins's earlier poem, bird and heart appear in conjunction, and the 'diver's dip' echoes the plummeting falcon of the earlier sonnet. Once again, Hopkins's use of the word 'imp' calls up the imagery of heart enjoined with heart: 'Love-laced!'

As in *The Wreck*, Hopkins's theme of divine union in 'The Windhover' is developed in conjunction with the metaphor of the mystical body. If the hidden image of the imping of wing with wing suggests the soul's engrafting into Christ, this theme is reiterated in an etymological play of word. Justus Lawler's reading of 'The Windhover' discusses the poem's surprisingly Francophonic diction, visibly seen in the vocabulary of 'dauphin', 'chevalier', 'minion' and 'silion'. Analysing Hopkins's use of the word 'achieve' Lawler writes:

> Its most obvious cognate is another French word, *chef*... which immediately evokes, first, various New Testament images for Christ,

for example, this conflation of English and French from Colossians 1:18: "And he is the head of the body the church, *le* chef..."[11]

As we have seen, Hopkins's title of 'Head' in *The Wreck* may be read with reference to Colossians 1.18. The title appears at that very juncture of the poem (stanza 28) where Hopkins suggests union through the mystical body of Christ, a foreshadowing of the perfect eschatological union of the soul with the divine. Here too, in Hopkins's most famous sonnet, it is this incorporation into Christ that is the subtext of the poem. The word 'achieve' relates 'The Windhover' to the religious and mystical paradigms central to *The Wreck*. 'Achieve' derives etymologically from the Anglo-French *achever*: 'to finish, from *a*-(from Latin ad-) + *chef* end, head; (to) reach'. By equating achieve(ment) and 'mastery' Hopkins evokes precisely such a finishing or perfecting; an end that is 'reached'. Again, this configuration is prefigured in stanza 28 of *The Wreck*. Hopkins's question, 'How shall I...reach me a place there' is answered by the naming of Christ as 'Head': the 'place' that is the mystical body in heaven, the perfection of the soul's ascent.

In *The Wreck of the Deutschland*, Hopkins's culminating apprehension of God is reached through an effort of the poet's own heart. It is, simultaneously, a recognition of the mind or heart as the place or habitation of divinity. In 'The Windhover', the 'imping' of soul with Christ, of heart with heart, is reiterated in a seemingly odd word – the 'thing' that is achieved or mastered. This deliberately odd word recalls the 'thing' seen in stanza 28 of *The Wreck*. In both cases this is the subject and object of heightened vision – it is the heart whose spiritual vision is the soul's union with the divine. In this contemplative apprehension, the heart is transformed into the very image of God; it becomes the thing itself.[12] As in *The Wreck,* divine union is specifically the achievement of the mind or heart. The 'mastery of the thing' is that fullest action of the mind described by Hopkins in his spiritual notes. It is a contemplative experience, the vision or knowledge of Christ and the Spirit in the heart. The divine apprehension described here uses the very language and metaphors of Hopkins's mystical vision in *The Wreck*. The flight of the windhover echoes the flight of Hopkins's dovewinged heart; what is seen or experienced is the majesty or glory that is the divine working in world and soul, bird and heart. Hopkins continues:

> ...the achieve of, the mastery of the thing!
>
> Brute beauty and valour and act, oh, air, pride, plume, here
>   Buckle! AND the fire that breaks from thee then, a billion
> Times told lovelier, more dangerous, O my chevalier![13]

Hopkins draws out his meaning of union with or engrafting into Christ through a further play of word. If both 'wimpling' (which hides the word 'imp') and 'achieve' carry an interior sense of incorporation into Christ, this underlying meaning is continued in Hopkins's use of the word 'buckle'. Perhaps the most analysed word in Hopkins scholarship, 'buckle', in its obvious meaning of enjoining, suggests too the mystical body of Christ into which the believer is engrafted. 'Buckle! AND...' emphasises this very sense of conjunction, the divine union of the soul with God, at once its end and beginning. The 'fire that breaks from thee' is the heart aflame with the love of God, and both 'thee' and 'chevalier' may be read as the heart now joined with God.[14] This is the bold and splendid vision of 'The Windhover'. The lesson learned from a bird in flight is that only a grafting or buckling of wing to wing, heart to heart, releases that breaking fire, which is 'a billion times told lovelier'. This is the 'ecstasy' of divine union and resurrection.

Hopkins's imagination moves easily from the heart-bird of emblematic literature to the heart aflame with love – an image common in baroque emblem books and in the spiritual literature of the sacred heart.[15] The buckling of the heart is that divine fusion by which it is set alight. The word suggests also the action of collapse or crumpling, intimating perhaps the wound of divine love. By this wound is the heart made 'lovelier'. Etymologically, 'buckle' derives from the Anglo French *bocle*, 'boss of a shield', related to the English word 'buckler', denoting a small shield. Given Hopkins's penchant for multiple meanings, 'buckle' may correspondingly be read in relation to the image of Christ as 'chevalier'. This pattern of imagery also relates to the final line of *The Wreck* where Hopkins writes – 'Our hearts' charity's hearth's fire, our thoughts' chivalry's throng's Lord'. The conclusion of Hopkins's ode evokes Christ as a chivalrous knight who shoots through the heart with fiery arrows. 'Chevalier', as used in 'The Windhover' is a cognate of 'chivalry', and the second stanza of the sonnet suggests the very image which closes *The Wreck*: the heart wounded and set alight by divine love.[16] In 'The Windhover', Hopkins's exclamation 'O my chevalier!' similarly evokes Christ as cavalier, who wounds the heart with his love. Interestingly, Lawler too relates the imagery of 'The Windhover' to *The Wreck*, suggesting that the bird's flight towards the eastern dawn relates to the final stanza of Hopkins's ode and the prayer that Christ will 'easter in us' in the 'crimson-cresseted east'.[17] What is at stake, as Lawler suggests, is a resurrection of sorts. But this is one specifically conceived through the action of Christ within and upon the heart. The next stanza continues:

> ...No wonder of it: sheer plod makes plough down sillion
> Shine, and blue-bleak embers, ah my dear,
> Fall, gall themselves, and gash gold-vermilion.[18]

If the second stanza of 'The Windhover' conveys the heart set alight by divine love, the third stanza, as Alan Heuser suggests, evokes the emblematic cross-plough in the field of the heart. As Heuser writes in the endnotes to his essay, *The Shaping Vision of Gerard Manley Hopkins*, 'The inscape in the outspread bird is the cross. The plough is the cross acting in the field of the heart. The cross-plough is familiar in emblem-literature...'[19] In other words, like the figure of the chevalier, the plough becomes the instrument or agent for the instressing of God in the heart. As we have noted, the words 'ah my dear' are generally interpreted as an allusion to Herbert's familiar reference to Christ in 'Love' (III). Lawler contests this, suggesting that the words refer to 'Hopkins/heart', and not to Christ. The parallel, Lawler argues, is between 'ah my dear' and 'O my chevalier' – both exclamations evoking the heart.[20] Both readings, however, are valid. The two readings converge, and their convergence is the very subject of the poem. Hopkins evokes in emblematic images the action of Christ within and upon the heart; the central metaphor of 'The Windhover' is the heart or soul conjoined with God. Turning to Herbert's 'Love' (III), we see that this in fact is the central conceit of the poem. Herbert's words 'ah my dear' despairingly address Christ, but the response received is an affirmation of God in the soul – 'Who made the eyes but I?' In the manner of Herbert's 'Love' (III), the visual act by which Hopkins perceives the windhover becomes itself a contemplative recognition of the inner presence of the divine.

Yet another emblematic trope employed in 'The Windhover' to portray divine action in the heart is the 'sounding' of the heart as a musical instrument. We considered earlier that the heart 'wrung' (or rung) in stanza 9 of *The Wreck of the Deutschland* derives from emblematic imagery of the heart as musical instrument.[21] Here, once again, Hopkins employs this emblematic metaphor in his description of the heart-bird that is '*rung* upon the rein of a wimpling wing [my italics].' The phrase suggests both musical sound and string, especially when read against the preceding description of the windhover sweeping on a 'bow-bend'. The implied imagery of 'rein' and 'bow' links these two lines of the sonnet; at one level, what is heard is the ringing out of music played upon the 'bow' of an instrument. A further play of sound continues this meaning, for the phrase 'bow-bend' perhaps plays at the famous 'Bow bells', the bells of the Church of St. Mary-le-Bow in London. This sound play recurs further in the poem, when Hopkins describes the 'fire that breaks from thee then, a billion / Times told lovelier...' The poet's use of the word 'told' as a play on 'tolled' is suggested by Gardner, who nevertheless advises caution in the searching out of puns and echoes in Hopkins's poetry.[22] Yet there is a case to be made in 'The Windhover' for Hopkins's synaesthetic account of the flight of the heart-bird as divine music in the soul. The peculiar conjunction of musical metaphor is also echoed in another poem of 1877, 'As kingfishers catch fire...' In this well-known poem, Hopkins similarly describes the flight of a kingfisher as it catches the light of the sun, setting these tremors of light against the auditory ringing of stones. Hopkins writes, 'Stones ring; like each tucked string tells, each hung bell's / Bow swung finds tongue to fling out broad its name'. Here, the ringing of sound and the imagery of 'string', 'bell' and 'bow' repeat the metaphors of 'The Windhover', as do the accompanying images of fire and flame. What Hopkins describes in the 'Kingfishers' sonnet is the 'dealing out' of the inner self, housed in the heart. Similarly, in an unfinished poem fragment, Hopkins writes even more explicitly of 'these heart-song powerful peals' (Fragments, 141). In 'The Windhover', the central trope of the heart-bird works in Hopkins's imagination to generate further emblematic images; the heart set alight bursts also into sound. This conflagration of images is symptomatic of the emblematic imagination that underwrites many poems of the period; as in *The Wreck*, 'The Windhover' repeats the ascent of the heart conceived in emblematic figures.

The heart-imagery of Hopkins's 1876 ode is continued in another 1877 poem, 'Hurrahing in Harvest'. The poem begins with a description of harvest fields at the end of summer. What is described as an experience of natural beauty is progressively revealed as mystical experience, and the soul's ascent is once again a recognition of Christ in the heart.

> Summer ends now; now, barbarous in beauty, the stooks rise
> Around; up above, what wind-walks! What lovely
> Behaviour
> Of silk-sack clouds! Has wilder, wilful-wavier
> Meal-drift moulded ever and melted across skies?
>
> I walk, I lift up, I lift up heart, eyes,
> Down all that glory in the heavens to glean our Saviour;
> And, eyes, heart, what looks, what lips yet gave you a
> Rapturous love's greeting of realer, of rounder replies?...[23]

In the eucharistic grain of the harvest fields and 'meal-drift' of clouds, Hopkins sees an image of Christ.[24] In order to do so, to 'glean' the Saviour, Hopkins must lift up heart and eyes. Then, inverting this order, he addresses eyes and heart, in an attempt to understand a response that is glimpsed and heard. Hopkins asks: 'what looks, what lips yet gave you a / rapturous love's greeting of realer, of rounder replies?' Hopkins's wording here at the end of the second stanza is deliberately and irreducibly ambiguous. This ambiguity is central to the meaning of the poem: 'love's greeting' is both the rapture of Hopkins's own heart in its knowledge of Christ and the image of Christ that greets Hopkins from within the landscape he sees. Lawler notes that these 'realer, rounder replies' suggest the circular imagery that is the classic mystical and poetic imagery of fulfilment.[25] The word 'reply' is etymologically linked with the Latin *replicare*, 'to fold back', 'to make a legal replication'; this idea of 'replication' is at the core of Hopkins's meaning. Hopkins's important inversion of 'heart, eyes' / 'eyes, heart' presents a mirror image, suggesting the eyes, heart or soul as a mirror to and reflection of Christ. This inversion is also a circularity of exchange: no longer does Hopkins look *on* a landscape; rather, the recognition of Christ in the landscape turns the vision around so that it is Christ who looks out at Hopkins, from within the world, and more importantly, from within himself. It is this realisation that emboldens the heart –

> And the azurous hills are his world-wielding shoulder
> Majestic–as a stallion stalwart, very-violet-sweet!–
> These things, these things were here and but the beholder
> Wanting; which two when they once meet,
> The heart rears wings bold and bolder
> And hurls for him, O half hurls earth for him off under his
> feet.

'Behold' etymologically derives from the Middle English 'to keep' and from the Old English *behealdan*, from 'be-' + *healdan* 'to hold'. The soul does not only recognise Christ, but also will 'hold' him within itself. Hopkins's now-familiar imagery of the winged heart suggests more than the soul rearing Plato's spiritual wings in response to beauty;[26] the image is again consciously or subconsciously linked with the imping of the heart to Christ. This is the rapturous meeting Hopkins describes. A further cue to this reading lies in the use of the word 'O', which suggests that circularity of fulfilment seen in the first part of the poem. This circularity is now specifically conjoined with the heart. 'O half hurls' describes the heart's momentum as it meets its maker, much as in 'The Windhover' the words 'O my chevalier' evoke Christ-in-the-heart. This is the heart's mystic exaltation; and the twice repeated 'hurl', describing the motion of the winged heart, repeats the heart's ascending prayer in *The Wreck of the Deutschland*.[27] As we have seen, the word 'hurl' may be linked with the Latin *ejaculari* and Augustine's conception of ejaculatory prayer. Here in 'Hurrahing in Harvest', as in Hopkins's other poetry, the exclamations of 'O,' 'Oh' and 'Ah' become the expression of ejaculatory prayer – the mystical prayer of the heart. These are the silent sighs of the spirit, the 'unspeakable groanings' described in Romans 8.26 (AV, 'groanings which cannot be uttered'). This is a key text in Augustine's formulation of ejaculatory prayer, and one that underwrites Hopkins's heart-centred mysticism. Hopkins's interpretation of Romans 8.26 emphasises the circularity of God and man, and the activity or energy of the spirit in the soul.

> For prayer is the expression of a wish to God and, since God searches the heart, the conceiving even of the wish is prayer in God's eyes (see

> Rom. viii. 26, 27)... correspondence itself is on man's side not so much corresponding as the wish to correspond, and this least sigh of desire, this one aspiration, is the life and spirit of man... ...And even the sigh or aspiration itself is in answer to an inspiration of God's spirit and is followed by the continuance and expiration of that same breath which lifts it, through the gulf and void...to do or be what God wishes his creature to do or be.
>
> (30 December, 1881)[28]

Hopkins traces the cycle of inspiration and aspiration, the sighing of desire or love that brings the soul to union with the divine. What the Greek Fathers understand through the doctrine of the energies is echoed in Augustine's prayer of the heart. Hopkins similarly describes the inspiration of God's spirit as the beginning of the soul's future perfection. The operation of the Holy Spirit in the soul enables its participation in divinity. For Hopkins, like Augustine, the unutterable groans of the spirit are heard above all in the heart; the words 'O', 'Oh' and 'Ah' are for Hopkins the heart's sighs of desire, the aspirations by which the soul is raised up to the divine and itself deified. This is the rapture described in 'Hurrahing in Harvest'; the winged heart, which 'O half hurls', is the heart raised up to God in contemplative celebration. Hopkins's 'Os', 'Ohs' and 'Ahs' signify the heart's ascending prayer; man's 'reply' to God's inspiration is the word/Word spoken in the heart. In another poem of the period, 'The Valley of the Elwy', Hopkins similarly employs an emblematic and mystical vocabulary to suggest the heart as the place of the creature's 'completion' in God. Hopkins writes:

> Lovely the woods, waters, meadows, combes, vales,
> All the air things wear that build this world of Wales;
> Only the inmate does not correspond:
>
> God, lover of souls, swaying considerate scales,
> Complete thy creature dear O where it fails,
> Being mighty a master, being a father and fond.[29]

Describing God as a 'lover of souls', Hopkins reflects on his compassionate judgements and on the divine compensation of human failing. The completion of the creature is in the hands of God and Hopkins's image of swaying scales recalls emblematic engravings. In the *Schola Cordis,* Harvey's engraving entitled 'The Weighing of the Heart' shows the human heart being weighed in a set of scales, with the accompanying proverb 'The Lord pondereth the heart' (Prov. 21.2).[30] Hopkins again suggests the heart as the place and purchase of divine grace, using an increasingly familiar vocabulary. In 'The Windhover', Hopkins's words 'ah my dear' evoke the self or heart as joined with God. Here too,

Hopkins's invocation to God to 'complete thy creature dear O where it fails' hints at the heart as the place of this completion. The word 'dear' is itself implicitly linked with Hopkins's imagination of the heart, and functions as an index of the heart itself. At the same time, Hopkins's 'O' portrays again the heart's 'sighs' of desire (cf. Rom. 8.26), in its yearning for divine union. Scripture teaches that the spirit completes the creature where it fails: 'for we know not what we should pray for as we ought' (Rom. 8.26), but the spirit intercedes on behalf of humankind, reconciling souls to God. God works in the heart through the operation of the spirit, perfecting the creature and raising souls to himself. Hopkins's emblematic inscapes reinforce this idea of God as saviour of souls and restorer of hearts. Such an inscape is perhaps behind the deliberately alliterative, emphatic ending of the poem, which draws the attention of the reader to the closing word 'fond'. Etymologically, the word derives from the Old French *fons,* or *font* and Hopkins's closing image subtly recalls emblematic engravings of the divine spring in the heart, the living waters of the soul.[31] A similar configuration of metaphor and imagery may be seen in 'Ribblesdale', a poem that Hopkins explicitly connects with Romans 8 by attaching the scriptural quotation, 'For the earnest expectation of the creature waiteth for the manifestation of the sons of God' (Rom. 8.19 AV). Here, it is the whole of creation Hopkins speaks for.

> Earth, sweet Earth, sweet landscape, with leaves throng
> And louched low grass, heaven that dost appeal
> To, with no tongue to plead, no heart to feel;
> Thou canst but only be, but dost that long –
>
> Thou canst but be, but that thou well dost; strong
> Thy plea with him who dealt...
>
> ...And what is Earth's eye, tongue, or heart else, where
> Else, but in dear and dogged man? –Ah, the heir
> To his own selfbent so bound, so tied to his turn,
>
> To thriftless reave both our rich round world bare
> And none reck of world after, this bids wear
> Earth brows of such care, care and dear concern.[32]

Lawler argues that the poem shows nature as replacing man in giving God glory. Noting that the 'creation' of Romans 8.19 is understood by all commentators as 'nature', Lawler suggests that Hopkins's use of the word 'long' is a pun on 'the creature *longing* for the manifestation of the sons of God'.[33] But while at one level the poem contrasts earth's 'strong...plea' with man's 'selfbent' and 'thriftless' spoiling, the undergirding imagery of the text yet suggests a belief in humankind as nature's 'dearest...clearest selved spark'.[34] Hopkins's hidden allusions and etymological wordplay move against the surface meaning of the poem, instead expressing a vision of creation ultimately reconciled to God through the human heart. Earth's 'eye, tongue, or heart' is found only in 'dear and dogged man': the 'heir'. Against Hopkins's explicit reference to Romans 8, the word 'heir' may be linked with Romans 8.16–17:

> For the Spirit himself giveth testimony to our spirit, that we are sons of God. And if sons, heirs also; heirs indeed of God, and joint heirs with Christ...that we may be also glorified with him.

The word 'heir' suggests again the working of the spirit, by whom men and women are made children of God. Hopkins's interjection of 'Ah' suggests again the ascending sighs of the spirit in the heart. A series of synonymous words at the poem's conclusion continues this inscape of meaning. Hopkins's twice repeated 'care' is reiterated in the words 'reck' and 'concern', and his deliberate conjunction of 'care' and 'dear' is a cue to readers. Although there is no firm etymological link between the two words, Hopkins, by a simple chiming, uses 'care' to evoke '*caritas*' or 'charity'. This is the charity of God poured forth in the heart by the Holy Ghost, the charity by which human souls are adopted into divine sonship (cf. Rom. 5.5). The Latin '*caritas*' suggests dearness, deriving from '*carus*': dear, beloved, highly priced, costly. Hopkins's concluding words 'care and dear concern' gesture towards this inner meaning of 'caritas' as dearness or costliness. The final two stanzas of 'Ribblesdale' contain a number of words that emphasise this idea; 'heir', 'rich', 'bid', 'thrift', 'reave' and of course 'dear' may all be connected with the idea of cost. It is, Hopkins tells us, 'dear and dogged man' who is 'heir'. Hopkins's use of the word 'dear' as an index of the heart is perhaps made clearer in 'Ribblesdale', for the heart houses the gift of God's love, the 'dear' and precious gift of caritas. As Hopkins suggests in his reflections on Romans 8.26, all of creation aspires to God through the sighs of the Spirit in the human creature. This too is the hidden conclusion of 'Ribblesdale'. Hopkins's odd usage of the word 'brows' in the poem suggests a reading of 'expression'.[35] 'Earth brows of such care' because the human being is Earth's expression – her 'eye, tongue and heart'. Creation is reconciled to God through humankind; for although the man of 'Ribblesdale' is 'selfbent' and 'thriftless', he is yet the 'heir' to divine love. As Hopkins writes elsewhere, it is only man who can knowingly give God glory.[36] Earth's 'longing' for revelation can in truth only be felt in the human heart, through the *caritas* which is the heart's longing.

In 'The Leaden Echo and the Golden Echo', Hopkins continues this theme of the divine operation in the human soul. What we see once again is the persistence of a poetic vocabulary and imagery symptomatic of Hopkins's mystical imagining of the heart.

> Somewhere elsewhere there is ah well where! One,
> One. Yes I can tell such a key, I do know such a place,
> Where whatever's prized and passes of us...
> ...dearly and dangerously sweet
> Of us...
> ...fastened with the tenderest truth
> To its own best being and its loveliness of youth: it is an ever
>   lastingness of, O it is an all youth!...[37]

The 'place' Hopkins describes is one that is 'prized', 'dearly' sweet, fastened to its own 'best being'. It is the very place sought and found in *The Wreck*: the heart that is the dwelling place of divinity. 'Where, where, where was a place?' Hopkins asks in *The Wreck of the Deutschland*, and the answer is found in the flight of the heart to the heart of Christ. Now once again, Hopkins's vision of the heart is described through an abundance of metaphor that recalls Hopkins's earlier ode. The heart is a key, a place, an eternal youth; Hopkins's description of 'an everlastingness' suggests again the waters of the heart springing up to life everlasting (cf. Jn. 4.14). As Hopkins writes in 'God's Grandeur', this is the 'dearest freshness deep down things'. It is the divine spirit sighing at the heart of creation and in human hearts, bringing the world to God. This is the working of the divine energies. Breath, fire and water, all convey the motion and movement of being – being as *energeia,* participating in that best being that is Christ. Hopkins's exclamations are the heart's sighs as it reaches up to the divine: '*ah* well where!'; '*O* it is an all youth! [my italics]'. That these sighs are the soul aspiring to God is made clearer as Hopkins urges the man or woman to forsake outwards forms and turn to beauty's 'best being'. This is the inner beauty of the soul in its cooperation with the divine spirit.

> Resign them, sign them, seal them, send them, motion them
>     with breath,
> And with sighs soaring, soaring sighs, deliver
> Them; beauty-in-the-ghost, deliver it, early now, long before
>     death...
>   ...Give beauty back, beauty, beauty, beauty, back to God,
>       beauty's self and beauty's giver.

The relinquishing of visible beauty becomes, conversely, the recognition of true beauty. By returning beauty to God, its external forms are collapsed into the invisible 'self' of beauty that is the divine gift of the spirit. Nearly each word in this section of the poem is connected with the operation of the spirit: (re)sign, sign, seal, motion, breath, sighs. The 'beauty-in-the-ghost' is the Holy Ghost in the heart; through the 'soaring sighs' of the heart's ascent is beauty's self, the divine spirit, 'delivered' back to God. This is the ascent of man through the charity of God's love. This is 'God's better beauty, grace'.[38] Hopkins continues:

> ...what we had lighthanded left in surly the mere mould
> Will have waked and have waxed and have walked with the
> wind what while we slept,
> This side, that side hurling a heavyheaded hundredfold
> What while we, while we slumbered...

Hopkins contrasts what is 'lighthanded left' with what 'hurls a heavyheaded hundredfold'. The ways of men, on 'this side', are opposed to the ways of God. Hopkins perhaps implicitly draws on the metaphor of the mystical body, contrasting the members of this earthly body with Christ who is head – at once in heaven and on earth, and in the hearts of men. 'Hurls' is Hopkins's characteristic description of the heart ascending to God (the word is used in this context in *The Wreck*, 'The Windhover' and 'Hurrahing in Harvest'). Here, Hopkins's use of the verb is again linked with the heart as the place of the divine indwelling – a meaning also suggested in Hopkins's description of the 'mere mould'. 'Mere' derives from the Latin *merus*, having no admixture, pure. This purest mould of man, his 'best being' or type is Christ in the heart; the divine element of the soul. What men and women lightly leave behind 'in surly the mere mould' wakes, waxes and walks with the wind. This divine part of the soul sleeps in the creature yet 'wakes' in God; held 'lightly' by men it weighs heavy with God, 'hurling a heavyheaded hundredfold'. Hopkins's words perhaps echo the description of the heart's beauty in 'The Windhover' – not a 'hundredfold' but 'a billion times told lovelier'. As in the earlier poem, Hopkins suggests again the beauty of the heart raised up to God; beauty returned and restored to its true self. Interestingly, what is described as 'dearly and dangerously sweet / Of us...' can also be connected with 'The Windhover's description of the heart's 'dangerous' and 'lovelier' fire. In both poems, 'dangerous' perhaps suggests the now obsolete meaning of 'danger' as 'reach' or 'range' – the heart's mystical journey of ascent, through the divine energies of the spirit. So, Hopkins asks:

> O then, weary then why should we tread? O why are we so
> haggard at the heart, so care-coiled, care-killed, so fagged,
> so fashed, so cogged, so cumbered,
> When the thing we freely forfeit is kept with fonder a care,
> Fonder a care than we could have kept it, kept
> Far with fonder a care (and we, we should have lost it) finer,
> fonder
> A care kept. – Where kept? Do but tell us where kept, where. –

Yonder. – What high as that! We follow, now we follow. –
    Yonder, yes yonder, yonder,
Yonder.

Once again, Hopkins contrasts the ways of men with the ways of God; what men and women 'freely forfeit' is kept with 'far with fonder a care'. The word 'heart', seen only once in the poem, appears here at the poem's conclusion in close conjunction with the word 'care'. Hopkins perhaps again uses both 'heart' and 'care' to suggest *caritas*: the heart as the seat of God's charity. The word 'care' occurs six times at the poem's close, and in four instances, Hopkins uses the phrase 'fonder a care'. The word 'fond' in its normative sense is synonymous with that other of Hopkins's indices of the heart: 'dear'. But the word evokes too a sacramental and emblematic imagery of the heart. In 'The Valley of the Elwy' Hopkins suggests the word 'fond' in its etymological context of '*fons*' or '*font*'. Charity is the gift given in baptism, and Hopkins's repeated conjunction of 'fonder' and 'care' suggests through semantic chiming and etymological play the *caritas* that is the inner fountain of divine spirit. This is the 'best being' described earlier in the poem, the gift of 'everlastingness' and 'all youth'. As the divine operation in the human creature, charity brings the soul to God. Both *from* and *of* God, charity is the means by which the heart ascends. As Hopkins tells us, what is 'kept with fonder a care' is 'kept far', 'high as that' – 'yonder'. This 'thing' is the heart seen in *The Wreck* and in 'The Windhover'. It is the heart in its vision and knowledge of the divine: 'finer, fonder'. Etymologically, 'finer' is connected with the Middle English *fin*, from Anglo-French, from Latin *finis* 'end, limit'. Hopkins suggests that man's best self is God's self in him; to this divine end the human creature aspires, ascending through the working of the spirit in the heart. This is the end of the soul's journey into God.

## Notes

1 The term is proposed by Walter J. Ong, as quoted by Lawler, *Hopkins Re-Constructed*, 209. Lawler explicates Ong's term as 'a common family… of images drawn from desultory readings, conversations, retreat sermons… to which Hopkins would have been exposed during the whole of his Jesuit life' (ibid.).
2 Bath, *Speaking Pictures*, 271.
3 See Chapter 7, n 4.
4 George Herbert, *The Temple: Sacred Poems and Private Ejaculations* (London: Pickering: 1844), 262. The 'Advertisement to The Synagogue' lays out over five pages the grounds for ascribing to Christopher Harvey the authorship of the 'Synagogue' (1640), and further suggests Harvey as the likely author of the *Schola Cordis*: 'Another work, probably by Ch. Harvie, is entitled "*Schola Cordis;* or the Heart of itself gone away from God; brought back again to him; and instructed by him, in 47 emblems, London,

printed for H. Blunden, at the Castle in Cornhill, 1647," 12 mo. pp. 196. In the edition of 1675 it is stated, that they were "written by the Author of the 'Synagogue' annexed to Herbert's Poems;" if so, this volume must be also ascribed to Christopher Harvey; it should, however, be observed, that it has been reprinted two or three times, within the last half century, and ascribed to Francis Quarles, but erroneously.' The Advertisement also notes that Harvey's emblems are taken from the earlier work of Benedictus Haeftenus published in Antwerp in 1635.

5 Herbert's connections to the emblem tradition are discussed in detail by Rosemary Freeman in *English Emblem Books.*

6 White, *Hopkins: A Literary Biography*, 283. White suggests that the immediacy of Hopkins's first-person singular opening echoes Herbert's conversational tone, and that Hopkins's fond address at the close of the poem – 'ah my dear' – is borrowed from his 'favourite' Herbert. Gardner, in his notes to an early poem of Hopkins, 'New Readings', notes that an Oxford friend (W. E. Addis) once said of Hopkins that 'George Herbert was his strongest tie to the English church,' *Poems,* 248, n 7.

7 See Chapter 7.

8 Quarles, 353. In order to retain clarity with regard to textual sources, I will continue to reference Harvey's emblems under the name of Quarles, as they appear in the 1866 edition of Quarles's *Emblems*. In Ode 38, which accompanies the emblem of the flying heart, the pattern of wings becomes visible when the six stanzas of the ode are seen together.

9 Hopkins, *Poems,* 69.

10 Ibid., 87–88.

11 Lawler, *Hopkins Re-constructed,* 189.

12 Ibid. Lawler too reads the 'thing' with reference to the heart and similarly suggests that Hopkins's heart achieves, like the Windhover, the transcendence of dualities; Lawler's emphasis however is on the balancing of the contemplative and active life by which the Christian chivalrous mission is fulfilled, 190–91.

13 Hopkins, *Poems,* 69.

14 Lawler, *Hopkins Re-constructed,* 191. Lawler too interprets 'thee' and 'chevalier' with reference to the heart, but does not relate this reading to the trope of the mystical body.

15 See Quarles, *Emblems,* 345. In 'The Inflaming of the Heart,' the final stanza of Harvey's ode petitions God to 'let then thy fire inflame / My cold heart so thoroughly...That I may / Ev'ry day...attending / All occasions of ascending, / Heaven upon earth begin.' (ibid., 347).

16 Lawler's reading of 'The Windhover' also draws attention to Hopkins's Franco-Latinate heart imagery, though he finds this imagery 'atypical' in Hopkins's poetry, *Hopkins Re-constructed,* 206. Lawler argues that the heart, which Hopkins generally evokes in his poems, has little in common – other than the red-yellow colours – with the Sacred Heart of traditional iconography or spiritual literature (ibid., 205) 'The Windhover', Lawler suggests, is an exception, and he imaginatively relates its heart-imagery to two people or events: the bloody martyrdom of the Jesuit Jean de Brebeuf in Canada in the seventeenth century and the figure of Joan of Arc, whom he believes broadly 'hovers over the entire poem' (ibid., 215).

17 Ibid., 184.

18 Hopkins, *Poems,* 69.

19 Alan Heuser, *The Shaping Vision of Gerard Manley Hopkins* (Hamden, CN: Archon Books, 1968), 111.

20 Lawler, *Hopkins Re-constructed,* 201.
21 Chapters 7 and 8.
22 Gardner, 'Introduction to the Fourth Edition,' in *Poems* by Hopkins, xxxii.
23 Hopkins, *Poems,* 70.
24 Heuser, *Shaping Vision,* 52.
25 Lawler, *Hopkins Re-constructed,* 181.
26 Cf. Heuser, *Shaping Vision,* 52.
27 See Chapter 6.
28 Hopkins, *Sermons and Devotional Writings,* 154–56. Cf. Lawler's discussion of Hopkins's interpretation of Rom. 8.26, *Hopkins Re-constructed,* 126.
29 Hopkins, *Poems,* 68.
30 Quarles, *Emblems,* 297.
31 Ibid., 324, 'The Watering of the Heart.'
32 Hopkins, *Poems,* 90–91.
33 Lawler, *Hopkins Re-constructed,* 129.
34 Hopkins, *Poems,* 'That nature is a Heraclitean Fire,' 105.
35 Perhaps this idea of Earth's 'expression' may also be linked with Hopkins's portrayal of Christ's features that emerge from the landscape described in 'Hurrahing in Harvest'. This image or reflection of Christ would above all be found in the heart stamped with the likeness of God.
36 Hopkins, *Sermons and Devotional Writings,* 239. Reflecting on the Principle or Foundation of the *Exercises,* Hopkins writes of the created world and its creatures, 'they make [God] known, they tell of him, they give him glory, but they do not know they do, they do not know him...This then is poor praise, faint reverence, slight service, dull glory. Nevertheless what they can *they always do.*' (ibid.) Hopkins's words, '*they always do,*' echo at one level his punning description of nature that 'dost that long –'; nature, whose hope of God is, without man, unchanging and unending.
37 Hopkins, *Poems,* 'The Leaden Echo and the Golden Echo,' 91–93.
38 Ibid., 'To What Serves Mortal Beauty,' 98.

# 10 The Paradise Within

*The Wreck of the Deutschland*, in Robert Bridges's famous words, stands like a 'dragon in the gate' at the entrance to the corpus of Hopkins's mature poetry.[1] But while *The Wreck* represents the beginning of a poetic method, it suggests also a spiritual end; one that is echoed in the best of Hopkins's later poems. Hopkins's most obscure composition is the product not only of a formidable literary endeavour, but also the spiritual achievement of a mind that has mastered the exercise of contemplative activity and has 'seen' God. In his reflections on Hopkins's religious life Humphry House writes, '[Hopkins] was not by training likely to become a mystic: nor by nature. There is nothing in the poems to show that he felt that immediate and personal presence of God'.[2] On the contrary, this is the very subject of Hopkins's longest and most imposing poem, whose portrayal of the immediate experience of God necessitates the reconsideration of a question that has disappeared from Hopkins scholarship – what Dennis Sobolev calls the 'problem of mysticism'.[3]

*The Wreck of the Deutschland* records Hopkins's spiritual journey to union with God. The implied progress of *The Wreck*, as in the *Schola Cordis* emblems it employs, is the threefold mystical way of purgation, illumination and union. This is not a matter of demarcated structure, but of affective experience portrayed in the poem. The spiritual stages reflected in *The Wreck* are often merged or out of sequence (Hopkins's brief mystical encounter with the divine occurs not at the end of the poem, but three-quarters of the way through). Nevertheless, they are present and fundamental to Hopkins's spiritual and mystical project. At one level, Hopkins's use of this submerged structure relates generally to his representation of the progress of Christian life. The inner narrative of *The Wreck* is one of spiritual journey, drawing heavily on the theology of baptism and Christian initiation. Yet the mysticism of the *Song of Songs* and of Hopkins's other scriptural and patristic sources reiterates the contemplative underthought of *The Wreck*. This mystical dimension of Hopkins's ode is seen in its application of the mystagogic catecheses of the early church, its invocation of Augustine's contemplative theology and its incorporation of a baroque emblematic imagery that draws on Bonaventure's *Itinerarium* and the threefold mystical way. Hopkins's influences all point to a central preoccupation with divine union and the vision of God – achieved through the sacraments and mystical body of Christ, and by the soul's contemplative ascent. Many of the poems that follow *The Wreck* continue these mystical concerns in their implied emblematic imagery and recurrent interest in charity as a motif of the soul's ascent.

Hopkins's sensibility leads him to reunite the soul's religious progress with the exercise of mystical contemplation (the medieval threefold division is anticipated in the last three stages of Augustine's seven grades of the soul, *tranquillitas, ingressio* and *contemplatio*).[4] In his study of the *Spiritual Exercises,* Hopkins sought to reconcile Ignatius's discursive methods with the *scala mystica* and the contemplative tradition from which Ignatian meditation partly derives. Written after the years of silence that followed Hopkins's conversion, *The Wreck* reflects the personal and religious development of a period for which there are few records. For almost nine years, from Hopkins's conversion in 1868 to 1877, there is little information on his personal and religious life. Other than a few letters to Bridges, there are only Hopkins's journals, which were reserved for non-religious notes and observations. Interestingly, Pick's study *Gerard Manley Hopkins: Priest and Poet* draws attention to the disappearance of Hopkins's religious notes on meditation. In an 1873 journal entry Hopkins writes, 'August 30–September 8-Retreat, of which there are notes in my meditation papers.' A year later another entry reads, 'There are some remarks on [the retreat] in my notes of meditation.'[5] Clearly, Hopkins designates a second journal or diary meant for religious thoughts and meditations; the loss or possible destruction of these religious notes is unfortunate, and perhaps curious. We may speculate that Hopkins perhaps destroyed these notes as he did his early poems. Much as he felt his literary efforts inappropriate to his religion and vocation, Hopkins would have been hesitant to provide evidence of a contemplative journey that did not remain fully within the parameters of Ignatius's prescriptive methods.

It is important to note that while St Ignatius himself is reserved or silent about mystical states, he does not in any way prohibit such experience. His reservation relates to his reluctance to consider such mystical states as unquestioned signs of perfection.[6] Ignatius's own mystical experiences at Manresa are in fact well known, but the *Exercises* are not meant as a complete manual of asceticism leading to mysticism. As Downes observes, 'Ignatius' goal was to give God more missioners; the mystics he left to God.'[7] As we noted in Chapter 2, the *Directory* to the *Exercises* strongly urges caution in relating the meditative methods of the Four Weeks to the traditional stages of mystical life:

> It would be a mistake if anyone were to suppose that having gone through the First Week he was perfectly and fully cleansed of sin; and

> after the Second and Third Weeks, perfectly illuminated; and at last, at the end of the Fourth Week, that he had attained to perfect union with God. For all these stages require much time and care and labour in rooting out faults, subduing passions and acquiring virtues.[8]

Nevertheless, the *Directory* acknowledges correspondences between the schedule of weeks and the *scala mystica*. The only study to evaluate Hopkins's poetry against this threefold spiritual structure emphasises the first stage, the purgative way. In his *Studies in Structure*, Robert Andreach evaluates the spiritual progression of the mystical or ascetical way in four modern authors, including Hopkins. In an attempt to avoid the controversial issue of the precise relationship between asceticism and mysticism, Andreach describes this spiritual progress largely in terms of the 'stages' or 'degrees' of spiritual life, rather than the 'ascetic' or 'mystic way'. (He does, however, also use the terms 'purgative', 'illuminative' and 'unitive', as well as the 'degree of beginners', 'degree of proficients' and 'degree of the perfect'.) Andreach points out that even spiritual writers who insist on the distinction between asceticism and mysticism acknowledge the intimate relation between the two. He refers his readers to Father Parente, who asserts that 'an ascetic is always an ascetic; the mystic is a mystic only when actually engaged in some form of mystical experience. At other times he must practice virtue, deny himself, pray like every ascetic.'[9] Elsewhere Parente writes, 'mysticism is not a substitute for asceticism, except in contemplation...In everything else the ascetical life of the soul continues unchanged.'[10]

Despite a theoretical stance that chooses to view the subtle differentiation between ascetical and mystical theology as unimportant Andreach asserts that with regard to Hopkins's poetry, the term 'ascetic' is more accurately applicable than 'mystical'. Hopkins, Andreach writes, is 'pre-eminently a poet of *ascetical theology*, of "prayer, patience, alms, vows" (No. 32).'[11] He argues that while the language and imagery of Hopkins's early poetry are characteristic of that associated with mystical writings, this early work is neither authentically ascetic nor genuinely mystical. Poems like the early 'Nondum' display an impatient, youthful desire to experience 'infused contemplation', but Andreach describes this tendency as pseudo-mysticism.[12] As Sobolev suggests, the term 'pseudo-mysticism' is misleading, yet we may agree with Andreach's observation that these early poems reflect a desire to experience something that has yet not been experienced.[13] But while Andreach suggests that Hopkins's later poems never move beyond the 'illuminative' stage, Hopkins's early interest in contemplative experience can be seen in a more rigorously developed and interiorised form in *The Wreck* and later poems. Hopkins's *The Wreck of the Deutschland* not only presents a spiritual awakening and purgation, but also a movement from asceticism to mysticism that builds on Hopkins's insights into Ignatian and patristic theology.

So while Hopkins's spiritual journey is made through a practice based on Ignatius's *Exercises*, a subtle dissatisfaction can sometimes be sensed in Hopkins's writings. As Hopkins reflects in his *Commentary*, 'The only class of people St Ignatius contemplates as making the Exercises or as reading these rules are the second...they are in the Purgative Way and penitents at any rate now.'[14] The rules to which Hopkins refers are Ignatius's 'Rules for the Discernment of Spirits'. In this section, Ignatius lays out guidelines by which the exercitant may identify the affections excited in the soul by the operation of the spirit. The second rule, with which Hopkins is specifically concerned, is directed to 'those who go on earnestly purifying themselves from their sins, and advancing from good to better in the service of God our Lord'.[15] As Hopkins goes on to observe, all of the remaining rules elaborated by Ignatius in this section are essentially commentaries on Rule 2.[16] Hopkins's cursory remarks are in fact a broad comment on the theoretical foundations of the *Exercises*. The *Exercises,* as Hopkins understands them, are predominantly addressed to those in the purgative stage of spiritual life. By contrast, Hopkins's search for spiritual perfection, combined with his patristic study, would likely have led him to forge a meditative path that relocates the Ignatian method within a contemplative tradition. This attempt at reconciliation is seen in Hopkins's notes on the *Exercises*, where he relates Ignatius's 'Three Methods of Prayer' to the threefold mystical way.

> Three Ways of Praying: "Tres modi" – These three ways of praying correspond to the purgative, illuminative, and unitive stages respectively in a general sense. The third is prayer of the affections (L. R.).[17]

Hopkins's observations on Ignatian methods of prayer immediately follow his notes on the saint's 'Contemplation for Obtaining Love', which proves central both to Hopkins's poetics and his conception of the self. Hopkins's observations here relate to a theory of affective prayer that he elaborates in various sections of his *Commentary.* This is a method of prayer that moves beyond the 'purgative' and 'illuminative' way, to the *unio mystica.* Hopkins's understanding of this affective mode of prayer is predicated on his understanding of God's working or operation in the soul through the Spirit. Amongst the three powers of the soul, the human will is analogised to the Holy Spirit, and Hopkins's reflections on affective prayer are expectedly found in two primary sections of his commentary. These are his notes on 'Personality, Grace and Free Will' and on Ignatius's 'Contemplation for Obtaining Love', the 'contemplation of the Holy Ghost'.[18]

Affective prayer is defined as a 'form of mental prayer in which the affection of the heart (and the will) have a much larger share than the considerations of the intellect'.[19] It is, in other words, the heart's prayer, and Hopkins's conception of affective prayer as exemplifying the 'unitive' way may be understood through his interpretation of Romans 8.26–27. Hopkins's interpretation of this Pauline text, like his interpretation of Ignatius's 'Third Method' of prayer, emphasises divine union or the 'correspondence' of God and man. In the last chapter, we read Hopkins's detailed reflections on the 'unspeakable groans' of the Spirit who 'searches hearts' (Rom. 8.26–27). By Hopkins's interpretation, the operation of the spirit in the soul relates to that 'sigh or aspiration' – that slightest '*wish* to correspond [my italics]' – that is yet the 'life and spirit of man.'[20] This 'sigh of correspondence', Hopkins argues, links or begins to link the imperfect present with the perfect future.[21] This 'aspiration' ultimately 'lifts' the creature to God. But, Hopkins asserts, even this slight work of correspondence on the part of the creature is only a response to God's 'inspiration'. Hopkins's language of 'aspirations' is at one level connected with the language of ejaculatory prayer inaugurated by Augustine and continued by mystical writers such as François de Sales. For writers of the sixteenth and seventeenth centuries, this form of affective prayer is the foundation of mystical theology, bringing the soul into the immediate presence of the divine. Hopkins too clearly understands such 'aspiration' as the raising up of the soul. By means of this ascending prayer of the heart, which is the 'answer' or 'correspondence' to God's grace, the soul is lifted from one pitch of being to another, and ultimately to identification with Christ. This ascent is the function of that mode of grace, which Hopkins calls

> elevating...this is truly God's finger touching the very vein of personality, which nothing else can reach and man can respond to...by bare acknowledgment only...the aspiration in answer to his inspiration. Of this I have written above and *somewhere else long ago.* (my italics)[22]

I would venture that Hopkins's allusion to an earlier treatment of this theme refers to *The Wreck of the Deutschland.* Critics such as Downes have connected God's 'finger' in stanza 1 of *The Wreck* with Hopkins's discussion of elevating grace, but the full import of this relation is not appreciated. Hopkins's theological discussion of the operation of grace leads him to his most famous, radically mystical assertion. For Hopkins, grace is any divine action that carries the creature to its salvation. On God's part, this is 'divine stress, holy spirit, and, as all is done through Christ, Christ's spirit'; on the side of the creature this is 'action, correspondence... *actio salutaris*'. This, Hopkins declares, is 'Christ in his member on the one side, his member in Christ on the other...Christ *being me* and me being Christ'.[23] The mystical nature of this statement seems undeniable and we have already read this passage in the light of the Eastern conception of divine activity and the synergy between God and man. Some critics, however, contest the 'mysticism' of Hopkins's position. Analysing this very passage, Sobolev argues that while Hopkins clearly emphasises a divine presence in the soul, which enables spiritual ascent,

> nowhere does [Hopkins] suggest that divine presence is open to direct sensory perception or spiritual contemplation. It is by means of elaborate theological analysis rather than direct meditation that the presence of Christ within the soul can be detected. Consequently, this conception is not mystical. It is [an] analytical, rather than mystical, discussion of the elevating action of grace and the dialectics of faith...[24]

However, if Hopkins's 1881 notes on elevating grace are read as the theoretical analysis of a subject treated five years earlier in *The Wreck*, then the poem's application of patristic contemplative theology must vitally shape our understanding of this discussion. Beginning with the touch of God's 'finger', *The Wreck* leads up to a mystical encounter that is simultaneously experienced as the operation of the spirit in the heart and a vision of God 'seen' in a flash of light. From the vantage point of *The Wreck*, Hopkins's description of the elevating action of grace can be understood as fundamentally mystical and unitive. By the sighs of the spirit in the heart, the soul ascends to God. Appropriately, Hopkins's theological discussion in fact goes on to specify that this elevating grace is 'especially the grace of the Holy Ghost', as given at Pentecost.[25] What I am suggesting is that the 'prayer of the affections', which Hopkins describes as 'unitive', is a *way* of praying in the spirit or perhaps by the spirit, whose elevating presence in the soul, *when truly felt*, grants a contemplative experience of God. Such an experience, in Hopkins's words, can be responded to by 'bare acknowledgment only'.[26] By the 'aspiration' which is the right response to God's elevating grace, the individual may attain to a brief mystical experience of identification with Christ. This is a 'correspondence' with the divine, the 'touch' or 'vision' of God, which foreshadows the final glorification of the soul.

Contrary to Sobolev's argument, it is precisely through a meditative process, and specifically through the 'prayer of affections' that the *unio mystica* is achieved. The divine presence in the soul is grasped not through a process of intellectual analysis, but through an affective ascent that is the operation of God's spirit. Hopkins's theory of affective prayer essentially develops the conception of *caritas*, whose mystical import may be understood with reference to Augustine. *Caritas* is the love of God poured out in the heart by the Holy Ghost (Rom. 5.5), and of all the patristic writers, it is Augustine who most extensively discusses the nature of love. For the fourth-century Father, both love and knowledge are key to the soul's ascent to the mystical *visio Dei*.[27] As McGinn explains, God's love enters the soul and imparts both a knowledge of God and a '*desiderium*, or longing for God, that functions as a new eye of the soul...This new way of "seeing" is in us, but is not of us...its operation is from God himself.'[28] *Caritas*, then, is the heart's vision, by which the soul ascends to divine union. As we have seen, St Paul's famous Hymn to Love describes the perfection of *caritas* as the contemplation of God;[29] 'We see now through a glass in a dark manner; but then face to face... And now there remain faith, hope, charity, these three: but the greatest of these is charity.' (1 Cor. 13.12–13). The 'aspiration' or 'sigh of correspondence' that Hopkins describes as the operation of the spirit in the soul replicates the operation of charity. By this aspiration, the creature is lifted to God in a movement that 'begins to link the imperfect present to the perfect future.' In *The Wreck of the Deutschland*, Hopkins's intimation of contemplative vision develops the personal experience of divine presence which opens the poem. Hopkins's evocation of God's 'finger' in the opening stanza of *The Wreck* signifies the mystical operation of elevating grace, the grace of correspondence that is the operation of the Holy Ghost or charity, conforming the soul to God.

As McGinn points out, for many mystical writers following Augustine charity results from the immediate experience of God.[30] In the medieval Augustinian theology of St Bonaventure, charity is associated with the 'unitive' stage of the threefold mystical way; for Bonaventure, this threefold progression describes both the normal progress of Christian life and the contemplative journey of the soul. As Pierre Pourrat writes:

> That is the discovery of St. Bonaventure...In the purgative way come conversion and purification from sin; in the illuminative way the soul is enlightened as to God and Christ and itself, and tries to imitate the Lord; in the unitive way it is united to God by charity, and abandons itself to the exercise of holy love.[31]

Hopkins's portrayal of elevating grace draws on the mystical conception of charity to develop a theory of contemplative affective prayer. Beginning with the experience of elevating grace as the touch of the divine, *The Wreck* is composed as what Hopkins himself describes as the 'unitive' 'prayer of the affections'. Through this method of prayer, the experience of the poem is not one of meditation, but of contemplation. The perfection of charity is the contemplation of God, and in later poems, Hopkins's increasing emphasis on the motif of charity draws out the narrative of mystical ascent at the heart of Hopkins's 1876 ode. It is the philosophical theology of the early Fathers that underwrites Hopkins reflections on the 'Contemplation for Obtaining Love'. What Hopkins's notes on Romans 8.26–27 describe as 'correspondence' is understood by the poet as the 'communication' between the divine and human, which is the work of the spirit. So, we return to where we began – to Hopkins's notes of December 8, 1881, which reflect on Ignatius's directive to meditate on the divine indwelling and divine labour within all created things – above all, the human heart. Hopkins writes:

> This...is the contemplation of the Holy Ghost sent to us through creatures. Observe then it is on love and the Holy Ghost is called Love ('Fons vivus, ignis, *caritas*'); shewn 'in operibus,' *the works of God's finger* [my italics]...consisting "in communicatione" etc, and the Holy Ghost as he is the bond and mutual love of Father and Son, so of God and man; that *the Holy Ghost is uncreated grace and the sharing by man of the divine nature and the bestowal of himself by God on man* [my italics]...Again in Pt. 2 'templum', in 3. 'operatur' as above, in 4. 'a sole...radii, a fonte aquae' ('*Fons* vivus, *ignis*') (Dec. 8, 1881) All things therefore are charged with love, are charged with God and if we know how to touch them give off sparks and take fire, yield drops and flow, ring and tell of him.[32]

These lines are often quoted in Hopkins criticism, but shorn of their patristic and mystical context. Like the early Fathers, Hopkins suggests that the interior presence of God in the soul is indeed open to sensory perception and to spiritual contemplation: the divine charge in all things may be felt '*if we know how to touch them*'.

*The Wreck of the Deutschland* is best understood through the 'Contemplation for Obtaining Love' because the poem is a contemplation of love as the divine activity at work in creation – the communication of the human and the divine. The touch of God's finger with which the poem opens is the mystical activity of elevating grace, bringing the soul into correspondence with God. *The Wreck of the Deutschland* is Hopkins's incantational, mystical prayer of the heart; a hymn to divine love. The poem begins and ends with that divine operation by which the soul is conformed to God. Beginning with the touch of God's 'finger' Hopkins's ode culminates with an evocation of the 'heart's charity', which exemplifies the *unio mystica*.

35

> ...Let him easter in us, be a dayspring to the dimness of us...,
> be a crimson-cresseted east,
> More brightening her, rare-dear Britain, as his reign rolls,
> Pride, rose, prince, hero of us, high-priest,
> Our hearts' charity's hearth's fire, our thoughts' chivalry's throng's Lord.

As Hopkins writes in his *Commentary*,

> The Trinity made man after the image of Their one nature but They redeem him ('*faciamus* redemptionem') by bringing into play with infinite charity Their personality...One of Them therefore makes Himself one of that throng of persons, a man among men, by charity to bring them back to that union with themselves which they have lost by freedom and even to bring them to a union with God which nothing in their nature gave them.[33]

## Notes

1 Bridges's notes in *Poems*, 2nd ed., (1930; omitted from 3rd ed.), quoted in Schneider, *Dragon in the Gate,* 201 n.
2 Humphrey House, 'A Note on Hopkins's Religious Life,' (Chicago, IL: Loyola University Press, 1951), 110, quoted in Sobolev, 'Hopkins and the Language of Mysticism,' 1.
3 Sobolev, 'Hopkins and the Language of Mysticism,' 1.
4 Dom Cuthbert Butler, *Western Mysticism: Augustine, Gregory, and Bernard on Contemplation and the Contemplative Life* (1922; repr., Mineola: Dover Publications Inc., 2003), 28.
5 Pick, *Gerard Manley Hopkins,* 30.
6 Downes, *Ignatian Spirit,* 183 n 37 (cf. Pierre Pourrat, *Christian Spirituality,* vol. III). Downes draws attention to the influence of Thomas a Kempis' *Imitation of Christ* on Ignatius, describing it as 'one of the most important devotional books in the long tradition of Christian perfection' (134). It was at Manresa that Ignatius encountered the Spanish edition of the *Imitation* and was greatly moved by it; not surprising that during his composition of the Exercises after Manresa that his admiration of Kempis should be strongly reflected (134).
7 Ibid., 183 n 41.
8 Pick, *Gerard Manley Hopkins*, 28.
9 Fr. Parente, *The Mystical Life* (St Louis, 1956), 50, quoted in Robert J. Andreach, *Studies in Structure: The Stages of the Spiritual Life in Four Modern Authors* (London: Burns and Oates, 1964), 3.
10 Fr. Parente, *The Ascetical Life,* rev. ed. (St Louis, 1955), 235, quoted in Andreach, *Studies in Structure,* 3.
11 Andreach, *Studies in Structure,* 22.
12 Ibid., 24.
13 Sobolev, 'Hopkins and the Language of Mysticism,' 7.
14 Hopkins, *Sermons and Devotional Writings,* 205.
15 Ibid., 203.
16 Ibid., 205.
17 Ibid., 208. See *The Spiritual Exercises of St Ignatius Loyola*, ed. Halcyon Backhouse (London: Hodder and Stoughton, 1989), 56–60. Ignatius's Three Methods of Prayer immediately follow the 'Contemplation for Obtaining Love'.
18 Ibid., 195.
19 Fr. Parente, *The Ascetical Life,* 115 quoted in Andreach, *Studies in Structure,* 36. Interestingly, Andreach relates this mode of prayer to the second stage of spiritual life, but this is clearly not the case for Hopkins.

20 Hopkins, *Sermons and Devotional Writings,* 155.
21 Ibid., 156.
22 Ibid., 158.
23 Ibid., 154.
24 Sobolev, 'Hopkins and the Language of Mysticism,' 4.
25 Hopkins, *Sermons and Devotional Writings*, 158.
26 Cf. Fr. Parente's comments on the passive role of the soul in contemplative experience, Andreach, *Studies in Structure,* 3.
27 McGinn, *Foundations of Mysticism,* 258.
28 Ibid., 258.
29 Ibid., 71.
30 Ibid., 261.
31 Pierre Pourrat, *Christian Spirituality*, 4 vols; *Later Developments: Part I, From the Renaissance to Jansenism,* III, trans. W. H. Mitchell (Westminster, 1953), 8–10, quoted in Andreach, *Studies in Structure,* 7.
32 Hopkins, *Sermons and Devotional Writings*, 195.
33 Ibid., 171–72.

# Bibliography

## Books

Allsopp, Michael and Downes, David, eds. *Saving Beauty: Further Studies in Hopkins*. New York: Garland Publishing Inc., 1994.

Andreach, Robert J. *Studies in Structure*. London: Burns and Oates, 1964.

Astell, Ann W. *The Song of Songs in the Middle Ages*. Ithaca, NY; London: Cornell University Press, 1990.

Athanasopolous, C. and Schneider, C., eds. *Divine Essence and Divine Energies: Ecumenical Reflections on the Presence of God in Eastern Orthodoxy*. Cambridge: James Clarke & Co., 2013.

Bainvel, Jean, SJ. *Devotion to the Sacred Heart: The Doctrine and Its History*. London: Burns, Oates and Washbourne Ltd., 1924.

Bergonzi, Bernard. *Gerard Manley Hopkins*. London: Macmillan, 1977.

Bath, Michael. *Speaking Pictures: English Emblem Books and Renaissance Culture*. London: Longman, 1994.

Bender, Todd K. *Gerard Manley Hopkins: The Classical Background and Critical Reception of His Work*. Baltimore, MD: The Johns Hopkins Press, 1966.

Bernard of Clairvaux. *On the Song of Songs 1*, trans. Kilian Walsh O.C.S.O. *Cistercian Fathers Series: Number Four*. Kalamazoo, MIs: Cistercian Publications Inc., 1981.

———. *On the Song of Songs II*, trans. Kilian Walsh O.C.S.O. *Cistercian Fathers Series: Number Seven*. Kalamazoo, MI: Cistercian Publications Inc., 1983.

———. *On the Song of Songs III*, trans. Kilian Walsh O.C.S.O. and Irene M. Edmonds. *Cistercian Fathers Series: Number Thirty-One*. Kalamazoo, MI: Cistercian Publications Inc., 1979.

———. *On the Song of Songs IV*, trans. Irene Edmonds. *Cistercian Fathers Series: Number Forty*. Kalamazoo, MI: Cistercian Publications Inc., 1980.

Bradshaw, David. *Aristotle East and West: Metaphysics and the Division of Christendom*. Cambridge: Cambridge University Press, 2005.

Brilioth, Yngve. *The Anglican Revival: Studies in the Oxford Movement*. London: Longmans, Green and Co., 1925.

Brown, Charles Francis, ed. *The Roman Breviary Restored by the Sacred Council of Trent*. London: Burns, Oates & Washbourne, ltd, 1936–1937.

Brown, Daniel. *Gerard Manley Hopkins*. Tavistock, UK: Northcote House, 2004.

———. *Hopkins' Idealism: Philosophy, Physics, Poetry*. Oxford: Clarendon Press, 1997.

Bump, Jerome. *Gerard Manley Hopkins.* Boston, MA: Twayne Publishers, 1982.

Burnaby, John. *Amor Dei: A Study of the Religion of St Augustine.* London: Hodder & Stoughton, 1938.

Butler, Dom Cuthbert. *Western Mysticism: Augustine, Gregory and Bernard on Contemplation and the Contemplative Life.* Repr. of 2nd ed., E. P. Dutton and Co., London, 1926. New York: Dover Publications, 2003.

Cayré, Fulbert. *La contemplation augustinienne: Principes de spiritualité et de théologie*, 2nd ed. Paris: Desclée, 1954.

Chadwick, Henry. *Early Christian Thought and the Classical Tradition. Studies in Justin, Clement and Origen.* Oxford: Clarendon Press, 1966.

Chadwick, Owen, ed. *The Mind of the Oxford Movement.* N.p.: Adam and Charles Black, 1960.

Chadwick, Owen. *The Spirit of the Oxford Movement: Tractarian Essays.* Cambridge: Cambridge University Press, 1990.

Chavasse, C. G. R. *The Bride of Christ: An Enquiry into the Nuptial Element in Early Christianity.* London: Faber and Faber, 1940.

Clarke, Elizabeth. *Theory and Theology in George Herbert's Poetry.* Oxford: Clarendon Press, 1997.

Cotter, James. *Inscape: The Christology and Poetry of Gerard Manley Hopkins.* Pittsburgh, PA: University of Pittsburgh Press, 1972.

———. "Augustine's Confessions and 'The Wreck of the Deutschland.'" In *Saving Beauty: Further Studies in Hopkins*, eds. Michael E. Allsopp and David A. Downes. New York: Garland Publishing, Inc., 1994.

———. "The *Song of Songs* and 'The Wreck of the Deutschland'". In *Gerard Manley Hopkins and Critical Discourse*, ed. Eugene Hollahan. New York: AMS Press, 1993.

Dodsworth, W., Keble, J., Marriott, C., Pusey, E. B., Richards, W. U. and Williams, I. *A Course of Sermons on Solemn Subjects.* 2nd ed. Oxford: John Henry Parker, 1847.

Downes, David A. *Gerard Manley Hopkins: A Study of His Ignatian Spirit.* New York: Bookman Associates, 1959.

Danièlou, Jean S. J. *The Bible and the Liturgy*, ed. Michael A. Mathis, C.S.C. London: Darton Longman and Todd, 1960.

Dickson, Donald R. *The Fountain of Living Waters: The Typology of the Waters of Life in Herbert, Vaughan, and Traherne.* Columbia: University of Missouri Press, 1987.

Dominique, M., trans. *A New Beginning: Tertullian, Cyril, and Augustine on Baptism.* Leominster, UK: Gracewing, 1998.

Elliott, Mark. *The Song of Songs and Christology in the Early Church.* Tubingen: Mohr Siebeck, 2000.

Farris, J. and Taliaferro, C., eds. *The Ashgate Research Companion to Theological Anthropology.* Farnham, UK: Ashgate Publishing Ltd., 2015.

Fish, Stanley. *The Living Temple: George Hebert and Catechizing.* Berkeley: University of California Press, 1978.

Freeman, Rosemary. *English Emblem Books.* London: Chatto and Windus, 1948.

Heijke, J., ed. *St. Augustine's Comments on "Imago Dei" (An Anthology from All His Works Exclusive of the De Trinitate).* Worcester, MA: Holy Cross College, 1960.

Herbert, George. *The Temple 1633. A Facsimile.* Menston, UK: The Scolar Press Ltd., 1968.

———. *The Temple: Sacred Poems and Private Ejaculations.* London: Pickering: 1844.

Heuser, Alan. *The Shaping Vision of Gerard Manley Hopkins.* Hamden, CT: Archon Books, 1968.

Höltgen, K. J. "Henry Hawkins: A Jesuit Writer and Emblemist in Stuart England." In *The Jesuits: Cultures, Sciences, and the Arts 1540–1773*, ed. J. W. O'Malley, S. J., et al. Toronto, ON: University of Toronto Press, 1999,

———. Introduction to *The Devout Hart* by Henry Hawkins, S. J. London: The Scolar Press, 1975)

Hopkins, G. M. *The Sermons and Devotional Writings of Gerard Manley Hopkins*, ed. Christopher Devlin, S. J. London: Oxford University Press, 1959.

———. "The Wreck of the Deutschland." In *The Poems of Gerard Manley Hopkins*, ed. W. H. Gardner and N. H. MacKenzie. Oxford: Oxford University Press, 1970.

———. *The Collected Works of Gerard Manley Hopkins*, Vol. 1 *Correspondence* 1852–1881, ed. R. K. R. Thornton and C. Phillips. London: Oxford University Press, 2013.

———. *The Collected Works of Gerard Manley Hopkins*, Vol. 2 *Correspondence* 1882–1889, ed. R. K. R. Thornton and C. Phillips. London: Oxford University Press, 2013.

———. *The Collected Works of Gerard Manley Hopkins*, Vol. 3 *Diaries, Journals, and Notebooks*, ed. Lesley Higgins. London: Oxford University Press, 2015.

———. *The Collected Works of Gerard Manley Hopkins*, Vol. 4 *Oxford Essays and Notes*, ed. Lesley Higgins. London: Oxford University Press, 2006.

Jacobs, Nathan. "Created Corruptible, Raised Incorruptible: The Importance of Hylomorphic Creationism to the Free Will Defense". In J. Farris and C. Taliaferro, eds. *The Ashgate Research Companion to Theological Anthropology.* Farnham: Ashgate Publishing Ltd., 2015.

Jager, E. *The Book of the Heart.* Chicago, IL: University of Chicago Press, 2000.

Jeffrey, David Lyle, ed. *A Dictionary of Biblical Tradition in English Literature.* Grand Rapids, MI: William B. Eerdmans Publishing Co., 1992.

Johnson, Margaret. *Gerard Manley Hopkins and Tractarian Poetry.* Aldershot: Ashgate, 1997.

Johnson, Wendell Stacy. *Gerard Manley Hopkins: The poet as Victorian.* Ithaca, NY: *Cornell University* Press, 1968.

Jowett, *Benjamin. The Interpretation of Scripture and Other Essays.* London: Routledge, 1906.

Karrer, Otto, ed., Wydenbruck, N. trans. *St. Francis of Assisi: The Legends and Lauds.* London: Sheed and Ward, 1947.

Keating, John E. *The Wreck of the Deutschland: An Essay and Commentary*, Research Series VI, Vol. LI, No. 1. Kent, OH: Kent State University, 1963.

Kennedy, Robert, Paffenroth, Kim and Doody, John, eds. *Augustine and Literature.* Lanham, MD: Lexington Books, 2006.

Ker, Ian. "From Oxford to Liverpool: The Conversion and Poetry of Gerard Manley Hopkins." In *The Catholic Revival in English Literature, 1845–1961: Newman, Hopkins, Belloc, Chesterton, Greene, Waugh.* Notre Dame, IN: University of Notre Dame Press, 2003.

Kittel, Gerhard, ed., Bromiley, Geoffrey, trans. *Theological Dictionary of the New Testament.* Vol. IV. Grand Rapids, MI: Eerdmans Publishing Co., 1968.

Landow, George. *Victorian Types, Victorian Shadows: Biblical Typology in Victorian Literature, Art, and Thought.* Boston, MA: Routledge & Kegan Paul, 1980.

Lataste, Marie. *The Life of Marie Lataste, Lay-Sister of the Congregation of the Sacred Heart. With a Brief Notice of Her Sister Quitterie.* London, 1877.

Lawler, Justus. *Hopkins Re-Constructed: Life, Poetry and the Tradition.* New York: Continuum, 1998.

Lichtmann, Maria. *The Contemplative Poetry of Gerard Manley Hopkins.* Princeton, NJ: Princeton University Press, 1989.

Loomis, Jeffrey B. *Dayspring in Darkness: Sacrament in Hopkins.* Lewisburg, PA: Bucknell University Press, 1988.

Lossky, Vladimir. *The Mystical Theology of the Eastern Church.* New York: St Vladimir's Seminary Press, 1976.

Louth, Andrew. *The Origins of the Christian Mystical Tradition: From Plato to Denys.* Oxford: Clarendon Press, 1981.

Marceau, William. *The Eucharist in Théodore de Bèze and St. Francis de Sales.* Lewiston, NY: E. Mellen Press, c1993.

Martin, P. M. *Mastery and Mercy. A Study of Two Religious Poems: "The Wreck of the Deutschland," by G. M. Hopkins, and "Ash Wednesday,"* by T. S. Eliot. London: Oxford University Press, 1957.

Martin, Philip. "'Christens Her Wild-Worst Best': The Experience of the Nuns and the General Significance of the Wreck." In *Readings of the Wreck: Essays in Commemoration of the Centenary of G. M. Hopkins' The Wreck of the Deutschland*, ed. Peter Milward, S. J. and Raymond Schoder, S. J. Chicago, IL: Loyola University Press, 1976.

Martin, Robert B. *Gerard Manley Hopkins: A Very Private Life.* New York: G. P. Putnam's Sons, 1991.

Martz, Louis. *The Paradise Within: Studies in Vaughan, Traherne, and Milton.* New Haven, CT: Yale University Press, 1964.

Martz, Louis L. *The Poetry of Meditation.* New Haven, CT: Yale University Press, 1962.

Matter, E. Ann. *The Voice of My Beloved: The Song of Songs in Western Medieval Christianity.* Philadelphia: University of Pennsylvania Press, 1990.

McGinn, Bernard. *The Foundations of Mysticism.* Vol. 1, *The Presence of God: A History of Western Christian Mysticism.* New York: Crossroad, 1991.

McGrath, Alister E. *Christian Theology: An Introduction.* Oxford: Blackwell, 1994.

McGuckin, John, ed. *The Westminster Handbook to Origen.* Louisville, KY: Westminster John Knox Press, 2004.

Miller, J. Hillis. *The Disappearance of God: Five Nineteenth-Century Writers.* Urbana: University of Illinois Press, 2000.

Milroy, James R. D. *The Language of Gerard Manley Hopkins.* Belfast, UK: Queen's University Belfast, 1977.

Milward, Peter. *A Commentary on G.M. Hopkins' the Wreck of the Deutschland.* Tokyo: Hokuseido Press, 1968.

Muller, Jill. *Gerard Manley Hopkins and Victorian Catholicism.* New York: Routledge, 2003.

Newman, J. H. *Apologia Pro Vita Sua & Siex Sermons*, ed. Frank Turner. New Haven, CT: Yale University Press, 2008.

———. *An Essay in Aid of a Grammar of Assent*, ed. I. T. Ker. Oxford: Clarendon Press, 1985.

———. *Certain Difficulties Felt by Anglicans in Catholic Teaching Considered, in a Letter Addressed to the Rev. E.B. Pusey, D.D., on Occasion of His Eirenicon of 1864, and in a Letter Addressed to the Duke of Norfolk, on Occasion of Mr Gladstone's Expostulation of 1874*. N.p.: Pickering, 1876.

———. *Lectures on the Doctrine of Justification*. 3rd ed. London: Rivingtons, 1874.

Nixon, Jude V. *Gerard Manley Hopkins and His Contemporaries: Liddon, Newman, Darwin and Pater*. New York: Garland Publishing, Inc., 1994.

Ong, Walter J., SJ. *Hopkins, the Self, and God*. Toronto, ON: University of Toronto Press, 1986.

Origen. *Homilies on Genesis and Exodus*, trans. Ronald E. Heine. Vol. 71, *The Fathers of the Church*. Washington, DC: The Catholic University of America Press, 1982.

———. *The Song of Songs Commentary and Homilies*, trans. R. P. Lawson. Vol. 26, *Ancient Christian Writers: The Works of the Fathers in Translation*. New York: Newman Press, 1956.

Peters, F. E. *Greek Philosophical Terms: A Historical Lexicon*. New York: New York University Press, 1967.

Pick, John. *Gerard Manley Hopkins: Priest and Poet*. 2nd ed. London: Oxford University Press, 1966.

Phillips, Catherine. *Gerard Manley Hopkins and the Victorian Visual World*. Oxford: Oxford University Press, 2007.

Philo, of Alexandria. *Two Men of Alexandria: Philo…Origen… Some of Their Shorter Sayings and Incidental Side Issues*, trans. Herbert Gaussen. London: Heath Cranton, 1930.

Plotkin, Cary H. *The Tenth Muse: Victorian Philology and the Genesis of Poetic Language of Gerard Manley Hopkins*. Carbondale: Southern Illinois University Press, 1989.

Praz, Mario. *Studies in Seventeenth-Century Imagery*, $2^{nd}$. ed. Rome: Edizioni di Storia e Litteratura, 1964.

Pusey, Edward B. "Scriptural Views of Holy Baptism." In *Tracts for the Times*, Vol. II for 1834–5, No. 67. London: J. G. & F. Rivington, 1839.

———. *Sermons During the Season from Advent to Whitsuntide*. Oxford: John Henry Parker, 1848.

Quarles, F. *Emblems, Divine and Moral; The School of the Heart; and Hieroglyphics of the Life of Man*. London: William Tegg, 1866.

Reardon, Bernard M. G. *Religious Thought in the Victorian Age: A Survey from Coleridge to Gore*. 2nd ed. London: Longman, 1995.

Reid, Duncan. *Energies of the Spirit*. Atlanta, GA: Scholars Press, 1997.

Roberts, Gerald, ed. *Gerald Manley Hopkins: The Critical Heritage*. London: Routledge & Kegan Paul, 1987.

Rowell, Geoffrey. *The Vision Glorious*. Oxford: OUP, 1983.

Saint Ambrose. *St Ambrose Theological and Dogmatic Works*, trans. Roy J. Deferrari. Vol 44, *The Fathers of the Church*. Washington, DC: The Catholic University of America Press, 1963.

Saint Augustine. *The Confessions of St Augustine*, ed. Ernest Rhys, trans. Edward B. Pusey. London: J. M. Dent & Sons, 1907.

———. *Confessions*, trans. Vernon J. Bourke. In *The Fathers of the Church*, Washington, DC: Catholic University of America Press, 1966.

———. *Enarrationes in Psalmos* xxxvii. In *Corpus Christianorum Series Latina*. Turnhout, Belgium: 1956.

———. *Like as the Hart: Enarratio Super Psalmum XLI*, translated by an unknown sixteenth century writer, ed. Dom G. D. Schlegel. In *Sources Chrétiennes*, ed. P. de Lubac, SJ and P. Danièlou, SJ. Oxford: Blackfriars Publications, 1947.

———. *Soliloquies; and Immortality of the Soul with an Introduction*, translation and commentary by Gerard Watson. Warminster, UK: Aris & Phillips, 1990.

———. *The Trinity*, trans. Stephen McKenna. In *The Fathers of the Church*, ed. Roy J. Deferrari. Washington, DC: The Catholic University of America Press Inc., 1963.

Saint Ignatius of Loyola. *The Spiritual Exercises of St. Ignatius of Loyola*, ed. Halcyon Backhouse. London: Hodder and Stoughton, 1989.

Schneider, Elisabeth. *The Dragon in the Gate: Studies in the Poetry of G. M. Hopkins*. Berkeley: University of California Press, 1968)

Sobolev, Dennis. *The Split World of Gerard Manley Hopkins: Essay in Semiotic Phenomenology*. Baltimore, MD: Catholic University of America Press, 2011.

Sprinker, M. *A Counterpoint of Dissonance: The Aesthetics and Poetry of Gerard Manley Hopkins*. Baltimore, MA; London: Johns Hopkins University Press, 1980.

Storey, Graham. *Gerard Manley Hopkins*. Windsor, ON: Profile, 1984.

Sulloway, Alison. *Gerard Manley Hopkins and the Victorian Temper*. London: Routledge & Kegan Paul, 1972.

Tertullian. *On Baptism*, trans. Rev. S. Thelwall. Whitefish, MT: Kessinger Publishing, 2008.

Theodore of Mopsuestia. *Commentary of T. of M. on the Sacraments of Baptism and the Eucharist*, trans. Alfred Mingana. Cambridge: Woodbrooke Studies VI, 1933.

Thomas, Alfred, SJ. *Hopkins the Jesuit: The years of training*. London: Oxford University Press, 1969.

Trench, R. C. *Synonyms of the New Testament*. 11th ed. N.p.: Kegan Paul, 1890.

Verheylezoon, Louis, SJ. *Devotion to the Sacred Heart: Object, Ends, Practice, Motives*. London: Sands and Company, ltd., 1955.

Wagner, G. *Pauline Baptism and the Pagan Mysteries: The Problem of the Pauline Doctrine of Baptism in Romans VI. 1–11, in the Light of Its Religio-Historical "Parallels"*, trans. J. P. Smith. N.p.: Oliver & Boyd, 1967.

Weatherby, Harold. *Cardinal Newman in His Age: His Place in English Theology and Literature*. Nashville, TN: Vanderbilt University Press, 1973.

Wedderburn, A. J. M. *Baptism and Resurrection: Studies in Pauline Theology Against Its Graeco-Roman Background*. Tubingen: Mohr, c1987.

———. *Beyond Resurrection*. London: SCM, 1999.

Weyand, N., ed. *Immortal Diamond: Studies in Gerard Manley Hopkins*. London: Sheed & Ward, 1949.

Wheeler, Michael. "Hopkins: *The Wreck of the Deutschland*." In *Death and the Future Life in Victorian Literature and Theology*. Cambridge: Cambridge University Press, 1990.

White, Norman. *Hopkins: A Literary Biography*. Oxford: Clarendon Press, 1992.

Williams, A. N. *The Divine Sense: The Intellect in Patristic Theology*. Cambridge: Cambridge University Press, 2007.

Williams, Watkin Wynn. *Studies in St Bernard of Clairvaux*. London: Society for Promoting Christian Knowledge; New York: Macmillan Co., 1927.

### Articles

Milward, Peter. "Devotion to the Sacred Heart" (Part II). *The American Ecclesiastical Review* no. 148 (1960).

Virkar Yates, Aakanksha. "G.M. Hopkins and Tractarian Theology: The Doctrine of Baptismal Regeneration." *International Journal for the Study of the Christian Church* vol 12, no. 3–4 (2012 Special Issue: The Church and Literature): 263–278.

Virkar Yates, Aakanksha. "The Heart's Bower: Emblematics in Gerard Manley Hopkins's 'The Wreck of the Deutschland' (1876)." *Literature and Theology* vol 22, no. 1 (2008): 32–47.

Virkar Yates, Aakanksha. "The Light Unchangeable: Hopkins and Augustinian Contemplation." *Literature and Theology* vol 27, no. 1 (2013): 65–80.

Virkar, Aakanksha J. "Gerard Manley Hopkins and the *Song of Songs*." *Victorian Poetry* 45, no. 2 (2007): 195–207.

Woolf, R. "The Theme of Christ the Lover-Knight in Medieval English Literature." *The Review of English Studies* vol 13, no. 49 (1962).

### Online

Bump, Jerome, "Hopkins' Imagery and Medievalist Poetics." *Victorian Poetry* 15 no. 2 (1977). http://pao.chadwyck.co.uk.ezproxy.sussex.ac.uk/articles.

Cotter, James. "Hopkins and Augustine." *Victorian Poetry* 39, no. 1 (2001). http://muse.jhu.edu.ezproxy.sussex.ac.uk/journals/victorian_poetry/v039/39.1cotter.html.

Farrell, A. P., SJ, trans. "Rules of the Prefect of Lower Studies." In *The Jesuit Ratio Studiorum of 1599*. Washington, DC: Boston College Libraries, Digital Library Projects, 1970. www.bc.edu/bc_org/avp/ulib/digi/ratio/ratio_web.html.

King, Peter. "Duns Scotus on the Common Nature". *Philosophical Topics* 20 (1992), 11. http://individual.utoronto.ca/pking/articles/Scotus_on_Common_Nature.pdf

Knight, Kevin, ed. *New Advent Catholic Encyclopedia*. www.newadvent.org/cathen/.

Luzvic, Stephanus. *The Devout Hart or Royal Throne of the Pacifical Salomon. Composed by F. St. Luzuic S. I. Translated Out of Latin into English. Enlarged with incentive by F. St Binet of the Same S. and Now Enriched with Hymnes by a New Hand*. Early English Books Online, 1634. http://eebo.chadwyck.com.

Saint Augustine. *The Confessions of Augustine: An Electronic Edition*. Ed. James J. O'Donnell, http://ccat.sas.upenn.edu/jod/conf/.

Saint François de Sales. *Introduction to Devout Life*. Christian Classics Ethereal Library, Calvin College. www.ccel.org/ccel/desales/devout_life.

Saint Thomas Aquinas. *Summa Theologica*, trans. The Fathers of the English Dominican Province, 1947. www.sacred-texts.com/chr/aquinas/summa/sum496.htm.

Sobolev, Denis. "Gerard Manley Hopkins and the Language of Mysticism." Conference on Christianity and Literature, 22 June 2004. www.encyclopedia.com/doc/1G1-125407680.html.

# Index

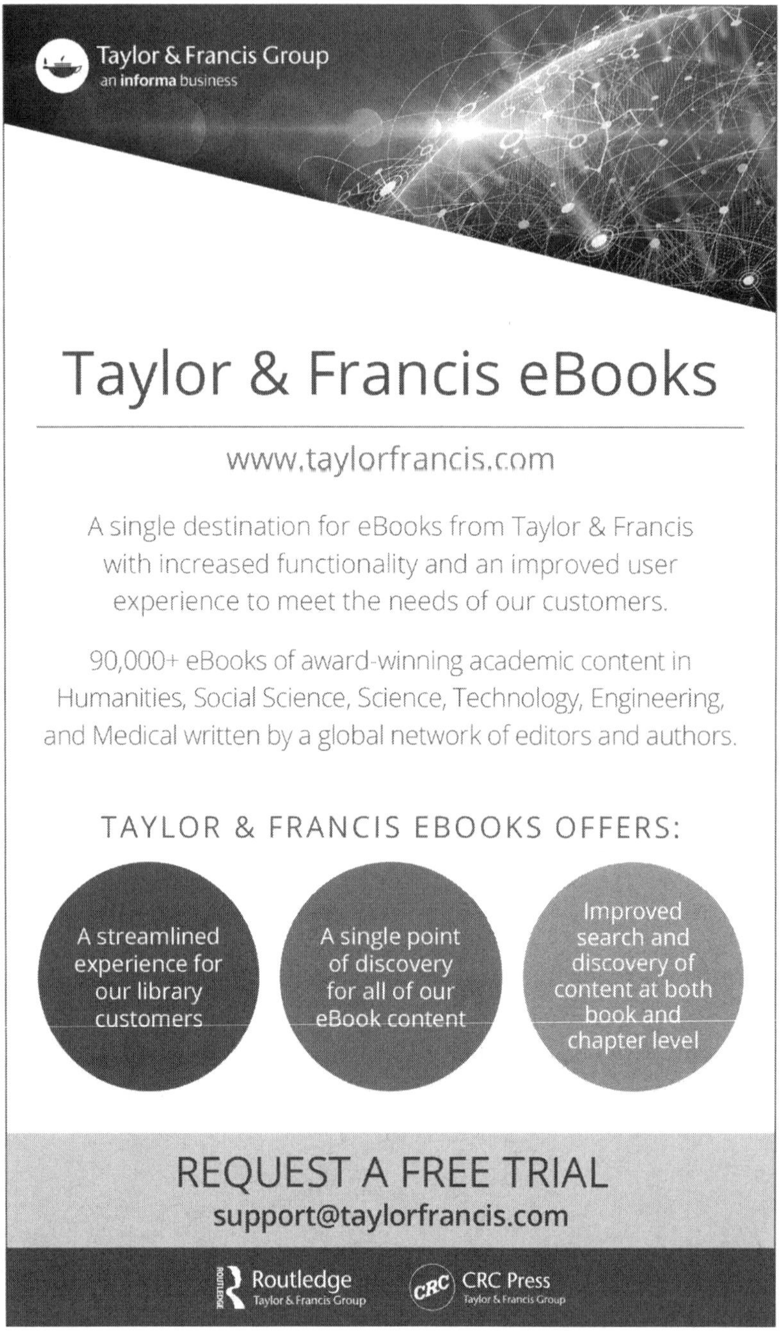